# Praise for *Teaching Psychology*

'Both new teachers and seasoned ones wi
of the enterprise we call "teaching psychol
make them more effective instructors who          ... ways that make
learning last.'

*Diane F. Halpern, Claremont McKenna College*

'This volume is likely to become an indispensable handbook for tertiary
psychology educators who are genuinely interested in improving student
learning outcomes.'

*Jacquelyn Cranney, University of New South Wales*

'This book is edited and written by some of the leading practitioners of the
area who are, and have been, closely involved in encouraging the development of psychology teaching and learning in Higher Education. I would
recommend that all those concerned with improving our Psychology
degrees should be using this source book of ideas, recent developments,
useful contacts, helpful suggestions and references.'

*Peter Banister, Manchester Metropolitan University*

# Teaching Psychology in Higher Education

*Edited by*

Dominic Upton

and

Annie Trapp

 **BPS BLACKWELL**

This edition first published 2010 by the British Psychological Society and Blackwell Publishing Ltd
© 2010 Blackwell Publishing Ltd

BPS Blackwell is an imprint of Blackwell Publishing, which was acquired by John Wiley & Sons in February 2007. Blackwell's publishing program has been merged with Wiley's global Scientific, Technical, and Medical business to form Wiley-Blackwell.

*Registered Office*
John Wiley & Sons Ltd, The Atrium, Southern Gate, Chichester, West Sussex, PO19 8SQ, UK

*Editorial Offices*
350 Main Street, Malden, MA 02148-5020, USA
9600 Garsington Road, Oxford, OX4 2DQ, UK
The Atrium, Southern Gate, Chichester, West Sussex, PO19 8SQ, UK

For details of our global editorial offices, for customer services, and for information about how to apply for permission to reuse the copyright material in this book please see our website at www.wiley.com/wiley-blackwell.

The right of Dominic Upton and Annie Trapp to be identified as the authors of the editorial material in this work has been asserted in accordance with the UK Copyright, Designs and Patents Act 1988.

Wiley also publishes its books in a variety of electronic formats. Some content that appears in print may not be available in electronic books.

Designations used by companies to distinguish their products are often claimed as trademarks. All brand names and product names used in this book are trade names, service marks, trademarks or registered trademarks of their respective owners. The publisher is not associated with any product or vendor mentioned in this book. This publication is designed to provide accurate and authoritative information in regard to the subject matter covered. It is sold on the understanding that the publisher is not engaged in rendering professional services. If professional advice or other expert assistance is required, the services of a competent professional should be sought.

Library of Congress Cataloging-in-Publication Data is available for this title.

HB: 9781405195508
PB: 9781405195492

A catalogue record for this book is available from the British Library.

Set in 10.5/13pt Minion by SPi Publisher Services, Pondicherry, India
Printed in Singapore by Ho Printing Singapore Pte Ltd

The British Psychological Society's free Research Digest e-mail service rounds up the latest research and relates it to your syllabus in a user-friendly way. To subscribe go to www.researchdigest.org.uk or send a blank e-mail to subscribe-rd@lists.bps.org.uk.

1   2010

# Contents

# Notes on Contributors

**Jacqui Akhurst** has a PhD in psychotherapy from Rhodes University, South Africa. She is a principal lecturer at York St John University, in York, England, and previously worked for the Higher Education Academy Psychology Network. She was formerly a senior lecturer in psychology in KwaZulu-Natal, South Africa, and lectured postgraduates there for more than a decade. She coordinated a master's programme for trainee educational psychologists for nine years and also contributed to modules for trainee counselling and clinical psychologists. Her research interests are in the fields of community psychology, student development in higher education and career psychology.

**Douglas A. Bernstein** completed his bachelor's degree in psychology at the University of Pittsburgh in 1964, then his master's and PhD in clinical psychology at Northwestern University. His current interests are focused on the teaching of psychology and towards efforts to promote excellence in that arena. He is chairman of National Institute on the Teaching of Psychology and he founded the APS Preconference Institute on the Teaching of Psychology. He was also the founding chairman of the Steering Committee for the APS Fund for the Teaching and Public Understanding of Psychological Science, and he is on the steering committee for the European Network for Psychology Learning and Teaching (Europlat). His has won several teaching awards, including the APA Distinguished Teaching in Psychology Award in 2002.

**Andy P. Field** is Reader in Experimental Psychopathology at the University of Sussex. He has published over 50 research papers and has written or edited nine books (and contributed to many more) including the bestselling textbook *Discovering Statistics Using SPSS: And Sex and Drugs and Rock 'n' Roll*, for which he won the British Psychological Society book award in 2007. His uncontrollable enthusiasm for teaching statistics to psychologists has led to teaching awards from the University of Sussex (2001) and the British Psychological Society (2006).

**Mark Forshaw** is a Principal Lecturer in Psychology at Staffordshire University. Amongst his published works is *Your Undergraduate Psychology Project: A BPS Guide*, the first book ever to be aimed at students completing psychology project research. He is a Chartered Health Psychologist, a Chartered Scientist and has various roles within the BPS and other professional bodies.

**Susan Hansen** is Senior Lecturer in Psychology at Middlesex University in London. She is passionate about the effective teaching and supervision of qualitative research methods, and recently edited a special issue of *Qualitative Research in Psychology* on Teaching Qualitative Methods. She has research interests in the application of conversation analysis to social problems and is currently engaged in qualitative work in broadly forensic contexts, including police–citizen interactions which involve the use of force, or threats of force, prison-based treatment groups for convicted sex offenders, and case conferences for professionals working with survivors of sexual assault.

**Kathy Harrington** is Director of the Write Now Centre for Excellence in Teaching and Learning, based in the Psychology Department at London Metropolitan University, which develops evidence-based methods and materials to support students' learning and writing development within disciplines (www.writenow.ac.uk). Prior to this she coordinated the Assessment Plus project on improving writing and assessment in psychology (www.writenow.ac.uk/assessmentplus). She conducts research and has published on student learning, writing and assessment in higher education. Specific areas of interest include the use of assessment criteria to promote staff–student dialogue, peer tutoring in academic writing, the role of Web 2.0 technologies in enabling collaborative learning and writing, and facilitating students' writing development through discipline-based teaching.

**Caprice Lantz** began her career as Clinical Projects Manager in Biological Psychiatry at the National Institutes of Mental Health, Bethesda, Maryland. Not long after moving to the UK in 2004, she joined the Higher Education Academy Psychology Network where she focuses her efforts developing resources and coordinating events for new and inspiring staff, enhancing the employability of students and leading work on a variety of other projects to support teaching in the discipline. She greatly enjoys teaching and working with students, serves as a guest lecturer at local universities and teaches psychology for the Centre of Lifelong Learning at the University of York.

**Stephen E. Newstead** is Emeritus Professor of Psychology at the University of Plymouth where he has worked for more than 30 years, including a spell as Vice-Chancellor. However his main love was (and still is) teaching and research, where his interests range from cognition (thinking and reasoning) to education (the psychology of student learning and assessment). He has had a number of roles in the British Psychological Society, including serving as President, and in 1999 received the BPS Award for Distinguished Contributions to the Teaching of Psychology.

**Peter Reddy** graduated from Aston University in 1977 and has taught psychology there since 1992. Before this he was a social worker, a counsellor and an A-level psychology teacher. He is interested in research in student learning including topics in assessment, e-learning and employability. He teaches on outcome research in psychotherapy and on a range of other topics in applied and social psychology. He is a member of the HEA Psychology Network Advisory Board, the BPS Division of Teachers and Researchers in Psychology committee and is secretary of the European network for Psychology Learning and Teaching.

**Annie Trapp** is Director of the Higher Education Academy Psychology Network and a founding member of EUROPLAT, a European network to support psychology education. She has been involved in a wide range of teaching and learning initiatives relevant to psychology education. In addition to editing the journal *Psychology Learning and Teaching*, she has written a number of book chapters and articles relating to psychology education and presented workshops on psychology education across the world.

**Dominic Upton** is Head of Psychological Sciences and Chair of Health Psychology at the University of Worcester. He is a Fellow of the British Psychological Society and was recently awarded a National Teaching Fellowship. His specialist interests are in the learning and teaching of psychology. He has published widely both on this topic and on studies relating to more specific issues in health psychology.

# Foreword

OK ... looking at your responses to the question I think
I'll go through that section again

Psychology is in danger of becoming a victim of its own success. Over the last two decades or so, the subject has grown immensely in popularity in the UK, both at university and secondary school level, to the extent that it is now one of the most popular subjects at both levels. In addition, the subject is taught to a wide range of other disciplines, spanning business, education and health, and has spawned enormous media interest, both factual and fictional.

But with success come problems. There are those who brand psychology as a 'Mickey Mouse' subject, not worthy of study at degree level. Others question whether it is right to produce so many psychology graduates when only a minority become professional psychologists. Students themselves will no doubt increasingly question the economic benefits of such a degree, especially as they are likely to have to contribute more and more to their education in the form of fees. Many universities have used psychology as a cash cow, using the income generated to prop up less popular disciplines, but this backfires when the funding bodies reduce the amount each student receives to reflect what is actually spent on them. This latter reflects another problem, that of whether psychology should be a laboratory-based science, with concomitant resources, or whether it is more of a social science.

None of these problems will be easily solved, and many of them will depend on factors outside the control of psychologists themselves. However, one thing that psychology lecturers can do is to ensure that they teach their students in the best possible way. Hopefully this book will provide a stimulus to the continuous improvement of teaching and learning in psychology.

A friend of mine, the late Tony Gale, used to say that it is difficult to teach psychology badly. He argued that the subject matter – ourselves – was intrinsically interesting to most students and that it should be very difficult to extinguish this interest. Further, psychology teachers' knowledge and understanding of issues such as motivation, learning, memory, assessment, social interaction, cognitive processes and individual differences should presumably allow them to use that knowledge in practical teaching sessions and ensure that their teaching is effective. In other words, teaching is a branch of applied psychology.

I am sure that a large number of psychology teachers use these inbuilt advantages to good effect and ensure that the subject matter is both fascinating and well taught. But I am equally sure that this is not universal – as many psychology students will no doubt attest. In this short Foreword, I want to discuss the reasons why this is, and at the same time indicate why I think the present book is very timely.

I suspect that one reason why psychology teachers do not always apply their knowledge of psychology principles to their teaching is because the relevance is not always clear, and in some cases may be almost impossible to use to advantage. As just one illustration, psychologists know a lot about individual differences, and that ability to learn depends on cognitive ability, learning style, motivation and a range of other factors. However, knowing this does not mean that it is easily applied to students. For example, we now know that there are significant and relevant differences between deep and surface learners. The former are more interested in a conceptual understanding of the information and how it relates to what they already know, while the latter tend to focus on simply memorising the facts. However, knowing this does not really help when faced with a class of 100 students;

you may know that there will be both types of learners in the room, but how can you adapt your teaching style to suit both of them? In fact, no one really tries to do this; instead, they make a value judgement that deep learning is best and try to encourage this in students, for example by having an assessment system that rewards deep learning (though this is more difficult than it might sound). It is less straightforward to know how to adapt teaching to differences in ability, aptitude, personality, and the like.

Another reason why psychology teachers do not apply psychological research knowledge to their own teaching is that the relevant facts are not always easily accessible, and in some cases may be of dubious validity. I remember when I first started teaching in the 1970s I was blessed with a deep knowledge of the psychology of learning; but this knowledge had more to do with rats learning in mazes than with students learning in my classes. There *was* a literature on human learning, though it was not voluminous and I was not overly familiar with it. There has since then been a massive growth in this literature, but that brings with it other problems in that it is almost impossible to keep up with one's own specialism, never mind keeping up to date with the rest of psychological research.

An additional reason for not being aware of all the research on teaching and learning is that much of it is carried out in disciplines other than psychology. Education, business, medicine and health are particularly rich sources of research on teaching and learning. To give one example, a favourite study of mine is on the so-called 'Dr. Fox effect' (Natfulin, Ware & Donnelly, 1973). In this study, professional educators from a variety of backgrounds (including some psychologists) were presented with a lecture given by an outside speaker (the eponymous Dr. Fox). Dr. Fox was in fact an actor without any expertise in the area of the seminar, and he was instructed to give a short, entertaining, but content-free presentation. Afterwards, the students were asked to rate his presentation, and most of them gave it a positive rating (in some cases extremely so). This study has proved irresistible to those who think that student evaluations (or 'happy sheets') give little or no insight into the true quality of teaching. Indeed, the idea that student ratings reflect little other than the charisma of the lecturer has passed into the folklore of higher education.

In common, I suspect, with most other psychologists, I was unaware of this research until some time after it had been published. My own awareness came through the much later investigations by psychology researchers such as Abrami, D'Apollonia and colleagues (see, for example, the review by D'Apollonia & Abrami, 1997). The follow-up research has shown that the phenomenon is much more complicated than it first appeared. It seems that the personality and expressiveness of the lecturer can indeed have an influence on students' ratings, but so too does the content. And when it comes to the effectiveness of the lecture in enhancing student learning, there is evidence that content is more important than charisma. Furthermore, it can also be argued that any effect of lecturer personality on ratings is not a bias but a genuine effect, in that lecturers who are friendly and helpful to students may not just receive higher ratings but may actually be more effective at helping students learn.

This brings us to another issue: the quality of the research which is carried out on teaching and learning. The original Dr. Fox study, while important and provocative, was flawed in a number of ways. It was carried out on a small number of graduate students, who were given a short seminar (the details of which were not presented), and who were given a non-standardised rating instrument invented for the purpose. Perhaps most crucially, there was precious little indication of the nature of the talk and the actor giving it, and just how free the talk was from content. It was left to follow-up researchers to tease out the effects of content, personality and other factors.

Psychologists (and others) may also be too ready to accept received wisdom and not to apply their research skills to separate myth from reality. If I may use an example from my own research, in the early 1990s we carried out research on student cheating (e.g. Newstead, Franklyn-Stokes & Armstead, 1996). This was, to our knowledge, the first time this topic had been systematically investigated in the UK or indeed in Europe. In contrast, there was a massive literature in the USA going back several decades. This meant that it was easy to rationalise things to the effect that this was a North American problem and that it would not happen this side of the Atlantic (it would not be cricket, would it?)

Our research gave lie to this assumption, and demonstrated that cheating (or academic dishonesty) is every bit as common in the UK as in the US. We like to think that our research has inspired others to investigate this issue further and has prompted universities and quality assurers to take the issue seriously. But this was only because we were willing to accept that the problem might be more widespread than previously thought and carry out research into a difficult and politically sensitive area.

I believe that psychologists can help themselves in a number of ways. They can carry out high-quality research into teaching and learning; they can ensure that their own practice is based on the best available research evidence; they can critically evaluate the research carried out by others to ensure that it is methodologically sound; they can help separate myth from reality in teaching and learning; and they can disseminate good practice. None of this will ensure that psychology will overcome the problems outlined at the beginning of this Foreword, but by putting our own house in order we can help protect ourselves from external criticism.

This is why I believe that the current book serves a useful and important purpose. It brings together a group of authors committed to good practice and outlines ways in which teaching and learning in psychology can be improved. My hope is that it will inspire psychology educators to review their own practice, to explore and apply existing research evidence and to carry out high quality research of their own in this area.

## References

D'Apollonia, S. & Abrami, P.C. (1997). Scaling the ivory tower Part II: Student ratings of instruction in North America. *Psychology Teaching Review, 6,* 60–76.

Natfulin, D.H., Ware, J.E. & Donnelly, F.A. (1973). The Doctor Fox lecture: A paradigm of educational effectiveness. *Journal of Educational Psychology, 71,* 856–865.

Newstead, S.E., Franklyn-Stokes, B.A. & Armstead, P. (1996). Individual differences in student cheating. *Journal of Educational Psychology, 88,* 229–241.

Stephen E. Newstead
Emeritus Professor of Psychology,
University of Plymouth

# Preface

The thinking behind this book was a result of a conversation in the winter of 2007. One of us (DU) had just received a National Teaching Fellowship and was bathing in the warm glow of congratulatory comments, messages and e-mails. One of these, however, had a sting in the tail with its enquiry of 'what now?' It then struck home that despite the accolade, little had been achieved – the next step had to be taken; there had to be a taking stock of the developments in psychology teaching. Where better to get assistance in this quest than with the other one of us (AT) who, as Director of the Higher Education Academy – Psychology Network, had a host of contacts, information, resources and insight. Our discussions suggested that between us we would value taking forward a project exploring psychology teaching in higher education (HE) and that others would similarly appreciate such a development.

The number of students studying psychology in higher education is increasing year on year (see Table 0.1) and its popularity is increasing in the pre-tertiary education sector as well. This growth in student numbers shows no sign of decreasing and it may be that the number of students in HE will grow with the increasing popularity of GCSE and A-Level psychology studies and the desire of students to continue their studies at postgraduate level. Of course this increasing number of undergraduate students will result in an increasing number of graduates seeking employment, either as psychologists or in some other career or progressing onto postgraduate studies.

This increasing number of students, graduates and workers rely on successful higher education provision. This text seeks to assist in this development by providing material for all psychology lecturers to develop their professional involvement, to try and facilitate best practice, but most importantly to provoke interest and engagement with teaching and learning of psychology in higher education.

**Table 0.1** Number of psychology undergraduates studying psychology

| Year | Number studying for UG degree (full-time) | Number studying for UG degree (part-time) |
|------|------|------|
| 2000/2001 | 21,285 | 2,060 |
| 2005/2006 | 43,200 | 14,180 |
| 2007/2008 | 44,625 | 14,215 |

*Source:* Compiled from HESA statistics, available online at www.hesa.ac.uk

The chapter topics selected are designed to do this for the key aspects of teaching psychology in HE as we see them today (July 2009). These topics may not have been the ones we would have selected two or three years ago, and they may not be the ones we would have selected if we were producing this text next year, such is the dynamic nature of psychology, psychology education and the climate in which universities operate. But they are the ones that are most relevant today and that we believe, gazing into our (admittedly rather hazy) crystal ball, are going to be relevant for many years to come.

The eleven chapters selected for this text are designed, as we have mentioned, to be guidelines and signposts for the reader to try and improve their practice (either at an individual or institutional level) and we hope that they will all be of use.

The book starts with chapter 1 (where else?) which sets the provision of psychology in the UK in the broader context of higher education within Europe. Trends and policies within the European higher education are explored as a means to understanding changes within our own universities. Some similarities and differences in provision between countries are explored and the relatively untapped potential to learn from others and share practice is highlighted.

The growth and increased diversity of the student population present a variety of challenges for the psychology educator. In chapter 2, a broad range of student issues are explored including students in large groups, independent learning, international students, ethical issues and student employability.

We continue exploring similar issues in chapter 3 where common misconceptions are examined from both a student and teacher perspective. For students, misconceptions may arise as a result of the media and an uninformed view of employment opportunities as well as with the course content. As teachers, we are reminded that we need to be aware not only of student misconceptions, but also of our own misconceptions relating to students and learning within higher education.

In chapter 4, we explore how psychological techniques can be applied to the teaching of psychology. There are a range of psychological concepts and techniques that may be appropriate and that are probably well known to teachers, but they may fail to integrate them into their practice. So why is this? What techniques may be appropriate and how can psychology teachers integrate them into their practice? Why do so few psychology teachers take the opportunity to apply their disciplinary knowledge to evaluate the effectiveness of their teaching?

In chapter 5, curriculum design is explored. Some broad-based principles are discussed and presented that may be applied to curricula, whether this be based at a module level or a programme level. In this chapter some principles, specific techniques and frameworks are proposed that, it is suggested, may stretch the students and make them more of capable, all-round individuals. This may take the student and the lecturer out of their comfort zone but this will be beneficial to both parties in the long term.

Chapter 6 highlights an area of the psychology degree curriculum that may be one of the hardest to engage students in – statistics. Although this topic is an essential underpinning of all psychology degrees, and psychological science full stop, it is often the subject that students struggle with the most. It is also probably one of the topics that some lecturers also struggle with. In this chapter, Andy P. Field presents some novel and adventurous techniques that could assist the lecturer in engaging the student in statistics.

Student research is also discussed further in the next chapter, chapter 7, when Mark Forshaw and Susan Hansen outline some issues surrounding supervising research projects. As is pointed out, the research project is a unique and fundamental element of the psychology undergraduate degree and brings with it some particular challenges that need careful consideration by the tutor.

Chapter 8 considers the assessment of students, highlighting developments in research and ways in which assessment can promote student learning. It outlines some of the challenges for the design of effective assessments and provides examples of ways in which these challenges can be addressed.

Chapter 9 reflects on the changing landscape of postgraduate psychology education for psychologists and the increase in professional community-based practice. The lack of research around postgraduate learning and the lack of training to prepare teachers, and supervisors, for postgraduate teaching are discussed alongside considerations of how to design training that will foster appropriate skills and attributes.

Of course psychology is taught across a range of other courses outside of psychology departments. In chapter 10, issues arising from teaching psychology to non-psychologists are discussed, in particular the need for psychologists to take an active role in the development of a psychology curriculum for non-psychologists. Furthermore, there is a need to consider the unique characteristics of the student cohort and how they may differ from the single honours student.

Chapter 11 concludes and summarises the material presented in the text and offers some guidance on 'what next' – what can psychology lecturers do for their students now and in the future? What changes in the external environment will impact on the student learning experience and what will the psychology lecturer have to deal with?

At the end of the book we present some resources for the psychology lecturer – web-based journal articles and paper-based material that the lecturer (whether new or long-term in post) may find of use.

Overall, we hope that you find this book useful and informative and a guide for your practice both now and in the future. This book is geared towards psychology lecturers at all stages of their careers – from those wishing to enter lecturing, those new lecturers and those who have been engaged in lecturing for a number of years but wish to enhance their practice. It is not a manual of tips or a series of laws that have to be followed by all. It is intended to be a series of thought-provoking chapters that will intrigue, stimulate and provoke. In short, we hope that by the end of the text it will inspire more questions than provide answers: a task to which any good psychology lecturer should aspire!

# Acknowledgements

This project has been a major undertaking for both of us and has involved us in reading and reviewing a considerable number of research and review papers, along with encouraging, cajoling and supporting our fellow contributors. All of us have tried to encompass the literature from both an academic and a practitioner basis. Obviously we thank the researchers, educators and policy makers for all this work and the contributions they have made to the current knowledge base. However, as will become apparent, there is still considerable research work to be undertaken and policy and practice developments to be discussed, argued over and progressed.

On a more personal level, several key colleagues have supported us during the writing of this text. Firstly, we must thank Doug Lawrence for the cartoons which we hope have been amusing but also include an element of truth (but not too much!). Many thanks also to the team at Wiley-Blackwell for helping us through this project. We also thank those involved in the production of this text – the designers and production editors for enhancing the text with some excellent features which we hope have provided guidance, direction and added value to all readers. Finally, we extend our thanks to all the individual authors for their excellent contributions, and our apologies for the nagging!

Finally, we must offer thanks and acknowledgements to those who have provided support for us both at work and at home. We want to thank our colleagues at the Higher Education Academy Psychology Network and the University of York (Annie) and at the University of Worcester (Dominic) for their help, advice, friendship and practical guidance. Finally, Dominic would like to thank his family: his children – Francesca (his favourite), Rosie and Gabriel – for keeping out of the way, and Penney for not. Similarly, Annie thanks Nick for being there, their children for welcome distractions and Kipling and Jemima for their utter lack of interest.

# 1

# Individual Differences
## *Psychology in the European Community*

## Annie Trapp and Dominic Upton

I know tuition fees include lectures ...but if you
give a really good lecture do you expect a tip ?

This chapter covers the following areas:

- a brief introduction to the European Higher Education Area (EHEA);
- the effect of EHEA policy on university structures;
- shifting values around the purpose of higher education;
- recognition of similarities and differences in psychology education and professional psychology across the EHEA;
- opportunities for collaboration in psychology education across Europe.

Psychology is a popular area of study across Europe. In 2005 there were at least 310,000 registered psychology students in the 32 member countries of the European Federation of Psychology Associations (Honkala, 2006) and this is before we consider the large number of students studying psychology within other discipline areas, such as medicine, the health sciences, education, engineering, neuroscience and computer science.

The nature of psychology education and training in the UK is shaped, in part, by policies emerging from the establishment of the European Higher Education Area, national government policy and national workforce priorities, as well as more local institutional and professional strategies. The intention of this chapter is to provide readers with a brief tour of European higher education policy in order to locate psychology education within a context that is broader than the immediate environment of our own departments and institutions.

## The European Higher Education Area

It is ten years since European Ministers of Education provided a vision for the creation of a European Higher Education Area (EHEA) by 2010. The framework for achieving this vision is commonly referred to as the Bologna Process which is summarised in Box 1.1.

### Box 1.1   The Bologna Process

*The Bologna Process* aims to facilitate mobility by developing tools to promote transparency in the emerging European Higher Education Area thereby allowing degree programmes and qualifications awarded in one country to be understood in another.

*Three Degree Cycle*
Two basic degrees, bachelor and master, have been adopted now by every participating country; sometimes in parallel to existing degrees during a transition period, sometimes replacing them completely. Typically, a bachelor degree requires 180–240 ECTS credits and a master's programme between 90–120 ECTS credits depending on the discipline. This allows for a flexible approach in defining the length of both bachelor and master's programmes. In the third cycle, European PhD programmes are not defined by ECTS credits.

*The European Credit Transfer and Accumulation System (ECTS)*
Credits reflect the total workload required to achieve the objectives of a programme – objectives which are specified in terms of the learning outcomes and competences to be acquired – and not just

## Box 1.1 (*Cont'd*)

through lecture hours. It makes study programmes easy to read and compare for all students.

### The Diploma Supplement
Compulsory for every graduate (since 2005), the Diploma Supplement is a tool which is attached to a higher education diploma and describes the degree's qualification. It is designed to provide a standardised description of the nature, level, context, content and status of the studies that were successfully completed by the graduate.

### Quality Assurance
The Bologna Process includes the promotion of European cooperation in quality assurance as one of its ten objectives. Common requirements for national systems have been defined at European level to improve the consistency of quality assurance schemes across Europe.

### Recognition
The recognition of qualifications is essential to allow students to study at different institutions in different countries. The Council of Europe's Lisbon Convention seeks to ensure that holders of a qualification from one European country have that qualification recognised in another and refers to the Diploma Supplement.

### Joint Degrees
Joint degrees (degree programmes involving periods of study at multiple institutions) provide innovative examples of inter-university cooperation. In recent years, many countries have adapted legislation to enable joint degrees to be awarded, and at European level an amendment to the Lisbon Recognition Convention was adopted in 2005 to facilitate the recognition of joint degree qualifications.

*Source*: Information adapted from the European University Association website, www.eua.be/bologna-universities-reform/bologna-basics/

Forty-six European countries have now signed up to this voluntary agreement, resulting in considerable structural reforms within universities in order, amongst other things, to implement a three-cycle degree system. This is a radical change for many institutions necessitating a reduction of five-year

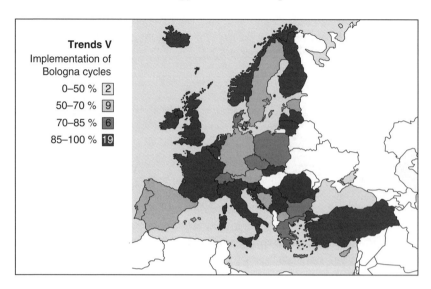

**Figure 1.1**   Implementation of Bologna cycles
*Source*: Trends V: Universities shaping the European Higher Education Area, European University Association, 2007

first degrees to typically a three-year format (180–240 ECTS) followed by a second (master's programmes, 90–120 ECTS). Figure 1.1 illustrates the percentage of universities in each country that had adopted the Bologna recommendations in 2007. A consequence of this reform is that over half of European universities have reviewed their curricula entirely, using the Bologna reforms to implement a more student-focused approach and to introduce new quality procedures (European University Association, 2007).

Although Bologna compliance does not stipulate a required length for master's programmes, two years is the norm in most European universities although in the UK the master's degree is typically one year in length. This disparity is not well understood outside the UK but is defended internally through claiming equivalence in terms of learning outcomes. In addition, some UK master's degrees are not intended as traditional research-intensive programmes designed to prepare students for a PhD and a career in academia but are intended to provide high-level professional skills required for specialised employment within the workplace.

The Bologna vision creates wide-ranging challenges for tertiary education across Europe including issues around quality assurance, equity and expectations as set out in Table 1.1.

**Table 1.1** Main challenges in tertiary education

| Domain | Main challenges |
|---|---|
| **Steering tertiary education** | Articulating clearly the nation's expectations of the tertiary education system. Aligning priorities of individual institutions with the nation's economic and social goals. Creating coherent systems of tertiary education. Finding the proper balance between governmental steering and institutional autonomy. Developing institutional governance arrangements to respond to external expectations. |
| **Funding tertiary education** | Ensuring the long-term financial sustainability of tertiary education. Devising a funding strategy consistent with the goals of the tertiary education system. Using public funds efficiently. |
| **Quality of tertiary education** | Developing quality assurance mechanisms for accountability and improvement. Generating a culture of quality and transparency. Adapting quality assurance to diversity of offerings. |
| **Equity in tertiary education** | Ensuring equality of opportunities. Devising cost-sharing arrangements which do not harm equity of access. Improving the participation of the least represented groups. |
| **The role of tertiary education in research and innovation** | Fostering research excellence and its relevance. Building links with other research organisations, the private sector and industry. Improving the ability of tertiary education to disseminate the knowledge it creates. |
| **The academic career** | Ensuring an adequate supply of academics. Increasing flexibility in the management of human resources. Helping academics to cope with the new demands. |
| **Links with the labour market** | Including labour market perspectives and actors in tertiary education policy. Ensuring the responsiveness of institutions to graduate labour market outcomes. Providing study opportunities for flexible, work-oriented study. |
| **Internationalisation of tertiary education** | Designing a comprehensive internationalisation strategy in accordance with country's needs. Ensuring quality across borders. Enhancing the international comparability of tertiary education. |

*Source*: Adapted from OECD, 2008c

The underlying message behind these challenges reflects a slow but purposeful transformation of higher education policy across Europe. In essence, the transformation represents a shift from education as personal development and self-fulfilment to education as an investment for economic development. Biesta (2006) traces this shift through and concludes that 'In about three decades, then, the discourse of lifelong learning seems to have shifted from "learning to be" to "learning to be productive and employable"' and 'the reduction of funding for those forms of learning that are considered not to be of any economic value'. The impact of this political intent on universities both in terms of how they are managed, the work of their academics and the purpose of university education is discussed further by Krejsler (2006).

Students too have concerns about what they see as the gradual commercialisation of higher education across Europe, claiming that Bologna amounts to the 'Anglo-Saxonisation' of established European state education systems. In December 2008, around 250,000 Spanish students protested, occupying university buildings, blocking train lines and interrupting senate meetings across the country, fearing that Bologna reforms in Spain will result in the introduction of tuition fees; a new degree structure that would not allow the necessary flexibility to continue working during term time; and fears that the new shorter degrees will devalue the worth of their first degrees, forcing them to complete an often-expensive master's degree. In France during 2008, election talk of making admission to universities more selective than the current open admissions policy for high school baccalaureate holders led student activists and others to deride the plans as an 'Americanisation' of French higher education (WENR, 2009).

The Organization for Economic Co-operation and Development (OECD, 2008a),[1] however, reports that threats to academic freedom and pressure on institutions to use public funds to benefit society as a whole requires a reconceptualisation of what comprises academic work: 'academic freedom needs to be framed within institutions' obligation to society … and the creation of closer relationships between tertiary education and the external world, greater responsiveness to labour market needs; enhance social and geographical access to tertiary education … in order to provide high-level occupational preparation in a more applied and less theoretical way.' The Improving Access to Psychological Therapies programme within the UK provides an apposite example of this approach. Such programmes may challenge traditional disciplinary and professional boundaries and set fresh entry qualifications designed to meet the needs of a new professional workforce.

Although European policy is directed towards increasing access to higher education there is still considerable variation in national policy with regard to how students are funded. However, average spending per tertiary student in most European countries is now well below half the level in the United States with funding for tertiary education in many countries barely keeping up with increased student numbers. In some countries, for example, Hungary, the Netherlands, Sweden Belgium, Germany and Ireland, the expenditure per tertiary student has fallen over the past 10–15 years whereas in the Nordic countries there is still high public spending on tertiary education (OECD, 2008b; see Figure 1.2).

The degree of funding support that students in tertiary education receive is variable but can be summarised as:

- No or low tuition fees but quite generous student support systems in countries such as Denmark, Finland, Iceland, Norway, Sweden, the Czech Republic and Turkey.
- High level of tuition fees and well-developed student support systems in countries such as the UK and the Netherlands.
- A low level of tuition fees and less developed student support in countries such as Austria, Belgium, France, Ireland, Italy, Poland and Spain. These countries have relatively low financial barriers to entry to tertiary education combined with relatively low subsidies for students, mainly targeted to specific groups.

In order to fulfil the EHEA's policy of increasing student and staff mobility, considerable efforts are being made to harmonise higher education national qualification frameworks across Europe and to align national quality assurance mechanisms within higher education. This work is being undertaken by the European Association for Quality Assurance in Higher Education (ENQA). Their standards and guidelines (ENQA, 2009) acknowledge systems based on subject review and accreditation as well as systems based on institution-led quality assurance with a focus on quality enhancement such as in the UK. Although commonplace in the UK, the appointment of external examiners as a mechanism for quality assurance and enhancement is not widespread across Europe.

Some discipline areas have endeavoured to introduce agreed EHEA subject benchmarks in the form of subject and general competences or learning outcomes. This is sometimes referred to as the Tuning process named after a pilot project called 'Tuning Educational Structures in Europe' set up in 2000. The project aimed at identifying points of reference for generic and

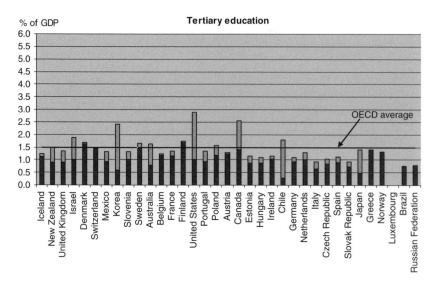

**Figure 1.2**   Expenditure on educational institutions (tertiary education) as a percentage of GDP (2005), public (lower bar), private (higher bar)
*Source*:  OECD Online Education database: www.oecd.org/education/database

subject-specific competences of first-cycle graduates across a wide range of subject areas, although psychology was not one of them. The Tuning process should not be confused with the work undertaken to establish an agreed set of competences for professional psychologists by the EuroPsy project described later in this chapter.

Another aspect of unified European policy is widening access to higher education with the aim of increasing the proportion of the European population trained in higher level skills. In 1995, 37 per cent of a cohort went into university-level programmes whereas it is now 57 per cent on average across OECD member countries. In some countries, such as Australia, Finland, Iceland, Poland and Sweden, as many as three out of four school-leavers set out to take a degree. Nonetheless, as UK educators will be aware, widening access across socio-economic classes is a difficult policy to implement and participation in higher education as measured by the socio-economic status of students' fathers reveals that substantially more students are likely to be in higher education if their fathers have completed higher education.

Within the UK, policies to implement widening participation have led to a large increase in pre-degree courses, including foundation degrees,

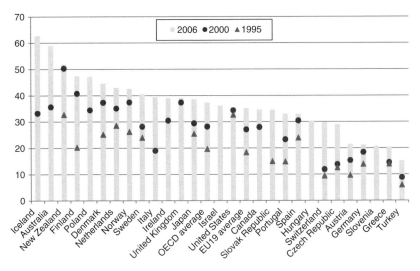

**Figure 1.3** Tertiary-type A graduate rates in 1995, 2000 and 2006 (first-time graduation)
*Source*: OECD Online Education database: www.oecd.org/education/database

access courses and provision through the Open College Network. At the time of writing over 87 psychology courses with a higher education qualification are being taught in UK colleges of further education, thereby fulfilling a need to provide local access points to higher education for more students.

Across the EU there is considerable variation in admission requirements to tertiary education. For example, in Slovenia students must reach 90 per cent in the state university entrance examination in order to be accepted to study psychology, whereas currently in France there is open access to the university system and, in the case of psychology, students are not 'filtered' until the second year of their master's degree. As a consequence French psychology students represent a quarter of all European students in psychology (Schneider, 2009). This is however set to change as in 2009 the French government announced their intention to base selection to universities on school results and to introduce student fees. National differences in admissions policy will naturally have an effect on student retention and graduation rates as shown in Figure 1.3 which illustrates the variation in graduate rates across OECD countries in 1995, 2000 and 2006.

With regard to student and staff mobility, many European university students already choose to spend some time studying abroad. To date two million students have benefited from EU Lifelong Learning Programme Erasmus grants, and the European Commission hopes to reach a total of three million by 2013. The number of international students studying in Germany, Switzerland and the United Kingdom is high, with more than 30 per cent second- and third-cycle degrees awarded to international students, whereas in Slovenia, Slovakia, Spain, Norway and Estonia the figure is less than 2 per cent.

Unsurprisingly, the language spoken and used in instruction is an essential element for students choosing to study in a foreign country and English is the most popular choice. In response to this demand, an increasing number of institutions in non-English-speaking countries, including Malta, Turkey, Denmark and other northern European nations, now offer psychology courses in English in order to attract foreign students. In the current economic climate there is a trend for students to study close to home but it is not impossible to imagine a time when variable tuition fees across Europe motivate more students to study outside their own country. The benefits to students undertaking a course of study outside their own country are well understood in terms of the importance to the economy (Bone, 2008), preparing students to work in an increasingly multicultural and interdependent world (Shiel, Williams & Mann, 2005) and promoting mutual understanding and respect for people of different cultures. Despite these advantages student mobility within Europe, particularly at bachelor level, is regarded as low. Reasons for this include comparability of academic experience, language problems and cultural norms. The latter can affect mobility as illustrated in Roales-Nieto's study showing that only 15.6 per cent of Spanish students were at universities located in provinces outside their familiar residence (Roales-Nieto, 2007). Similarly, a recent survey in the UK (National Union of Students, 2008) showed that 31 per cent of students are motivated to choose their university because it was close to home (53 per cent of these were from socio-economic group DE).

There are still many obstacles for academic staff wishing to move around the EHEA, including issues related to immigration, social security protection for mobile individuals, recognition of study and work periods abroad and lack of financial incentives. There may also be difficulties in relation to different methods of teaching and assessment, language skills and discipline-specific factors such as national subject benchmarks or core curriculum areas for accredited courses. Despite these difficulties many staff find teaching abroad an enriching and rewarding experience.

# The Psychology Curriculum in Europe

Across Europe the discipline of psychology has developed within the bounds of national histories, philosophies and experimental approaches. We should not therefore be surprised that within and between countries psychology is located across a wide range of university departments including education, philosophy and science with corresponding differences in curricular content and emphasis. Unlike the UK, national subject benchmarks for psychology undergraduate education do not exist in most European countries and there is considerable autonomy for psychology departments to define their own curriculum. Newstead and Makinen (1997) noted the difficulty in building up an accurate representation of psychology curricula but reported a degree of similarity across a small sample of European countries. Karandeshev (2007) describes the different frameworks for teaching psychology in the UK, Germany, Italy, Greece, France, Russia and Norway and some further information can be gleaned from books and articles providing overviews of psychology in different countries (e.g. Bagdona *et al.*, 2008; Biruski *et al.*, 2007; Iliescu, Ispas & Ilie, 2007; Latak, 2006; Sexton & Hogan, 1992). Where psychology is taught to other professional groups, information is much harder to come by. Even within the UK there is little agreement on ways in which psychology should or could contribute to the competencies required in different professions (for example, medicine, nursing, teacher education, law).

A shared knowledge of issues relating to psychology education including the diversity of curricula, curriculum design, lecturer autonomy, teaching methods and student issues within psychology education across Europe does not yet exist. A recent survey of a few European colleagues reported here illustrates the range of psychology texts used in their first-year psychology courses (Table 1.2), the average size of a lecture in their first-year psychology courses (Table 1.3) and typical problems encountered by psychology students in their first year (Table 1.4). The first table, although of some passing interest, reveals little about the process of teaching whereas the second and particularly the third table provide more insight and suggest that psychology educators across Europe are facing similar challenges.

Across Europe it seems students may also face similar problems. Table 1.4 illustrates the most common problems for students in their first year of studying psychology across a range of universities.

**Table 1.2** Examples of introductory textbooks used for first-year psychology students within their institution

| Country of university | |
|---|---|
| Austria | Kastner-Koller, U. & Deimann, P. (Eds.) (2007) *Psychologie als Wissenschaft* (2nd edn). Wien. WUV. |
| Belgium | Brysbaert, M. & Dumoulin, F. (2006). *Psychologie*. Gent: Academia Press. |
| | Dumoulin, F. & Brysbaert, M. (2006). *Psychologie. Oefenboek. Vragen.* Gent: Academia Press. |
| | Dumoulin, F. & Brysbaert, M. (2006). *Psychologie. Oefenboek. Oplossingen.* Gent: Academia Press. |
| | The first book is a translation and thorough adaptation of the work of Roediger, Capaldi, Paris, Polivy & Herman (1996). The adaptation includes so many local research examples and research that it is now considered as an original psychology textbook. The last two are exercise books. |
| Bulgaria | Levy, L. (2009). *Introduction in psychology*. Paradigm |
| Cyprus | Greek books or translations |
| Czech Republic | Hunt, M. (2000). *Dějiny pschologie* [The Story of Psychology]. Praha: Portál. |
| | Nakonečný, M. (1995). *Lexikon psychologie* (1. vyd) Praha: Vodnář. Atkinsonova, R.L, Atkinson, R.C., Smith, D. & Bem, J. (1997). *Psychologie*. Portal Praha. Czech translation. |
| Finland | Gleitman, H., Fridlung, A.J. and Reisberg, D. (2004). *Psychology* (6th edn). New York: Norton. |
| France | No single introductory text book, each course give its own bibliography and may use its own textbook. |
| Germany | No single introductory text book, each course give its own bibliography and may use its own textbook. |
| Ireland | Martin, G.N., Carlson, N.R. & Buskist, W. (2007). *Psychology* (3rd edn). Harlow: Prentice Hall. |
| Norway | Martin, G.N., Carlson, N.R. & Buskist, W. (2007). *Psychology* (3rd edn). Harlow: Prentice Hall. |
| Portugal | Gleitman, H., Fridlung, A.J. and Reisberg, D. (2004). *Psychology* (6th edn). New York: Norton. |
| Romania | Zlate, M. (2000). *Introducere in Psihologie: capitolul despre Ipostazele psihicului* [Introduction to Psychology]. Iasi: Polirom. |
| Slovakia | No single introductory text book, each course give its own bibliography and may use its own text book. |

**Table 1.2** (*Cont'd*)

| Country of university | |
|---|---|
| Slovenia | Field, A. (2005). *Discovering statistics using SPSS*. London: Sage. Marjanovič Umek, L. in Zupančič, M. (ur.) (2004). *Razvojna psihologija* [Developmental psychology]. Ljubljana: ZIFF. Musek, J. (1999). *Uvod v psihologijo* [Introduction to psychology]. Ljubljana: Educy. Musek, J. (2005). *Predmet, metode in področja psihologije* [Topics and methods in psychology]. Ljubljana: Filozofska fakulteta. |
| Turkey | Kalat, J.W. (2009). *Biological psychology* (10th edn). Belmont, CA: Wadsworth. Feldman, R.S. (2006). *Understanding psychology* (8th edn). Boston: McGraw-Hill; Schaefer, R.T. (2008). *Sociology* (11th edn). Boston: McGraw-Hill. Warburton, N. (2004). *Philosophy: The basics* (4th edn). London: Routledge. Shaughnessy, E.B., Zechmeister, J.S., Zechmeister, J.J. (2005) *Research methods in psychology* (7th edn). New York: McGraw-Hill. |

**Table 1.3** The average size of a lecture in the first year for students studying psychology

| Country of university | Approximate size of lecture (number of students) in first year psychology programmes |
|---|---|
| Austria | 500 |
| Belgium | 600–700 |
| Bulgaria | 103 |
| Cyprus | 50 |
| Czech Republic | 60 |
| Finland | 100 |
| France | 40–500 |
| Germany | 100 |
| Ireland | 70 |
| Norway | 150 |
| Portugal | 200 |
| Romania | 150 |
| Slovakia | 60 |
| Slovenia | 70–80 |
| Turkey | 35 |
| UK | 100–150 |

**Table 1.4** The most common problems for students in their first year of studying psychology across a range of universities

| Country of university | The most common problems for students in their first year of studying psychology across a range of universities |
| --- | --- |
| Austria | Anonymity, disorientation, information overload. |
| Belgium | The courses in the field of statistics and research methodology. Adaptation to the university study regime. Independent study without external directions and support. Time management. Quantity of material to read and assimilate. |
| Bulgaria | The new way of organisation of education – too many disciplines, too much material, new methods of teaching and learning. Uncertainty in relation to the future. |
| Cyprus | Secondary schools do not teach psychology so students lack understanding of basic terms and come with misconceptions. |
| Czech Republic | Acclimatisation from secondary school. Different way of teaching. No strictly specified sources of information. Higher standards. More demanding. |
| Finland | Transition from a relatively prescribed high-school learning habits to a more independent and creative university learning process. |
| France | Independent learning, social networking, reading texts written in English, slow feedback on assessed work. |
| Germany | Statistics and Psychological Methods. Adaptation to independent, self-controlled learning and time management. |
| Ireland | Students find developing critical thinking skills a challenge. Student expectations of psychology as a subject do not always match up to the reality. Psychology is not taught in secondary schools and most students have only encountered the subject in the popular media. |
| Macedonia | Lack of translated resources. |
| Norway | Coming to grips with being in a university as opposed to high school. |
| Portugal | The adaptation to a different reality from high school in terms of classes, study habits and strategies, relations, etc. Difficulty for mature students in managing demands of work, home and study. |
| Romania | The difficulty of identifying the hidden variables which make up the psychological processes. Lack of research terminology and methodology to facilitate their understanding. Lack of translated resources. |
| Slovakia | Lack of literature (especially international), old literature. Orientation in new way of study. |
| Turkey | Culture shock. Studying resources written in English language. |

Opportunities to engage in collaborative ventures across Europe are on the increase. Some universities are building collaboration through the creation of joint courses. There is, for example, a European master's programme in sport and exercise psychology involving a consortium set up by 12 European universities. The programme is integrated into the national master's level degree programmes at the network universities, and involves a minimum of one-year full-time study consisting of jointly designed modules, including a common introductory reading package (10 ECTS); a two-week International Intensive Course where students from all the partner universities come to study together (10 ECTS); courses at home and abroad university (17 ECTS); a master's thesis (23 ECTS); and a study-abroad period of four to six months. The programme graduates are awarded a master's degree by their home university and, in addition, a European master's certificate is granted to the graduates. Other examples include a European master's programme in mathematical psychology involving universities from seven European countries and a European master's in Clinical Linguistics.

## Professional Psychology and Employability

National differences in psychology education and training create problems with professional recognition of qualifications between countries. Establishing comparability between qualifications, whether it be related to working or hiring someone from another country or establishing comparability of student qualifications, is made somewhat easier by the establishment of the European Network of National Information Centres on academic recognition and mobility (ENIC, 2009). Their national websites provide useful information on: national education bodies, the system of education, university education, post-secondary non-university education, recognised higher education institutions, policies and procedures for the recognition of qualifications, qualifications framework and diploma supplement information.

Work is also ongoing towards establishing the recognition of professional qualifications across the European Union (Directive 2005/36EC). The title or the profession of psychologists is now legally regulated in the majority of the EU member states and other EEA countries. According to Honkala (2006), legal regulation exists or legislation is in process in Austria, Belgium, Croatia, Cyprus, the Czech Republic, Denmark, Estonia, Finland, France,

Germany, Greece, Hungary, Iceland, Ireland, Italy, Luxembourg, Malta, Norway, Poland, Slovakia, Spain, Sweden, Switzerland, Turkey and UK. For a more recent review of legal regulations for psychology and psychotherapy in 17 European countries, see Van Broeck and Lietaer (2008).

In 2005, the European Federation of Psychology Associations (EFPA) ratified EuroPsy – the European Certificate in Psychology (Lunt & Poortinga, 2009) – which provides a benchmark of competences for independent practice. These are defined in the number of credit points to be gained at bachelor's and master's phases rather than a prescription of curricula content. Six countries (Finland, Germany, Hungary, Italy, Spain and the UK) trialled the procedures and issuing of EuroPsy certificates during 2006–2008 and it is intended that the EuroPsy certificate will be launched more widely across European countries in 2010.

A survey conducted by the EFPA (Honkala, 2006) estimated that the number of professional psychologists in Europe in 2010 will be around 371,000, representing a 27 per cent increase for the period 2005–2010, but to achieve a ratio of 1:1000 (already reached in seven European countries), an additional 550,000 psychologists would be required in the 31 European countries associated with European Federation of Psychology Associations.

At present the majority of professional psychologists in Europe work within health care although percentages range from 80 per cent in Norway to less than 20 per cent in countries where psychology is still an emerging profession such as Croatia, Latvia and Estonia. Similarly there are large differences in the proportion of psychologists working in other professional areas; for example, in Latvia over 65 per cent of psychologists work within education and, although in Italy there are few work or organisational psychologists, in Belgium and the UK they represent over 25 per cent of professional psychologists (Honkala, 2006).

The need for an increase in trained professionals to treat the mental health problems that affect one in four people has been identified in three reports from the World Health Organization: *Policies and practices for mental health* (WHO, 2008a); *Guidelines on mental health and psychosocial support in emergency settings* (IASC, 2007); and *Scaling up care for mental, neurological, and substance use disorders* (WHO, 2008b). Psychologists should be well placed to respond to this need although the competencies and level of training required are undetermined.

Given the need for mental health workers and psychologists across Europe, it is unfortunate that many countries do not have enough professional psychology employment opportunities for psychology graduates.

Although it is difficult to find reliable national estimates on the proportion of psychology graduates that succeed in finding employment as professional psychologists, anecdotal estimates range from 20–90 per cent. There is therefore an identifiable need to consider psychology education from the perspective of employment opportunities in a broader sense than the traditional professional areas. Some universities are already adapting to this agenda; for example, the University of Warsaw offers a range of psychology degrees closely aligned with particular work areas. The employability of psychology graduates is likely to become an increasing problem within Europe due to the perceived low status of graduates released into the job market at the end of a bachelor's degree. Reporting on a European meeting of major employers in the public and corporate sectors, Roberts states:

> I came away with the sense, however, that the new bachelor's degree still has a long way to go before it is accepted as an entrance qualification to higher level careers in the civil service, business and industry…. Hierarchical attitudes remain, but in place of the division between a university-educated elite and a shopfloor workforce with vocational qualifications, the new division is between holders of bachelor's and master's degrees. The latter can hope to access careers in the higher grades of the civil service and professional and managerial positions, while the former are likely to be confined to more technical and practical roles. There is still a view that graduates with a bachelor's degree haven't really finished their studies. (Roberts, 2008)

Even in the UK, where it is commonplace for graduates with a three-year degree to enter the workplace, the transferable skills that psychology graduates bring to the workplace are not well understood by employers.

## Support and Training for Psychology Education in Europe

Few European countries have organisations dedicated to supporting the teaching and learning of psychology. Notable exceptions are: the British Psychological Society, Division of Teachers and Researchers in Psychology and the Higher Education Academy Psychology Network in the UK; the Association des Enseignants-chercheurs en Psychologie des Universités in France; and the German Psychology Teachers Organisation. The European Federation for Psychology Teachers' Associations focuses on pre-degree psychology education.

In August 2007 a small group met in London to consider a network to support learning and teaching within the discipline of psychology in Europe. Further contacts were made, and in February 2008 representatives from psychology departments in 17 countries met in Florence followed by a meeting in July 2008 in Berlin with representatives from 22 countries. Although in an early stage of development, the European Network for Psychology Learning and Teaching (www.europlat.org) has as its aims:

- the enhancement of the quality of teaching and student learning in psychology;
- the development of scholarship relating to the teaching and learning in psychology.

## Conclusion

In this chapter I have attempted to set UK psychology education within the context of psychology education in the European Higher Education Area. Across Europe psychology educators are facing similar challenges. Many of these issues are not unique to psychology, for example, overreliance on the lecture, lack of opportunity to exchange practice, teaching as the poor relation to research, part-time staff, admission and selection policies, large class sizes and the increasing diversity of students. Other identified issues are more discipline specific, such as a lack of psychology teaching material, unrealistic student expectations about psychology, problems of student numeracy and literacy, professional development for psychology teaching and student employability. These issues, alongside the harmonisation of European higher education and together with the effectiveness of a discipline-based approach to supporting teaching and learning, provide a strong rationale for building networks and opportunities with psychology educators across Europe to learn from each other, to work on collaborative projects with their students and to share practice and resources.

## Key Messages

- University strategies have to operate within a European context.
- Universities are operating in an increasingly competitive environment.

- University education can develop employability skills that may be transferable across Europe.
- Teaching and studying abroad has benefits for both staff and students.
- There is a range of psychology content taught across Europe, but there are common issues, concerns and developments.

## Research Questions

1. What resources and training are needed to enhance psychology education across Europe?
2. What are the understanding, expectations and experiences of international staff and students?
3. How can we use technology to support integration of psychology education across Europe?
4. What is the impact of the three-cycle degree system on student employability?

## Note

1   The OECD member countries are: Australia, Austria, Belgium, Canada, the Czech Republic, Denmark, Finland, France, Germany, Greece, Hungary, Iceland, Ireland, Italy, Japan, Korea, Luxembourg, Mexico, the Netherlands, New Zealand, Norway, Poland, Portugal, the Slovak Republic, Spain, Sweden, Switzerland, Turkey, the United Kingdom and the United States. The Commission of the European Communities takes part in the work of the OECD.

## References

Atkinsonova, R.L, Atkinson, R.C., Smith, D. & Bem, J. (1997). *Psychologie*. Portal Praha.

Bagdona, A., Pociute, B., Rimkute, E. & Valickas, G. (2008). The history of Lithuanian psychology. *European Psychologist, 13*, 227–237.

Biesta, G. (2006). What's the point of lifelong learning if lifelong learning has no point? On the democratic deficit of policies for lifelong learning. *European Educational Research Journal, 5*(3 & 4), 169–180.

Biruski, D.C., Jerkovic, I., Zotovic, M. & Krnetic, I. (2007). Psychology in Bosnia and Herzegovina, Croatia and Serbia. *The Psychologist, 20*(4), 220–222.

Bone, D. (2008). *Internationalisation in HE: A 10-year review.* UK Higher Education International Unit. Retrieved on 13 January 2009 from: http://www.international.ac.uk/resources/Internationalisation-Bone.pdf

ENIC (2009). *The European network of Information Centres.* Retrieved on 13 June 2009 from www.enic-naric.net/index.aspx?s=n&r=g&d=about

ENQA (2009). *Standards and Guidelines for Quality Assurance in the European Higher Education Area – 3rd edition.* Retrieved on 13 June 2009 from www.enqa.eu/pubs_esg.lasso

European University Association (2007). *Trends V: Universities shaping the European Higher Education Area.* Retrieved on 16 February 2009 from www.eua.be/trends-in-european-higher-education/

European University Associaton (2008). *EUA Involvement in the Bologna process.* Accessed from www.eua.be/bologna-universities-reform/ on 16 February 2009.

Honkala, J. (2006). The present status and future prospects of the profession of psychologists in Europe: EU Directive and the European Diploma in Psychology. *European Psychologist 11*(1), 71–75.

Iliescu, D., Ispas, A. & Ilie, A. (2007). Psychology in Romania. *The Psychologist, 20*(1), 34–35.

Inter-Agency Standing Committee (IASC) (2007). *The Inter-Agency Standing Committee (IASC) Guidelines on mental health and psychosocial support in emergency settings.* Geneva: IASC.

Karandashev, V. (2007). International practices in the teaching of psychology: Europe. In S. McCarthy, S. Newstead, C. Prandini, V. Karandashev, C. Hutz & W. Gomes, (Eds.) *Teaching psychology around the world, Vol. 1* (pp.167–214). Newcastle, UK: Cambridge Scholars Publishing.

Krejsler, J. (2006). Discursive battles about the meaning of university: The case of Danish university reform and its academics. *European Educational Research Journal, 5*(3), 210–220.

Latak, K. (2006). Studying psychology in Europe. *The Psychologist, 19*(5), 297.

Lunt, I. & Poortinga, Y. (2009). Certification of psychologists in Europe: Implications for teaching psychology. In S. McCarthy, V. Karandashev, M. Stevens, A. Thatcher, J. Jaafar, K. Moore *et al.* (Eds.) *Teaching psychology around the world, Vol. 2.* Cambridge Scholars Publishing.

McCarthy, S., Karandashev, V., Stevens, M., Thatcher, A., Jaafar, J., Moore, K. *et al.* (2009). *Teaching psychology around the world, Vol. 2.* Cambridge Scholars Publishing.

National Union of Students (2008). NUS student experience report. Retrieved on 30 April 2009 from www.nus.org.uk/PageFiles/4017/NUS_StudentExperience Report.pdf

Newstead, S. & Makinen, S. (1997). Psychology teaching in Europe. *European Psychologist, 2*(1), 3–10.

OECD (2008a). *Trends shaping education – 2008 edition.* Organization for Economic Cooperation and Development. Retrieved on 19 June 2009 from www.oecd.org/document/58/0,3343,en_2649_35845581_41208186_1_1_1_37455,00.html

OECD (2008b). *Education at a glance 2008.* Organization for Economic Cooperation and Development. Retrieved on 16 February 2009 from www.oecd.org/edu/eag2008

OECD (2008c). *Tertiary education for the knowledge society, Vol. 1.* Retrieved on 19 June 2009 from www.oecd.org/document/35/0,3343,en_2649_39263238_360 21283_1_1_1_1,00.html

Roales-Nieto, J.G. (2007). Análisis de la Movilidad del Alumnado en los Estudios Universitarios de Psicología en España [An analysis of the student mobility in university degrees of psychology in Spain]. *International Journal of Psychology and Psychological Therapy, 7*(1), 73–117.

Roberts, G. (2008). 'Employability' on the agenda in Luxembourg. *This Month in Europe.* Issue 52, p.3. London: The UK Higher Education Europe Unit. Retrieved 4 June 2009 from www.europeunit.ac.uk/sites/europe_unit2/resources/This%20month%20in%20Europe%20Dec%2008.pdf

Roediger, H.L. III, Capaldi, E.D., Paris, S.G., Polivy, J. & Herman, C.P. (1996). *Psychology* (4th edn). St. Paul, MN: West.

Schneider, B. (2009). Training for psychologists in French universities: A look at the current debates in this sphere. In S. McCarthy, V. Karandashev, M. Stevens, A. Thatcher, J. Jaafar, K. Moore *et al.* (Eds.) *Teaching psychology around the world*, *Vol. 2*. Cambridge Scholars Publishing.

Sexton, V.S. & Hogan, J.D. (1992). *International psychology: Views from around the world*. Lincoln and London: University of Nebraska Press.

Shiel, C., Williams, A. & Mann, S. (2005). *Global perspectives and sustainable development in the curriculum: Enhanced employability, more thoughtful society?* Bournemouth Learning and Teaching Conference 2005: Enhancing Graduate Employability. Conference proceedings. Retrieved on 10 January 2009 from www.bournemouth.ac.uk/cap/documents/ConfProc2005.pdf

Van Broeck, N. & Lietaer, G. (2008). Psychology and psychotherapy in health care: A review of legal regulations in 17 European countries. *European Psychologist, 13*(1), 53–63.

WENR (2009, Jan./Feb.). Protests against Bologna. *World Education News and Review, 22*(1). Retrieved April 2009 from www.wes.org/ewenr

WHO (World Health Organization) (2008a). *Policies and practices for mental health – meeting the challenges*. Denmark: WHO.

WHO (World Health Organization) (2008b). *Scaling up care for mental, neurological, and substance use disorders*. Geneva: World Health Organization.

# Those We Serve?
## *Student Issues and Solutions*

### Caprice Lantz

I take pride in knowing the names of all my students
you are PSY/375/M

This chapter covers the following areas:

- issues in teaching large groups;
- working with diverse students;
- teaching sensitive topics;
- ethical issues in teaching;
- helping students think about and prepare for careers.

## What Student Issues?

Changes occurring in UK higher education (HE) in recent years have had a profound impact on the nature of the relationship between lecturers and students. The introduction of tuition fees has resulted in a more customer-like culture with students concerned about getting value for money. As well, the increasingly competitive job market and recent economic downturn have led students to be more concerned with employment opportunities, especially as many students today go to university to enhance their employment prospects.

Government initiatives have also impacted HE teaching. Drives toward widening participation, developing a more educated workforce and internationalisation have created far larger and more diverse campuses. Once elite, most institutions now cater to ever larger numbers of students with backgrounds reflecting most every variation of ethnicity, nationality, disability, sexual orientation and health status. Classes of students numbering in the hundreds now challenge lecturers not only because of sheer numbers but because of the increasing diversity of student needs.

Technological advances have also created new challenges by raising questions regarding what lecturers must do to reach the up and coming generation of students who some suggest have advanced technological skills and expectations (Prensky, 2001a, 2001b). Virtual learning environments, blogs and wikis, social networking sites, pod-casting, mobile phones and virtual reality games are just some of the technologies now impacting relationships with students.

This chapter provides an overview of student issues that impact teaching practice as well as some strategies and starting points for lecturers for addressing those issues. Whilst far from comprehensive, it approaches the most salient issues in teaching today, some of which are alluded to above and others which are of particular relevance to the discipline.

## Students, Students Everywhere

Lecturers have a variety of concerns about teaching large classes. Managing marking, gauging student understanding, dealing with incivilities, conducting group activities, maintaining student attention, and helping students to learn are just a few. Likewise students have concerns. Difficulty asking questions, getting to know other students, approaching lecturers, getting helpful feedback and feeling anonymous are some. These difficulties highlight the need for lecturers to consider issues around large group teaching in order to help students overcome these issues and get the most out of classes, but also to help themselves operate more comfortably and effectively in large group situations.

## *Student engagement in large groups*

Some lecturers may believe that it is difficult to do much of anything with large groups except lecture and may feel compelled to 'cover' as much as possible in the time allowed. However, research suggests that students' attention begins to drift after just 15 minutes (Biggs, 1999; Bligh, 1998). So while large groups may be more unwieldy, it is important to use a variety of teaching methods and activities which can help students pay attention and learn. As well, it is important not to cover too much which can actually interfere with learning (Bligh, 1998) and can lead students to adopt a shallow learning approach (Marton & Saljö, 1976).

Research suggests that lecturers should strive to do something different about every 15 minutes to help to improve students' concentration and learning. A change can be a period of silence which students use to ponder and consolidate material (Bligh, 1998), a change of media, a demonstration which involves a student, or it can be asking students to write about or discuss the preceding 10 minutes of the lecture (Lantz, 2009). Some lecturers use electronic voting systems (EVSs), also known as handsets or clickers, to both change activity and assess students' understanding of what has been presented. EVSs allow lecturers to pose questions that students then answer using electronic key pads. Aggregate answers display on a screen providing the entire class with interactivity and immediate feedback (Draper, 2008).

Some suggest that students who feel less connected to their lecturers and classmates tend to be less committed (Wolcowitz, 1984). Students who do not feel connected might find it easier to miss class, leave questions unasked (Lantz, 2009) or be more likely to cheat (MacDonald, 2008). Connecting with each student becomes increasingly difficult as class sizes grow; however, there are ways that lecturers can help students feel more connected. While it is probably impossible to learn student names when class sizes number in the hundreds, Biggs (1999) notes that learning and using just some student names helps all students feel more connected. Lecturers can also facilitate connectivity by using good eye contact which makes students feel individually recognised (Goss-Lucas & Bernstein, 2005). Arriving early and talking with different groups of students before class can also be helpful (Zakrajsek, 2007).

Students who arrive late, leave early, sleep, use mobile phones, talk during class or are otherwise disruptive can be problematic in any class but can be more of a problem in large classes. When encountering such behaviours, it is important to remember that there might be reasonable explanations for students' behaviour and not to automatically assume the worst. Students may sleep because they had to work late, be late for class because a child-minder did not arrive, or may be absent frequently because of unreliable transportation (Lantz, 2009). Behaviours such as these may signal a student that needs help rather than a reprimand; considering such explanations helps to facilitate a calm and reasonable approach to addressing such issues. As well, a number of techniques have been found to be effective in preventing such behaviours. For instance, Race (2005) suggests providing guidelines for students during the first class addressing phone use, late arrivals, early departures, talking, etc. Revisiting the concept of connectedness, social psychology research suggests people who feel anonymous feel less personally responsible, reinforcing the importance of forming connections with students in this case to mitigate these behaviours (Zakrajsek, 2007). Finally, Boice (2000) suggests that lecturers use pro-social motivators rather than threats and guilt to address behavioural issues (e.g. 'How can I help make that clearer for you?' or 'You can do better!').

### Assessment and feedback

According to the National Student Survey (HEFCE, 2007), students are more dissatisfied with assessment and feedback than other areas of teaching, which stands to reason as assessment and feedback techniques that work in classes of 30 do not work well at all in classes of 100+. However, a variety of options exists which can help lecturers to provide opportunities for formative assessment and feedback in reasonable timescales while keeping workloads manageable.

Goss-Lucas and Bernstein (2005) suggest assigning one-page papers which can be assessed quickly using scoring rubrics that reduce marking time and result in more valid and reliable feedback (Stevens & Levi, 2005). Zakrajsek (2007) suggests strategies for developing rubrics which include identifying the most important points to assess. Pro forma sheets that list assessment criteria with places for tick marks and comments can also save time. Providing group feedback by distributing and reviewing outlines of common mistakes, characteristics of quality answers, and commonly needed explanations directly after students hand in assessments provides some immediate feedback, saves time, and can increase learning (Race, 2005).

Self and peer assessment provide another option for large classes. While lecturers may think that such techniques are more appropriate for small classes, staff involved in Boud's (1995) study indicated that they spent about

75 per cent of the time preparing and administering the large-group self and peer assessment schemes that they would have spent using conventional marking methods. Boud noted that for small classes, conventional marking actually takes less time than self and peer assessment methods and that it is when classes are larger that time saving really increases. In addition to benefits in student learning, this technique might well lead to a reduction in tedium for lecturers who can replace stacks of marking with less onerous tasks.

Finally, some lecturers are using audio feedback (JISC, 2008) and electronic feedback (Denton *et al.*, 2008). While it is relatively early days for these technologies, some research suggests that they are time saving, preferred by students (who may favour hi-tech forms of feedback) and lecturers (Denton, 2003).

## Independent Learning

Fostering autonomous learning in students is a cornerstone of UK HE and with increased class sizes it is more important than ever to develop student autonomy early on. However, the increased diversity of student backgrounds makes this more challenging. Student attitudes and performance in self-directed learning situations are largely dependent upon previous experiences (Higgs, 1988). Students from backgrounds where traditional teaching and learning methods are common and students who have had negative experiences with independent learning will be more difficult to engage.

In an effort to encourage students in embracing autonomy, some lecturers may think that offering courses that provide maximum student autonomy are good. However, if students have little or negative experiences with this approach, it is likely to be counterproductive and may simply lead to more negative experiences (Boud, 1988) and student failure (Cornwall, 1988). However, there are several methods to introduce students to autonomous learning more slowly. For instance, Higgs (1988) advocates introducing self-directed learning using a rating tool that can spur small-group discussions in which students reflect on and discuss their learning behaviours. Also, discussing the benefits of self-directed learning (e.g. preparation for responding quickly to changing environments faced throughout life) can help students to understand why this is important (Boud, 1988).

Cornwall (1988) suggests providing students with a clear framework for autonomous learning which includes ensuring that there are clear goals, necessary materials and support available, understanding of the roles and responsibilities for lecturers and students, adequate preparation, possibilities to develop some requisite skills without fear of failure, and periodic checks which can indicate if changes to activities are needed. He notes that although encouraging autonomous learning involves a gradual weaning process which can prove challenging and takes time, it is well worth it to students in the long term as they are able to more effectively and independently manage their studies and lives.

## Students Come in All Shapes and Sizes

Today, the UK's widening participation agenda has opened the doors of HE institutions to nontraditional students, offering them valuable experiences and the chance to improve employment prospects and circumstances. Likewise, the UK's drive towards internationalisation has encouraged increasing numbers of international students to study in the UK. Widening participation and internationalisation bring with them many potential benefits for individuals as well as for society. Bringing together individuals from diverse backgrounds allows for the development of relationships between diverse students which can promote tolerance and mutual respect. However, this diversity challenges lecturers by requiring them to take into account a much wider array of backgrounds, skills and personal circumstances. Indeed some lecturers see these initiatives as a threat to traditional academic standards. However, others argue that they are important not only to promote diversity but to use as a tool for valuable learning (Swenson, 1982), relevant to an increasingly complex globalized world.

The following provides information and suggestions for working with different groups of students although this does not imply homogeneity in any group. Also, while it does not cover every student variation, the topics were chosen based on the most common concerns today and many suggestions apply across groups.

### Born with a chip (digital natives)

In 2001, Marc Prensky published two papers describing what he defined as the new generation of students, those who grew up with computers, video-games, digital music players, video equipment, mobile phones and other digital devices. Prensky suggested that this technology laden environment defined the generation, which he termed 'digital natives'. Prensky and others, who sometimes refer to this group as the 'net generation', 'I-POD generation', or 'millennials', suggest that these students think differently; are said to prefer multitasking and active learning; are able to take in and process information rapidly; and heavily use digital technologies to access information and interact with others (Frand, 2000; Oblinger, 2003; Prensky 2001a, 2001b).

It is no surprise that simultaneously, Prensky and others (Frand, 2000; Oblinger, 2003) suggested that a gap existed between digital natives and those termed 'digital immigrants' (e.g. those who learned to use technology later so were 'foreigners'). They also suggested that pedagogical models needed to be adjusted to teach this new generation effectively and suggested measures such as speeding up instruction and providing random access to information to cater for differences in how this new generation learn.

The concepts of generations and generational gaps are not new (e.g., Baby Boomers and Generation X), however, they can be problematic because they risk stereotyping large groups of people which some argue has happened with digital natives (Kennedy *et al.*, 2008). Likewise, educators may engage in an educational panic, jumping quickly into reforms based not on evidence but on assumptions (Bennett *et al.*, 2008).

Since 2001, researchers have been questioning the assertions made about digital natives and carrying out research to examine the arguments. What they have found is that today's students have a complex mix of backgrounds, skills, knowledge and preferences. A critical review of the evidence by Bennett *et al.* (2008) finds, for instance, that teenage internet and video-game use vary considerably based on such factors as socio-economic status and sex. Others have found the use of some technologies is not as prevalent as one might think. One study found, for instance, that use of social networking software such as Facebook was used by less than 25 per cent of students regularly while nearly 63 per cent had never logged in (Kennedy *et al.*, 2008). Also, students today are increasingly comprised not only of traditional-aged students but mature students who do not fit neatly into the digital native category (Lorenzo *et al.*, 2006). As well, cognitive psychologists suggest that multitasking, which many digital natives are reported to engage in and prefer, and which is endorsed for use in an educational context by Prensky and others, can contribute to losses in concentration and diminished learning (Rubinstein *et al.*, 2001; Sweller, 1988). Finally, preferences or styles of learning vary individually and can hardly be attributed to an entire generation (Bennett *et al.*, 2008). If much of what is being said about this new generation of students and the educational changes they should be ushering in is unsubstantiated, then what are the student issues of this generation?

## *Information quantity, quality and availability*

In his book, *Information Anxiety*, Wurman (2003, p.32) draws attention to the dramatic explosion of information now available by noting that 'a week-day edition of the *New York Times* contains more information than the average person was likely to come across in a lifetime in seventeenth-century England.' Halpern (2009) notes that because of this proliferation of information, and specifically information of variable quality, it is increasingly important to help students develop critical thinking skills in order to effectively evaluate sources and arguments. While we may think that students know what reliable sources of information are, some studies find otherwise. One (Lorenzo *et al.*, 2006) for instance notes that only 2 per cent of students use their library as a starting point when looking for information and 72 per cent rank internet search engines as their first choice.

The ready availability of information on the internet and students use of it for research has heightened concerns about plagiarism which are well founded. Roberts (2008) notes that, according to the Centre for Academic Integrity, academic misconduct increased threefold from 1999 to 2005. One survey found that out of 700 undergraduates surveyed, 25 per cent reported online cutting-and-pasting without citing sources and in another survey of 35,000 students, 36 per cent reported engaging in cut-and-paste plagiarism one or more times. Roberts also suggests that these studies may represent the lower limits of incidences since many students may be afraid to admit to such practices. Plagiarism and academic integrity, therefore, have been raised as central issues for many students in this new generation. Chapter 8 in this book provides a more detailed discussion.

## *Using technology in teaching*

While the concept of digital natives is not as widely applicable as some suggest, generally the younger generation tends to be more adept with technology and may benefit from, and be quite comfortable with, approaches that integrate it in teaching and learning environments. Furthermore, the proliferation and potential usefulness of technology in education cannot be denied and many educational research studies now focus on the effective use of technology in teaching. A recent study, for instance, found that the use of virtual reality technology to expose students directly to psychological treatments helped to develop student understanding of treatments (Stark-Wroblewski *et al.*, 2008). Another by Hove and Corcoran (2008) found that

*lectures online = higher grades*
*& not signif.*
*decrease in att.ce*

30                                    *Caprice Lantz*

making lecture presentation material available online led to an increase in student grades without significant decreases in attendance. Studies such as these contribute to the mounting body of evidence that supports the use of technology in teaching (e.g. Hewson & Charlton, 2007; White *et al.*, 2005) and hopefully it is such research that will inform further integrations (Bennett *et al.*, 2008).

### Multitasking

In line with the argument of Preskey and others, some students insist that they work more effectively and feel less stressed when multitasking which often occurs through the use of technologies (e.g. typing an essay while talking on a mobile, watching a YouTube video, and instant messaging a friend). A half a century ago, researchers began exploring how effectively the brain can deal with competing demands (e.g. Broadbent, 1958). Since then a body of mounting evidence suggests that multitasking is problematic. A summary of research from Bannister and Remenyl (2008) suggests that the effectiveness of the brain is substantially reduced during multitasking and leads to increased fatigue, an inability to recall details and raised stress and adrenaline levels. Other research (e.g. Rubinstein *et al.*, 2001) suggests that learning with attention divided does not support long-term memory and understanding, and that switching between tasks can reduce productivity by some 40 per cent.

While students may feel as if they are more productive and relaxed when multitasking, it may be more a case of them being accustomed to and therefore comfortable while multitasking than they would if confronted with silence or concentrating on a single task (Dzubak, 2008). Also, researchers have raised concerns about how overstimulation may result in a lack of relaxation and reflection time leading to excessive levels of anxiety which could result in other problems, some suggest attention deficit disorder. Entire books (e.g. DeGrandpre, 1999; Hallowell, 2006) have explored this idea of today's fast paced, overstimulated society and the potentially damaging effects it has on individuals.

Although technology can be useful in teaching and may be particularly appealing to some students, perhaps what is called for by lecturers is to help students take a step back and realise that, although they may be accustomed and even crave multitasking, it may be to their detriment on a number of levels. While students may say they enjoy it (some also enjoy smoking!), research suggests that often it is not to their benefit.

## You're from Where?

International students in the UK are considered those who have come from another country to study. They may have come from countries within or outside of the EU but their most important characteristic is that they come from different cultures and often English is not their first language (Trahar, 2008).

International students account for about 15 per cent of all students throughout UK universities; however, in some programmes they account for much larger percentages, making up, for instance, approximately 66 per cent of taught postgraduate level courses (UKISA, 2008). While the recruitment of international students has blossomed in recent years, lecturers who are unfamiliar with the unique issues that they bring can find working with them a challenge.

Although collectively referred to as 'international students', it is important to highlight that they are by no means homogeneous. Coming from a multitude of cultures, their experiences of teaching and learning environments vary substantially as do their more general concerns around studying in the UK. Becoming familiar with the pedagogy and issues of all of the cultures represented among international students may be quite impractical for lecturers (Biggs, 2003); however, a growing body of evidence exists outlining the issues faced by international students generally as well as strategies by which to address them (e.g. Caroll & Ryan, 2005). Limited research exists as well (e.g. Craig & Trapp, 2008; Higgins & Zheng, 2002) which may elucidate issues particular to psychology students.

### *Lack of representation*

Perhaps unsurprisingly, international students raise concerns regarding curriculum being UK-centric and not necessarily applicable to their home countries. While it stands to reason that courses taught in the UK would be more focused on UK practice, lecturers might consider ways to integrate more international perspectives by making use of the experiences of international students which could provide welcome perspectives for home students as well, as evidenced by the following comment. When asked about how the curriculum provides an international perspective, one psychology student noted that the curriculum is not 'opening avenues where we can compare and contrast or delve into the way that people work and the way that different cultures might approach psychology – which is what I am interested in' (Hyland *et al.*, 2008, p.15). Providing opportunities for students to discuss cultural differences related to content and inviting international students to describe what they find surprising or different from their home cultures might go a long way towards 'internationalising' the curriculum (Trahar, 2008).

Another important point with regard to UK-centric curriculum is that lecturers consider how approaches to curriculum in other countries might impact students' understanding. For example, the way in which cultural traditions frame depression in China is very different from the UK. This could interfere with student learning about the topic from a UK perspective (Higgins & Zheng, 2002). As discussed later in Reddy and Lantz's chapter on misconceptions, lecturers may wish to address these differences not only to help students feel as if the curriculum is more inclusive but to facilitate students in exploring differences which may be more likely to create lasting changes in students' perceptions of different topics.

## Loneliness and isolation

International students often report feelings of loneliness and isolation (UKCOSA, 2004). Being far from home and away from friends and family, entering a new culture, and potentially learning in a second language are just some of the challenges leading to such feelings. Related to this, international students note difficulty in forming relationships with home students (Hyland *et al.*, 2008) and a lack of mixing between cultures is well reported (e.g. UKCOSA, 2004). This not only has the potential to contribute to isolation, but it can potentially diminish international students' opinions of the UK as well as diminishing their overall experiences. The dearth in cross-cultural relationships experienced by students is an unfortunate loss for home students as well, who miss opportunities to learn about and appreciate diversity through interacting with students from other cultures (Pearce, 1998).

Some lecturers foster cross-cultural relationships and combat student loneliness by creating mixed cultural groups for classroom activities. However, it is important to do this with care as issues on both sides may impact students' receptiveness. For instance, some international students indicate that they are so overwhelmed with adapting to the UK that mixed cultural groups simply result in more unwelcome stress. Also, UK students sometimes report being wary of working with international students who they think might not have a grasp of English or be active contributors (Hyland *et al.*, 2008). Lecturers may therefore wish to consider when to allow students to form their own groups (which are often with those from the same culture) and when to direct group formation. Also, it is important to outline group members' responsibilities and establish grading policies that are fair to all group members. Trahar (2008) also suggests facilitating the planning of group meetings between classes which, to international students accustomed to heavier timetables, can seem long. This might also help to reduce loneliness and encourage preparation.

## Language

Lecturers in a recent focus group discussed the low standards of English accepted at some universities and lamented the consequences of admitting students who struggle with course requirements due to low-level English ability (Hyland *et al.*, 2008). However, even international students with reasonable English skills can struggle with lecturers who speak quickly and use idioms, proverbs, or humour which are unfamiliar to them. Simple awareness of language issues can help lecturers to check themselves and eliminate those things from their speech that might cause difficulty. Shortcomings in students' English skills might not be as easy to address; it is therefore important to be aware of and refer struggling students to appropriate support services. In some larger departments where English skills have been an issue, subject-specific credit-bearing modules to improve international students' language skills have had some success (e.g. English in Psychology) (Hyland *et al.*, 2008).

## Pedagogy

Some international students who undertake study in the UK undergo an academic culture shock when confronted with differences in pedagogy. For instance, many Chinese students view higher education as a didactic process in which the lecturer imparts knowledge to them whilst their roles are to passively listen and absorb (Foster, 2008). This approach is rather at odds with that promoted in the UK which encourages active learning, student independence, and planning one's own study. The following quotes illustrate other cultural differences.

I sometimes did not enjoy the discussion … because some discussion topics are vague and I found it difficult to talk … we Japanese are not given many chances to discuss in classrooms. (MSc psychology student, Japan) (Craig & Trapp, 2008, p.7)

The structure of exams was quite different to what I have previously done in the USA. Exams are normally a mixture of multiple choice, essay, short essay, or fill in the blank. Here all of my exams were essay-based. (MSc psychology student, US/Poland) (Craig & Trapp, 2008, p.10)

Differences in learning and teaching typically lead students to question their approaches to learning and attempt to change them, but each student reacts slightly differently and proceeds through the process of adjustment at different paces (Foster, 2008). While there are various techniques lecturers might use to address individual issues, one general piece of advice is to explain the reasoning behind pedagogical approaches used and to allow students time to discuss them and raise issues of concern (Trahar, 2008). A second is to use judgement in making allowances. For example, Trahar (2008, p.21) notes 'I have sought to achieve a balance between "telling" students what to read and recognising that being faced with an extensive reading list without any direction can be overwhelming for them. Highlighting those texts that are highly recommended and providing copies of essential reading can be extremely helpful and begin to diminish anxieties.'

## I Never Would Have Guessed

Government documents such as the Dearing Report promote inclusivity by extending the benefits of higher education to individuals from a variety of backgrounds. Inclusive access is a welcome advance in higher education institutions (HEIs). However, Skelton (1999) and others suggest that it falls short of addressing the 'lived experience' because adding numbers of diverse people to universities does not automatically remedy campus climate, culture and curriculum which, although inclusive in number, can reinforce stereotypes, prejudice and exclusivity.

Not a lot is known about the learning and teaching experiences of lesbian, gay, bisexual and transgender (LGBT) students. Epstein (1994) argues that it has been a neglected area partially because lecturers want to avoid it, viewing sexuality as private and not part of the public domain of education. Although sexuality may be in the private domain, LGBT students are faced with the issue of disclosure perhaps on a daily basis. For instance, while heterosexual students can openly talk about their boyfriends and girlfriends, LGBT students must continually make decisions as to whether or not to mention their partner. Therefore being LGBT is not just a private matter but very much impacts people's public lives.

According to a recent study of UK HE psychology lesbian and bisexual female students, there are many issues which highlight the need for concern. Study participants routinely feel isolated and noted that they do not find enough role models in the academic environment. They report experiencing homophobic attitudes, language and incidents. Regarding the content of the curriculum, these same students felt separated from the content, felt lesbians and bisexuals lacked visibility in research and content, and found content to be sexist and andocentric (Pearson & Smith, 2006).

A similar study of gay and bisexual males' accounts of their experiences had similar findings with some reporting that they felt they had to 'translate' course material to offset the psychological research's tendency towards heteronormative assumptions (Hodges & Pearson, 2008).

While some lecturers might think that LGBT students come to psychology looking for explanations as to their sexual orientations, researchers suggest this is not the case (Hodges & Pearson, 2008; Pearson & Smith, 2006). However, what some students do expect but do not find is a more progressive environment: 'I had this incredibly romantic idea of academia being … wonderfully liberal and I would never hear anything that would be remotely negative towards sexuality' (Smith *et al.*, 2006, slide 16).

One of the recommendations to help improve the experiences of LGBT students is awareness training for staff (Hodges & Pearson, 2008) but perhaps for students as well. Work in this area would be particularly appropriate for some psychologists given the subject matter (e.g. identifying and reducing stereotypes by encouraging empathy) (Clarke & Peel, 2007).

Smith *et al.* (2006) suggests that lecturers carefully consider their own values and beliefs concerning sexuality and other issues to identify their own potential biases. Lecturers might also consider ways to open up possibilities for small-group discussion of issues. Barker (2006) encourages LGBT lecturers to consider their own thoughts on disclosure. Heterosexual lecturers regularly use anecdotes about significant others. While LGBT lecturers may feel they put themselves in a vulnerable position by using similar anecdotes, not doing so may reinforce heterosexism and deprive LGBT students of much-welcomed role models.

Butler (2008) produced a short educational film, *Homoworld,* to help lecturers and students to gain a better understanding of the experiences of the

LGBT community. The film portrays the world as heterophobic, one in which being gay and lesbian is normal and heterosexuals are in a minority. This 17-minute DVD is available at no charge to UK psychology academics who wish to improve their own or their students' understanding of the experience of LGBT students.

## What's Nontraditional Anyway?

The massification of HE has transformed a once academically elite system into one that must cater to increasingly variable sets of students' skills and capabilities. While previously students were expected to have the ability to work independently and keep up with material in a more 'sink or swim' environment, the need to cater to differing levels of ability and life circumstances has become important in order to promote the retention of nontraditional (e.g. widening participation) students. Nontraditional students are generally thought to be those from low economic status or minority groups; disabled, mature, or first-generation university students; and refugees (Crosling *et al.*, 2008). While some suggest that this term is no longer appropriate since it refers to a highly diverse group that may soon outnumber traditional students, it is used here for convenience as many of the issues described impact across this group.

The rate of withdrawals in HEIs that have a greater proportion of nontraditional students has been increasing (Select Committee on Education and Employment (SCEE), 2001), suggesting that these students are more at risk of abandoning their courses before completion. Students withdraw for reasons such as poor academic skills, personal or financial pressures, lack of support and feelings of isolation (Zinkiewicz & Trapp, 2004). A student who is married and has children, for example, while often highly motivated, also needs family time and may encounter childhood illnesses or care issues making it difficult to meet academic obligations. Whilst early withdrawal is generally thought to be a negative outcome, it is not always. Some who withdraw early eventually study elsewhere (SCEE, 2001) and others go on to satisfying lives and careers without completing university.

While reasons for early withdrawal are many and often complex, some studies suggest that it is the nature of an institution's teaching and learning environment that is the deciding factor. For instance, when Davies (1999) compared students who had withdrawn with those who had not, there were not significant differences in incidence of personal problems, financial difficulties, or job and study conflicts. However, there were significant differences in perceptions of learning environments. Helpful and supportive teachers seemed to be most related to whether or not students were current or withdrawn. Laing and Robinson (2003) also suggest that the teaching environment is of primary importance.

Most HEIs today have adopted the Student Life Cycle model (HEFCE, 2001; Layer *et al.*, 2002) to meet the needs of students from widening participation backgrounds. The model includes initial stages of aspiration-raising and pre-entry support but more relevant here are the later stages which cover the support provided in the first term and moving through courses. The highest withdrawal times appear to be early in the first term and at the end of the first year so efforts are often concentrated during these times (Zinkiewicz & Trapp, 2004).

While departments may offer induction programmes targeting non-traditional students, lecturers also have an important role to play in retention through teaching practice. The following provides a few suggestions.

- As with international students, isolation is often an issue for nontraditional students. In addition to the suggestions above, Allen (2000) advocates encouraging students to join psychology-specific campus organisations as well as the British Psychological Society Student Members' Group or the Psychology Postgraduate Affairs Group.
- With life's competing demands, nontraditional students who often have timetabling issues appreciate flexibility in general but also through the provision of virtual learning environments (Newlin & Wang, 2002).
- As noted earlier, good practice suggests clearly outlining for students what is expected from them. This can be particularly helpful for students who have not been in educational settings for some time (Grover, 2006) and those with many time demands. This can also provide an opportunity to discuss dealing with time demands effectively and recognising the importance of non-academic responsibilities.
- As nontraditional students may lack confidence in academic skills, it is important to demonstrate confidence in their potential to succeed (Zinkiewicz & Trapp, 2004). Thanking students, even for minimal contributions, providing avenues for less confident students to be heard, and encouraging students who are evidently challenged by the subject matter are just some ways to do this.

## But There's No Lift

Although disabled students are considered nontraditional students, some of the unique issues that they bring to the classroom merit separate attention. The Disability Discrimination Act (DDA) (1995) defined a disability as any 'physical or mental impairment, a specific learning difficulty or health condition that has a substantial and long-term adverse effect on a person's ability to carry out normal day-to-day activities.' The DDA (1995), which was updated in 2005, requires that HEIs promote equality for disabled students across varying functions.

Today disabled students make up a greater proportion of HE students than in previous years. Statistics from the Higher Education Statistics Agency (HESA) as reported by the Improving Provision for Disabled Psychology Students (Craig & Zinckiewicz, in press) show that disabled students made up 2.6 per cent of all students in 1994/95 and this increased to 15.3 per cent in 2007/08. Also disabled psychology students make up a larger proportion of all students. In 2007/08, 8.8 per cent of psychology students declared a disability while in all other subjects 7.15 per cent of students declared disabilities. Out of the disabilities that students disclose, dyslexia is the most common for all students as well as for psychology students. However, many more psychology students declare mental health difficulties (10.6 per cent of the total declaring disabilities) than students in other subjects (5.39 per cent of the total). While there are more disabled psychology students than students in other subjects and particularly more with mental health issues, it is unclear if this is because psychology students are more likely to disclose or because more disabled students study psychology. Additionally, it is speculated that the number of disabled students is actually higher with some avoiding disclosure for fear of discrimination or other reasons (Craig & Zinckiewicz, in press). Regardless, however, statistics do provide an indication that there are substantial numbers of disabled students in psychology and there may be reason for this. Many psychology students, whether disabled or not, believe that psychology focuses on treating people with problems as opposed to being a scientific discipline. Therefore, it is likely that some students study psychology to gain insight into their disabilities and may assume that academic staff will be more sensitive and empathetic and offer more support than academics from other disciplines (IPDIPS, 2009). Such beliefs can lead students to have higher and quite possibly unreasonable expectations of psychology lecturers. The following quotes highlight this (Craig & Zinckiewicz, in press).

They are scientists, but don't appreciate the knowledge they have that explains my behaviour, and how they can help … It is very frustrating. (Student with learning difficulties)

I expected that psychology staff would have a deeper understanding of issues such as chronic pain frustration and the needs of an individual to be included. (Student with multiple sclerosis)

Such evidence suggests the need for psychology lecturers to become aware of good practice when working with disabled students, to consider how students might be helped to realign their expectations, and to ensure that they protect themselves from undue pressure from students.

Good practice from various sources suggests inviting disabled students to disclose their disabilities (e.g. Dittman, 2003; Craig & Zinckiewicz, in press) which can be done verbally as well as in a syllabus or website. Inviting students to disclose demonstrates openness to making adjustments and abiding by rules (Dittman, 2003). Johnson (2002) further suggests talking to disabled students, particularly those with more significant needs, about their preferences and past experiences. In this, way lecturers can tap into the students' knowledge and experience rather than making assumptions. He mentions, for instance, that lecturers sometimes assume that blind students read Braille when today screen readers are actually more common.

When inviting students to disclose, lecturers can also inform them of what to expect in terms of accommodation and support. While it is important to talk about what is provided, this also provides an opportunity to discuss what is not provided (e.g. lecturers are not therapists) and to direct students to appropriate providers.

The Improving Provision for Disabled Psychology Students (Craig & Zinckiewicz, in press) provides comprehensive information on a variety of disabilities in a psychology-specific context based on surveys and interviews with psychology and disability staff, and disabled psychology students. The following provides a sampling of ideas from this and other sources for lecturers who work with disabled students.

- While it is common for departments to require students to participate in psychological research studies, the reality is that study requirements (e.g. must not be colour-blind or dyslexic) can create barriers for disabled students. Help ensure departments offer enough opportunities for disabled students to participate in research (Craig & Zinckiewicz, in press).

- Disabled students can have difficulty in obtaining and completing placements due to problems of accessibility and confusion over who is responsible for helping them (Dittmann, 2003). Help to ensure that training sites accommodate the needs of disabled students.
- Become aware of the signs that might help to identify non-diagnosed disabled students. For instance, students who always hand in work late, write illegibly, listen without taking notes, and are late and disorganised might be dyslexic (Craig & Zinckiewicz, in press).

## Expecting the Unexpected

The emerging view of diverse student populations centres around recognising that 'difference is not an exception ... but something that happens in the natural course of things' (Striker, 1997, p.12). While it is perhaps impossible to be familiar with all possible barriers in teaching and learning, by applying the concept of inclusive practice, lecturers can work towards reducing barriers. Inclusive practice involves developing programmes of study from the outset that decrease potential barriers encountered by students whatever their age, ethnicity, disability, gender, race, religion, sexual orientation, economic status, or personal responsibility. This approach is most commonly viewed through the lens of considering the needs of disabled students which, it has been said, facilitates the development of good practice for all students. Developing inclusive approaches to teaching involves such practices as thinking through the core course requirements, assuming that one or more students will have limitations, avoiding making assumptions about students' abilities and helping to alleviate student anxiety by outlining academic practices used (Gravestock, 2009). The Higher Education Academy and the Psychology Network (2009) recently developed a series of e-bulletins on Inclusive Practice which provide a variety of suggestions for lecturers interested in taking this approach to teaching.

## Is That Ethical?

Lecturers are in positions of authority. New lecturers may doubt this authority, especially those who are close to students in age or younger or those who have limited teaching experience. Alternatively, some lecturers may feel as if they are more like students. Being active in online communities (e.g. Facebook), some may well be 'friends' with people who later became students which can blur relationship boundaries and, as a recent survey suggests, can be viewed quite negatively by students (Shepherd, 2008).

Whatever lecturers feel about their roles, being in a position of power comes with a responsibility to use that power wisely. The BPS (1993) notes that lecturers developing intimate relationships with students 'raise issues of conflict of interest, of trust, confidence and dependency in working relations and of equal treatment in teaching, learning and selection, assessment and research'. While some dual relationships may pass without harm, the risks are high and have the potential to compromise reputations, professional standings and judgement, as well as the mental health of students involved. Additionally, dual relationships may undermine lecturers' relationships with other students (BPS, 1993; Goss-Lucas & Bernstein, 2005).

Despite cautions not to get too close to students, it is important to be aware that at times students may need help that may seem to go beyond the remit of teaching. Students in all disciplines have problems; however, the possibility of them surfacing may be higher in psychology which may attract students seeking to work out their personal problems (Hogan & Kimmel, 1992) and because coursework may involve self-disclosures of a personal nature. Students may also be more likely to approach psychology lecturers in general with the misperception, as previously noted, that they have had clinical training (Haney, 2004).

While student problems may be more of a concern for psychology lecturers in general, new lecturers might be more likely to be approached by students in need if they are close in age and identity. This can be particularly problematic, given that they are least experienced in dealing with student problems and possibly more at risk for crossing boundaries inappropriately.

Whether new or experienced, lecturers must decide on the amount of listening they feel able and qualified to provide and to recognise when it is appropriate to refer students to campus support services (Perlman *et al.*, 2007) as it is unethical to attempt to provide treatment without appropriate qualifications. Haney (2004) suggests that, rather than providing support themselves, lecturers instead focus on identifying students with problems (e.g. those missing classes, not turning in coursework, struggling with assignments) and referring them to appropriate support.

Academic psychologists have recognised the difficulty lecturers have in making decisions around such ethical issues as student support. Haney (2004) discusses several models. One by Kitchener (1985) includes principles of autonomy, ensuring that no harm comes to students, having positive impact, and being fair and just. Haney also proposes one of her own which includes: documenting and reflecting on the concern, generating possible courses of action, consulting with colleagues and ethical boards, analysing courses of action for risks and benefits, and taking action as appropriate.

## You're Just Being Too Sensitive

As noted, psychology is laden with sensitive or controversial topics. Students (and lecturers) often have very strong feelings about these topics and this can lead to uncomfortable classroom situations. Topics such as sexuality, sexual orientation, gender roles, masturbation, ethnicity, religion, child abuse, abortion, rape, aggression, euthanasia, evolution, pornography, racism, prejudice, stereotyping, divorce, parenting, substance use, mental and physical health, and experimentation on animals all fall into the category of potentially sensitive topics (Poe, 2000).

There is much lecturers can do to prepare to teach sensitive topics. Flagging up the fact that sensitive topics will be covered in advance is widely recommended (Goss-Lucas & Bernstein, 2005; Poe, 2000; Russell *et al.*, 2008). This can be done at the beginning of a module (in the syllabus and verbally) as well as a few sessions before topics are to be addressed. Giving students advanced notice allows them to prepare. Lecturers might also ask students to anonymously submit questions or comments about topics in advance which can further students' thinking about topics and provide lecturers with discussion ideas (Brooke, 1999 as discussed in Goss-Lucas & Bernstein, 2005).

Developing ground rules for discussion is also important. Ground rules might include: respecting others' viewpoints, keeping discussions confidential, protecting the anonymity of people used as examples, considering self-disclosures carefully before making them, and noting that it is okay for students to keep their thoughts to themselves if they feel uncomfortable (Poe, 2000). It is also helpful to tell students in advance that some may feel uncomfortable or have emotional reactions and that it is OK to leave class if necessary. Taking time to introduce sensitive topics in this way also provides an opportunity for lecturers to highlight (sensitively) that they cannot serve as therapists but that students can talk through issues that might crop up with campus support services (Russell *et al.*, 2008).

Before teaching sensitive topics, lecturers must also prepare themselves by recognising their own strongly held views and ensuring their impact on teaching is kept to a minimum. As well, while some lecturers might be uncomfortable with various topics, it is important to be able to compartmentalise and to present material in a mature and straightforward way using appropriate terms (Goss-Lucas & Bernstein, 2005).

Research by Silvia (2006) as discussed in Russell *et al.* (2008) suggests additional strategies for addressing sensitive topics. They note that people tend to disagree when they feel that their attitudinal freedom is at risk. Also students may feel personally accused and therefore more defensive if they are part of a group that is being criticised (e.g. English whites being racist towards blacks). To mitigate the effects of potential threats on students, Russell *et al.* (2008) suggest explaining content in less dichotomous terms. For instance, if the lecturer is in the majority (e.g. white English male), he might disclose the ways in which the group he represents has privilege over others. This can help students to be more accepting of their own identity and feel less under attack.

Keeping emotional responses to a minimum can go hand-in-hand with raising the discussion level and helping students to think more critically. Some find it useful to have groups of students study several different viewpoints on a sensitive or controversial topic and then summarise and discuss them. Such approaches can lead to more evidence-based and balanced discussions and prevent emotional outbursts (Allen, 2000; Heuberger *et al.*, 1999).

## It's Not My Job – Or Is It?

Some academics believe that higher education is not vocational and is designed to educate students as opposed to train them for the workplace (Harvey & Knight, 2003). Some perhaps subscribe to intrinsic motivations and undoubtedly pursue careers in academia out of intellectual curiosity. Intrinsic motivation is to be respected and certainly some students take on further study due to such motivations. However, with widening participation and employability initiatives, higher education is becoming more a place where students go to improve their employment prospects and life circumstances. Furthermore, hefty tuition fees now make higher education a financial as well as a time investment and students increasingly expect a return on that investment.

While government initiatives encouraging widely available education are not beyond reproach, they do help students to become more capable of contributing to a world increasingly dominated by knowledge management as opposed to unskilled jobs (Harvey & Knight, 2003). Even academics who support student employability may believe that their responsibility is to the subject and that student employability should be supported by careers services. Whilst centralised careers services offices do provide support, they cannot provide all that students require. Careers offices are sometimes understaffed, serve students from a multitude of disciplines, not all of which they are able to become familiar with, and typically offer generic advice which, while helpful, can lack a disciplinary perspective that can help students to be more effective in career planning and job acquisition. In addition, some students are rooted in their departments and do not venture into careers offices and or take advantage of help available.

All of this may come as a surprise to new lecturers who might be buried under lecture preparation, delivery and associated marking as well as research work. Indeed academics in general are under pressure to respond to increasing numbers of government initiatives while shouldering the burden of heavy workloads. However, employability is no longer just a government initiative but a student concern that should really influence teaching.

Lecturers have the potential to play an important role in helping students prepare for careers. The positions of power that lecturers occupy extend far beyond assigning marks as most students respect and value lecturers' opinions. Therefore, they are well placed to influence students by helping them to begin thinking about careers. Sharing with them a few basic facts is a good start. For instance, many psychology students do not realise that only 20 per cent of students actually become psychologists whilst the majority go into other careers. Whilst many students begin their courses thinking they want to become psychologists, some later decide they want to work at the end of their first degree, psychology is not really for them, or postgraduate programmes are too competitive. Others simply study psychology because it is a broad subject and do not really know what they want to do. This non-vocational nature of the psychology course can make focusing in on a career a struggle for students (Lantz *et al.*, 2008). Lecturers who simply make students aware of such career issues early in their studies might provide the impetus for some to plan differently which could have a profound impact on long-term career outcomes.

Encouraging students to be involved in careers service programmes and inviting careers advisers to classes to provide short talks can also assist students to become engaged in the career preparation process. As well, most universities now offer some type of personal development planning (PDP) programme. PDP helps students to track their learning, progress and achievements to take charge of their personal and career development. PDP includes a variety of thinking and planning activities that can help them work out where they are, where they want to go, and what they need to do to get there (Higher Education Academy, n.d.).

A valuable resource designed for psychology students by the Higher Education Academy Psychology Network, *The psychology student employability guide* (Lantz *et al.*, 2008) outlines the benefits of PDP as well and describes how to use it. Written for students, this guide also includes psychology graduate employment trends, concerns for psychology graduates, emerging career areas, and a variety of career exercises and job search resources. It is available at cost for students through the Psychology Network and is downloadable at no charge from the website. Also available online is the guide *Enhancing the employability of psychology graduates* (Akhurst, 2003). Designed for psychology lecturers, this guide explains employability and provides a variety of suggestions for ways in which lecturers can begin to integrate employability into the curriculum.

## It's Just the Beginning

From increasingly large groups to students who are simply aiming for gainful employment, it is clear that there are many challenges facing UK HE lecturers. Whilst this chapter provides some starting points, it should be noted that research and support in general around teaching and learning has gained significant ground in recent years. The Dearing Report in 1997 (NCIHE) and the subsequent white paper, *The Future of Higher Education* (DfES, 2003), resulted in the creation of the Higher Education Academy and the Centres for Excellence in Teaching and Learning (CETL) (Higher Education Academy, 2009, February). The Higher Education Academy and its 24 subject centres champion the cause of teaching by recognising teaching excellence through the National Teaching Fellowship scheme and other awards, supporting teaching innovations through project funding, sponsoring events around teaching issues and innovations, and providing avenues for the dissemination of research into teaching. Institutions are also placing more emphasis on teaching with most now offering training courses leading to postgraduate certificates in teaching and learning and grants to support teaching and learning research and innovations.

Whilst it may be a challenging time for HE teaching, it is also a propitious time for teaching developments, and academic psychologists are well placed to contribute to this important area of research and practice development.

## Key Messages

- Research suggests that students in large groups can be engaged and actively learn when lecturers use a variety of innovative methods.
- While working with diverse student populations is more of a challenge for lecturers, if managed well, diversity can be a tool to enhance learning.
- Students and lecturers can have strong reactions to a wide range of psychological topics. Knowing the topics that provoke reactions, preparing for them in advance and handling them sensitively are key methods in avoiding uncomfortable situations and facilitating learning.
- Ethical standards can be tricky to navigate, however, lecturers have a responsibility to ensure they have a positive impact on students and that their treatment of them is fair and just (Kitchener, 1985).
- Contrary to what some might think, lecturers have an important role to play in helping students to consider their career goals.

## Research Questions

These may be at a high or a lower level:

1. What are the most effective methods by which to encourage independent learning in students?
2. Do students respond better to audio and electronic feedback than to more traditional forms of feedback?
3. How can student diversity be used to its best advantage to help students to learn about, tolerate and appreciate diverse perspectives?
4. What are effective methods by which lecturers can demonstrate to students the negative impact that multitasking has on learning?
5. How much of an impact do lecturers who embed employability-related content into their modules have on the career perceptions and outcomes of psychology students?

# References

Akhurst, J. (2003). *Enhancing the employability of psychology graduates.* Higher Education Academy Psychology Network. Retrieved on 27 January 2009 from www.psychology.heacademy.ac.uk/docs/pdf/p20050412_Enhancing Employability.pdf

Allen, M.J. (2000). Teaching non-traditional students. *APS Observer, 13.* Association for Psychological Sciences. Retrieved on 19 March 2009 from www.psychologicalscience.org/teaching/tips/tips_0900.html

Bannister, F. & Remenyl, D. (2008, September). *Multitasking: The uncertain impact of technology on knowledge workers and managers.* Paper presented at the 2nd European Conference on Information Management and Evaluation. Royal Holloway, University of London. Retrieved on 29 April 2009 from http://books.google.co.uk/books?id=uxI0QTPBkZQC&printsec=frontcover&source=gbs_summary_s&cad=0

Barker, M. (2006). Critical sexology: Sexual self-disclosure and outness in academia and the clinic. *Lesbian & Gay Psychology Review, 7*(3), 292–295.

Bennett, S., Maton, K. & Kervin, L. (2008). The 'digital natives' debate: A critical review of the evidence. *British Journal of Educational Technology, 39*(5), 775–786.

Biggs, J.B. (1999). *Teaching for quality learning at university.* Society for Research in Higher Education and the Open University Press.

Biggs, J.B. (2003). *Teaching for quality learning at university* (2nd edn). Buckingham: SRHE and the Open University.

Bligh, D. (1998). *What's the use of lectures?* Exeter: Intellect Books.

Boice, R. (2000). *Advice for new faculty members.* Boston: Allyn and Bacon.

BPS (1993). *Sexual harassment at work and the ethics of dual relationships.* Retrieved on 22 January 2009 from www.bps.org.uk/the-society/code-of-conduct/sexual-harassment-at-work-and-the-ethics-of-dual-relationships.cfm

Boud, D. (1988). *Developing student autonomy in learning.* New York: Nicholas Publishing.

Boud, D. (1995). *Enhancing learning through self-assessment.* London: Kogan Page.

Broadbent, D.E. (1958). *Perception and communication.* London: Pergamon.

Brooke, C. (1999). Feelings from the back row: Negotiating sensitive issues in large classes. *New Directions in Teaching and Learning, 77,* 23–33.

Butler, C. (2008). *Homoworld.* University of East London and Clevermax Productions/ Higher Education Academy Psychology Network.

Caroll, J. & Ryan, J. (Eds.) (2005). *Teaching international students: Improving learning for all.* Abingdon: Routledge.

Clarke, V., & Peel, E. (Eds.) (2007). *Out in psychology: Lesbian, gay, bisexual, trans, and queer perspectives.* Chichester, UK: Wiley.

Cornwall, M. (1988). Putting it into practice: Promoting independent learning in a traditional institution. In D. Boud (Ed.) *Developing student autonomy in learning* (pp.242–257). London: Kogan Page.

Craig, N. & Trapp, A. (2008). *A pilot study exploring the student learning experience from a disciplinary perspective.* Higher Education Academy Psychology Network. Retrieved on 10 May 2009 from www.psychology.heacademy.ac.uk/docs/pdf/p20081112_International_Project_Report.pdf

Craig, N. & Zinckiewicz, L. (in press). *Inclusion in psychology higher education.* York: Higher Education Academy Psychology Network

Crosling, G., Thomas, L. & Heagney, M. (2008). *Improving student retention in higher education: The role of teaching and learning.* London: Routledge.

Davies, P. (1999). *Student retention in further education: A problem of quality or of student finance?* Paper presented at British Educational Research Association Conference, University of Sussex, 2–5 September. Retrieved on 18 March 2009 from www.leeds.ac.uk/educol/documents/00001257.doc

DeGrandpre, R.J. (1999). *Ritalin nation: Rapid-fire culture and the transformation of human consciousness.* W.W. Norton and Company.

Denton, P. (2003). *Evaluation of the 'electronic feedback' marking assistant …* (pp.157–173). Proceedings of the 7th International Computer Aided Assessment Conference Learning and Teaching Development: Loughborough.

Denton, P., Roberts, M., Madden J., & Rowe P. (2008). Students' response to traditional and computer-assisted formative feedback: A comparative case study. *British Journal of Educational Technology, 39,* 486–500.

DfES (2003). *White Paper on Higher Education.* Retrieved on 27 January 2008 from www.dcsf.gov.uk/hegateway/uploads/White%20Pape.pdf

Disability Discrimination Act (DDA) (1995). Retrieved on 30 January 2009 from www.opsi.gov.uk/acts/acts1995/ukpga_19950050_en_1

Dittman, M. (2003). Improving accessibility in psychology programs. *Monitor on Psychology, 34*(1). Retrieved on 29 January 2009 from www.apa.org/monitor/jan03/accessibility.html

Draper, S. (2008). *Electronic voting systems and interactive lectures: Voting lobby.* Retrieved 12 January 2009 from www.psy.gla.ac.uk/~steve/ilig/

Dzubak, C.M. (2008). Multitasking: The good, the bad, and the unknown. *The Journal of the Association for the Tutoring Profession.* Retrieved on 10 May 2009 from www.jsu.edu/dept/edprof/atp/ejournal.htm#Multitasking:%C2%A0_The_good,_the_bad,_and_the_unknown. Also available at: www.myatp.org/Synergy_1/Syn_6.pdf

Epstein, D. (1994). *Challenging lesbian and gay inequality in education.* Buckingham: Open University Press.

Foster, M. (2008). *Enhancing the experience of Chinese students in UK higher education – lessons from a collaborative project.* London: Staff and Educational Development Association (SEDA).

Frand, J. (2000, Sept./Oct.). The information-age mindset: Changes in students and implications for higher education. *EDUCAUSE Review,* 15–24.

Goss-Lucas, S.G. & Bernstein, D.A. (2005). *Teaching psychology: A step by step guide*. London: Lawrence Erlbaum Associates.

Gravestock, P. (2009). *Inclusive curriculum practices*. Higher Education Academy and Psychology Network. Retrieved on 9 June 2009 from www.psychology.heacademy.ac.uk/networks/sig/icp.asp

Grover, C.A. (2006). Teaching and mentoring non-traditional students. In W. Buskist & S.F. Davis (Eds.) *The handbook of the teaching of psychology* (pp.149–152). Oxford: Blackwell Publishing.

Hallowell, E.M. (2006). *CrazyBusy*. New York: Random House.

Halpern, D.F. (2009, January). *Teaching and assessing critical thinking: Better thinking skills really can be a college outcome*. Presented at the Society for the Teaching of Psychology Online Conference: Reaching and Teaching Millennial Students.

Haney, M. (2004). Ethical dilemmas associated with self-disclosure in student writing. *Teaching of Psychology, 31*(3), 167–171.

Harvey, L., & Knight, P. (2003). *Briefings on employability 5: Helping departments to develop employability*. York Learning and Teaching Support Network and Graduate Prospects. Retrieved on 28 January 2009 from www.heacademy.ac.uk/resources/detail/Employability/employability282

Heuberger, B., Gerber, D. & Anderson, R. (1999). Strength through cultural diversity: Developing and teaching a diversity course. *College Teaching*, 47(3), 107–113.

Hewson, C. & Charlton, J. (2007). Comparing online and offline administration of multiple choice question assessments to psychology undergraduates: Do assessment modality or computer attitudes influence performance? *Psychology Learning and Teaching*, 6(10), 37–46.

Higgins, L.T. & Zheng, M. (2002). An introduction to Chinese psychology – It's historical roots until the present day. *The Journal of Psychology*, *136*(2), 225–239.

Higgs, J. (1988). Planning learning experiences to promote autonomous learning. In D. Boud (Ed.) *Developing student autonomy in learning* (pp.40–58). London: Kogan Page /Nichols Publishing Company.

Higher Education Academy (n.d.). *Personal Development Planning (PDP)*. Retrieved on 18 June 2009 from www.heacademy.ac.uk/ourwork/teachingandlearning/pdp

Higher Education Academy & the Psychology Network (2009). *E-bulletins on Inclusive Practice*. Retrieved on 9 June 2009 from www.psychology.heacademy.ac.uk/networks/sig/index.asp

Higher Education Academy (2009, February). *Reward and recognition of teaching in higher education*. Downloaded on 6 March 2009 from www.heacademy.ac.uk/assets/York/documents/resources/publications/Reward_and_Recognition_Interim.pdf

Higher Education Funding Council for England (HEFCE) (2001). *Strategies for widening participation in higher education: A guide to good practice*. Retrieved on 18 March 2009 from www.hefce.ac.uk/pubs/hefce/2001/01_36.htm

Higher Education Funding Council for England (HEFCE) (2007). *National student survey*. Retrieved on 9 June 2009 from www.hefce.ac.uk/pubs/rdreports/2008/rd12_08/

Hodges, I. & Pearson, C. (2008). Silent minority: Exploring British gay men's experience of the nature and content of psychology as a discipline. *Hellenic Journal of Psychology, 5*(1), 33–57.

Hogan, P.M. & Kimmel, A.J. (1992). Ethical teaching of psychology: One department's attempts at self-regulation. *Teaching of Psychology, 19*, 205–210.

Hove, M.C. & Corcoran, K.J. (2008). If you post it, will they come? Lecture availability in introductory psychology. *Teaching of Psychology, 35*(2), 1–5.

Hyland, F., Trahar, S., Anderson, J. & Dickens, A. (2008). *A changing world: The internationalisation experience of staff and students (home and international) in UK higher education*. Subject Centre of Education ESCalate and Languages, Linguistics and Aras Studies (LLAS). Retrieved on 10 May 2009 from www.heacademy.ac.uk/ourwork/learning/international

JISC (2008). *Audio Supported Enhanced Learning* (ASEL). Retrieved on 29 April 2009 from www.aselactive.com/About_ASEL

Johnson, D. (2002). Teaching students with disabilities. Excellence in teaching. PsychTeacher Electronic Discussion List (April). Retrieved on 29 January 2009 from http://teachpsych.org/resources/e-books/eit2002/eit02-04.pdf

Kennedy, G., Judd, T., Churchward, A., Gray, K. & Krause, K. (2008). First year students' experiences with technology: Are they really digital natives? *Australasian Journal of Educational Technology, 24*(1), 108–122.

Kitchener, K.S. (1985) Ethical principles and ethical decisions in student affairs. *New Directions for Student Services, 30*, 17–29.

Laing, C. & Robinson, A. (2003). The withdrawal of non-traditional students: Developing an explanatory model. *Journal of Further and Higher Education 27*(2), 175–185.

Lantz, C. (2009, January). *Large group teaching*. Higher Education Academy Psychology Network. Retrieved on 20 March 2009 from www.psychology.heacademy.ac.uk/docs/pdf/p20090128_Large_Group_Teaching.pdf

Lantz, C., Moysey, L., Dean, L., Tawse, I., & Duncan, A. (2008) *The psychology student employability guide*. Higher Education Academy Psychology Network. Retrieved on 27 January 2009 from www.psychology.heacademy.ac.uk/docs/pdf/p20080915_Employability_Guide.pdf

Layer, G., Srivastava, A., & Stuart, M. (2002). Achieving student success. *Student Success in Higher Education*, 11–33. Bradford: The University of Bradford.

Lorenzo, G., Oblinger, D. & Dziubam, C. (2006). How choice, co-creation, and culture are changing what it means to be net savvy. *EDUCAUSE Quarterly, 30*(1). Retrieved on 10 May 2009 from www.educause.edu/EDUCAUSE+Quarterly/EDUCAUSEQuarterlyMagazineVolum/HowChoiceCoCreationandCultureA/157434

MacDonald, R.G. (2008). *Why my students don't plagiarise: A case study.* Presentation at the 2008 3rd International Plagiarism Conference, Newcastle, UK.

Marton, F. & Saljö, R. (1976). On qualitative differences in learning: Outcome and process. *British Journal of Educational Psychology, 46,* 4–11.

NCIHE (the Dearing Inquiry) (1997). *Higher education in the learning society.* Norwich: HMSO.

Newlin, M.H. & Wang, A.Y. (2002). Integrating technology and pedagogy: Web instruction and seven principles of undergraduate education. *Teaching of Psychology, 29,* 325–330.

Oblinger, D. (2003, July/August). Boomers, Gen-Xers and Millennials: Understanding the new students. *EDUCAUSE Review,* 37–47.

Pearce, R. (1998). Developing cultural identity in an international school environment. In M. Hayden & J. Thompson (Eds.) *International education: Principles and practices* (pp.60–83). London: Kogan Page.

Pearson, C. & Smith, S. (2006, 8–9 June). *Diversity in higher education: Lesbian and bisexual psychology undergraduate's experiences of studying psychology.* Poster presentation at the Challenge of Diversity Conference, Galway, Ireland.

Perlman, B., McCann, L. & Kadah-Ammeter, T. (2007). Working with students in need: An ethical perspective. *APS Observer, 20*(11), 37–44.

Poe, E.R. (2000). Hitting a nerve: When touchy subjects come up in class. *APS Observer 13*(9), 18–19.

Prensky, M. (2001a). Digital natives, digital immigrants. *On the horizon.* MCB University Press, 9(5), Oct. Retrieved on 6 March 2009 from www. marcprensky.com/writing/Prensky%20-%20Digital%20Natives,%20 Digital%20Immigrants%20-%20Part1.pdf

Prensky, M. (2001b). Digital natives, digital immigrants: Do they really think differently? *On the horizon.* MCB University Press, 9(6) (Dec.) Retrieved on 6 March 2009 from www.marcprensky.com/writing/Prensky%20-%20Digital% 20Natives,%20Digital%20Immigrants%20-%20Part2.pdf

Race, P. (2005). *Making learning happen.* London: Sage Publications.

Roberts, T. (2008). *Student plagiarism in an online world: Problems and solutions.* London: IGI Global.

Rubinstein, J., Meyer, D.E. & Evans, J.E. (2001). Executive control of cognitive processes in task switching. *Journal of Experimental Psychology: Human Perception and Performance, 27*(4), 763–797.

Russell, B.S., Soysa, C.K., Wagoner, M.J. & Dawson, L. (2008). Teaching prevention on sensitive topics: Key elements and pedagogical techniques. *Journal of Primary Prevention, 29,* 413–433.

Select Committee on Education and Employment (SCEE) (2001) 6th Report. Retrieved on 19 March 2009 from www.publications.parliament.uk/pa/cm/ cmeduemp.htm

Shepherd, J. (2008, 30 September). Make friends before you start. *The Guardian*. Retrieved on 9 March 2009 from www.guardian.co.uk/education/2008/sep/30/students.facebook

Silvia, P.J. (2006). Reactance and the dynamics of disagreement: Multiple paths from threatened freedom to resistance to persuasion. *European Journal of Social Psychology, 36*, 673–685.

Skelton, A. (1999). An inclusive higher education? Gay and bisexual male teachers and the cultural politics of sexuality. *International Journal of Inclusive Education, 3*, 239–255.

Smith, S., Jessen, A., Hodges, I., Jobanputra, S. & Pearson, C. (2006, 8–9 June). *Mapping exclusion in undergraduate psychology: Towards a common architecture of the minority student experience*. Paper presented at the 4th Annual Conference on Teaching and Learning: Challenge of Diversity Conference, Galway, Ireland.

Stark-Wroblewski, K., Kreiner, D.S., Boeding, M.C., Lopata, A.N., Ryan, J.J. & Church, T.M. (2008). Use of virtual reality technology to enhance undergraduate learning in abnormal psychology. *Teaching of Psychology, 9*, 59–62.

Stevens, D.D. & Levi, A.J. (2005). *Introduction to rubrics: An assessment tool to save grading time, convey effective feedback and promote student learning*. Virginia: Stylus Publishing.

Striker, H.J. (1997). *A history of disability*. Ann Arbor: University of Michigan Press.

Sweller, J. (1988). Cognitive load during problem solving: Effects on learning. *Cognitive Science, 12*(2), 257–285.

Swenson, E.V. (1982). Faculty adaptation to changes in undergraduate psychology education during the eighties. *Teaching of Psychology, 9*, 59–62.

Trahar, S. (2008). *Teaching and learning: The international higher education landscape*. Lancaster: Subject Centre for Education ESCalate.

UKCOSA Council for International Education. (2004). *International students in UK universities and colleges: Broadening our horizons*. Report of the UKCOSA Survey. Retrieved on 10 May 2009 from www.ukcisa.org.uk/files/pdf/BOHsummary.pdf

UKISA (UK Council for International Student Affairs) (2008). *Higher Education Statistics*. Retrieved on 24 January 2009 from www.ukcisa.org.uk/about/statistics_he.php

White, F.A., Sartore, G., Gallate, J., Cartwright, A. & Curthoys, I. (2005). Digital videotaping (DVT): Evaluating an innovative mode of lecture delivery in psychology. *Psychology Teaching and Learning, 5*, 23–31.

Wolcowitz, J. (1984). The first day of class. In M.M. Gullette (Ed.) *The art and craft of teaching*. Cambridge, MA: Harvard University Press.

Wurman, R.S. (2003). *Information anxiety*. New York: Doubleday.

Zakrajsek, T. (2007). Effective teaching when class size grows. *Observer*. Association for Psychological Science. Retrieved on16 April 2009 from www. psychologicalscience.org/observer/getArticle.cfm?id=2169

Zinkiewicz, L. & Trapp, A. (2004). *Widening and increasing participation*. Higher Education Academy Psychology Network. Retrieved on 20 March from www. psychology.heacademy.ac.uk/docs/pdf/p20040422_widen_partic.pdf

# Myths, Maths and Madness
## *Misconceptions around Psychology*

### Peter Reddy and Caprice Lantz

I wear the mask for lecturing ... the students
feel happier if I conform to their stereotype of
a psychologist

This chapter covers the following areas:

- misconceptions about how to reach careers in professional psychology;
- the purpose of university education and the non-vocational tradition;
- psychology graduate employability – it is more than a good grade from a good university;
- reflection, self awareness and the psychology curriculum;
- teachers' misconceptions about students;
- students' misconceptions about learning and the transition from absolute to relative conceptions of knowledge;
- psychology as a subject:
  - confusion with psychoanalysis
  - confusion with clinical work

- the parts played by maths in statistics and by statistics in research
- biological connections
- psychology as a science
- psychology as *only* a science, science as *only* a given set of procedures
- psychology in isolation
- challenging students' misconceptions.

At the plenary session at the end of a psychology summer school, the Course Director summarised the week. It had been a great week she said, 128 research projects had been started, 21 lectures had been delivered and 2,000 meals eaten. Fortunately there had been little illness, no accidents and no deaths. There had been no births either, but it was possible that there had been a number of conceptions. There had, however, been 64,000 misconceptions. It's an old summer school joke, but the truth is that we all have misconceptions about psychology. It is a huge and constantly developing discipline and none of us can cover it all in depth. This chapter is about the misconceptions that undergraduates, or intending undergraduates, may have about psychology, and some ways of addressing them. Students may hold different misconceptions at different points in their studies and students' misconceptions have been well documented across many disciplines including psychology (Brown, 1983). While perhaps always a problem for teachers, the increasing diversity of students may bring increasingly diverse misconceptions as well as different levels of ability with which to combat them.

## Misconceptions and the Media

Misconceptions occur for a variety of reasons. The influence of the popular media is certainly one source, proffering inaccurate and partial reporting of research and some misrepresentation of psychology in television and film drama. The early 1990s' Granada television series *Cracker*, in which Robbie Coltrane played Fitz, a dysfunctional clinical psychologist anti-hero who nonetheless has brilliant insights into the minds of criminals, reinforced the stereotype of the psychologist as someone who can read minds, and popularised the added twist of criminal profiling. The flawed but glamorous Fitz is credited with fostering the boom in undergraduate psychology and is equally blamed for the illusion that every police force employs a criminal profiler. The reality is that the true specialists in solving crimes and catching criminals are detectives. Although there are one or two psychologists who advise on criminal profiling from time to time, a real 'cracker' would be a detective who used well-established policing methods, but might perhaps also be a psychology graduate. If students really want to solve crimes, it is worth reminding them that it is by no means unusual for psychology graduates to become police officers. The worlds of clinical and forensic psychology have their charm I am sure, but lack the glamour of *Cracker* and, hopefully, dysfunctional staff like Fitz. A less well-known psychology and media link comes from the UK version of the reality TV show *The Apprentice* with Sir Alan Sugar and his catchphrase 'you're fired'. The winner of the first series, Tim Campbell, is a psychology graduate. This is good for psychology students to know as it undermines the subject silo mentality that a degree subject is necessarily a career.

Misconceptions can also result from the use of intuitive logic. For instance, while it seems intuitive and logical that parents and infants begin to develop an attachment at birth, concepts that are counterintuitive can lead to misconceptions. For example it seems counterintuitive that negative correlations can be as strong as positive correlations and students can easily fall into the error of believing that negative correlations are weaker. Misconceptions sometimes come about through subjective experiences which then become stronger through confirmation bias. Stereotypes and prejudices are likely to fall into this category. Finally, colleagues teaching outside their areas of expertise might unknowingly pass on misinformation (Chew, 2006). A student objection undoubtedly heard by many may go something like this: 'But my A-level psychology teacher said it was true!'

## Psychology as a Career

One misconception could be called the BSc career fallacy. This is the expectation in the UK that graduation with a bachelor's degree in psychology confers entry to the profession of psychology in the same way that pharmacy and optometry degrees open the door to these professions. This in turn may rest on a misunderstanding of what undergraduate education is about.

The BSc career fallacy is an appealing idea to students and their parents. Psychology as an A-level and degree subject has expanded very rapidly in a generation and parents may be relatively unfamiliar with it as a subject or as a potential career. Professional careers probably remain a key parental ambition for their children and the professions can be ranked in status from medicine and law onwards. It may be entirely reasonable for both student and parents to assume (a) that psychology is a health profession, and (b) that graduate output and professional entry are roughly in equilibrium, as they generally are for health professions. Reality may therefore come as something of a shock. Only an estimated 20 per cent of UK psychology graduates (BPS, 2007) find their way into professional psychology. The bachelor's degree does not confer professional entry; it merely gets the graduate to the start line of the competition for entry. The range of professional specialisms may also be a surprise.

So, if most psychology students don't become psychologists what is the point of studying it? The question requires an answer about the point of undergraduate education as a whole, as well as an answer about what psychology graduates actually do for a living. Undergraduate education is generally non-vocational. Certainly some degrees are vocational and train students for specific careers – medicine and medically related degrees such as Pharmacy and Optometry spring to mind – but these are the exception rather than the rule. Psychology at undergraduate level is non-vocational, although of course at graduate level vocational courses exist to train for the psychology professions. Psychology is aligned with other non-vocational academic subjects such as history and sociology, rather than with vocational degrees such as medicine or vocationally oriented subjects such as Business Studies. Psychology lines up with Newman (Johnson, 2005) who argued that universities should aim for the education of the mind and the cultivation of understanding, rather than providing technical skills for the workforce or setting students to simply accumulate knowledge for its own sake. Universities, he suggested, should aim to develop students' critical faculties so that they can see things as they really are, get to the heart of the matter, discard irrelevance and detect poor arguments and sloppy reasoning. He argued that a student educated like this would be able to fill any post with credit and approach any subject without fear.

Some may think that a vocational degree is the best option because it leads clearly to a profession and a career. While this is true, and vocational degrees generally have better graduate employment figures, there are certain disadvantages. A vocational degree means that a vocational decision has had to be taken early. There is the risk of a poor decision leading to an unhappy student trapped in the wrong career and failing to prosper. Parents and others may push a bright youngster in the direction of the family business, or towards a career that has been chosen on their behalf. If the student eventually discovers that they are unsuited, or disinterested, the result can take quite some sorting out. The 19th-century author Robert Louis Stevenson is a famous example of someone who declined to enter the family engineering business (they built many of the lighthouses that still guard the Scottish coast) and escaped into writing.

Assuming that an early choice has been a good one, there may still be difficulties. There may be too few openings to accommodate all the graduates, and if a change in career is opted for, a vocational degree may not give the breadth of education of a non-vocational degree. Some vocational knowledge dates quickly and practitioners need agile minds and a commitment to continuing professional development (CPD) to keep up over a 40-year career. The all-round thinking skills promoted by a non-vocational degree may therefore be an excellent preparation for the less specific aspects of a professional career. It is also worth considering the long-term employment and reward prospects for a range of degrees. Many non-vocational subjects have good employment records, history and economics for example, as well as psychology. Patterns of employment are also changing as are the relative positions of managers and the professions. For example in the Health Service, managers lead and make decisions about employment, resources and service delivery to ensure that treatment targets are achieved by medical and health professionals. Recruitment has become increasingly graduate-based, and new graduate employment has emerged, for example in ITC.

So the reasons for studying a non-vocational degree, such as psychology, include high-level general education, training of the mind, development of mature judgment and reflection and general employability. This tradition did not start with Newman; medieval universities also taught students to reason and argue and to become able leaders and administrators, often in the Church. What has changed is the demand for these skills and competencies. We are now in a knowledge economy, there are far more jobs for those with graduate skills and competencies and far fewer tilling the soil, operating hand looms, bashing metal or assembling things by hand.

Students, along with most of us apart from careers advisers, know only about a few highly visible careers and employers. At university students need to find out about themselves, their competencies, what they are good at and what makes them happy. University is not just about academic work; it is also about personal growth and self-awareness. The traditional advice about what to study at university is to follow what interests you. Students will have access to large and well-resourced university careers services: some degrees have sandwich placement or internship work opportunities, and half the graduate jobs on offer are open to graduates of any discipline.

Students may fall into the false analogy that because only medical graduates can practice medicine, only business graduates can have business careers. The reality is far more interesting and diverse. In my university, academics teaching and researching in the psychology department include people with degrees in physics, medicine, biology and the social sciences, and the business school has more academics with psychology degrees, including the head of school, than the psychology department does. As we have said already, the discipline of psychology is very broad, psychology graduates contribute in many areas, and the discipline of psychology is not the same as the profession of psychology.

There are many avenues open to psychology graduates and some of them will be quite unknown to your students. Not all students go directly to a career that they stay in for their whole working life and they may want to try a few things before settling on a career that is right for them. The idea of a portfolio career is an interesting one. The emphasis is not on finding the single 'right' career but on building a raft of different employment experiences according to circumstances, interests, opportunities and personal development. This may be especially important for those who anticipate family care responsibilities and as most of our students are women we should ensure that a diversity of career patterns and choices are available as models. Examples might include a gap year, an undergraduate placement year as an honorary assistant clinical psychologist, three years in care assistant and two different assistant clinical psychologist posts, three years as a trainee clinical psychologist, four years as a clinical psychologist, a period of maternity leave and part-time work, a new post combining research, teaching and clinical work developing a new area of clinical practice, a senior post and perhaps a change of direction.

My career includes a year in youth work, two in social work, a few months of unsuccessful social research, four years in counselling and then a teaching qualification. After this I had three years of sessional teaching, a temporary college lectureship, then several permanent posts adding up to 16 years of A-level teaching ending in college management. I then switched back to teaching but in a university and took a further qualification. If I want to impress I can present this as a reasonably coherent portfolio, although really I feel that it includes several false starts. None of the experience has been wasted or is without value, however, and all of it contributes to who I am.

Portfolio careers, changes in direction and lifelong learning are becoming more common. Even for those staying in one career, though, an employer cannot be relied on to take responsibility for ushering their staff through career-long personal and professional development. An outstanding footballer *can* expect to be talent-spotted and whisked by their agent into the golden glow of a premier league salary, but outside such rare, cosseted and temporary situations, professional life is not like this. The boss will be impressed with those good at their jobs, and staff development opportunities and encouragement may be available, but graduates still need to take responsibility for their own career, personal and professional development. A career needs to be treated as if it were a personal business project. Being a professional means taking responsibility for initiating, monitoring and recording continuing professional development (CPD) whether in a health profession or in business. Strengths must be reinforced, weaknesses managed, knowledge, competencies, skills and experience reviewed and developed, change and new opportunities monitored and evaluated.

## What Do Psychology Graduates Do if They Do Not Become Professional Psychologists?

Lots and lots! Psychology graduates have an interesting and perhaps unique mix of skills and competencies. Psychology, it is sometimes said, has a long past but a short history. The concerns of psychology are as old as humanity but the contemporary discipline emerges in the second half of the 19th century as the application of the methods of science to the human mind and experience. In the ensuing 140 or so years this has not proved to be an easy or an uncontroversial application. Debates about science and methods have been central to the framing of the discipline, from introspection to the behaviourist exclusion of the study of the mind, its return in the cognitive revolution through to contemporary debates about neuroscience, social constructionism and evolutionary psychology. The result is that psychology graduates are well grounded in how to do research. This is also because psychological research, even at undergraduate level, is real research. There are few studies where the outcome is so well anticipated that unexpected results simply show that an error has been made. Results require analysis, thought and interpretation, perhaps rather more than in the physical sciences because of the nature of the subject matter. In researching our own mind, behaviour and experience, psychologists have to cope with participants that anticipate, interpret and react to their research and an inability to fully separate subject and object or to reliably distinguish fact from value.

Psychology graduates are therefore research literate. They can design, carry out, analyse, interpret and evaluate research, and can critically read research reports as well as writing their own. They will have at least some familiarity with a range of statistical procedures and a variety of research methods from more than one epistemological tradition. And if they can't do it all themselves, they will know someone who can. Most important of all, they know that there are generally not simple answers to complex problems. Their literacy extends to the weighing of evidence and the consideration of competing interpretations and theoretical accounts. Psychology encompasses the biological reality of the brain, the social construction of meaning and its representation in the mind.

The upshot is that while psychology students may begin their studies expecting to be given a cut-and-dried set of facts about the subject, they gradually come to a much more sophisticated, provisional, relative and perhaps value-based understanding of psychological knowledge and how it is formed. Indeed this enshrines the distinction between school and university put forward by Humboldt 200 years ago. He suggested that schools do and should present material as agreed, accepted and established knowledge, but that the appropriate stance for a university is to treat scholarship in terms of not yet completely solved problems, whether in research or teaching (Elton, 2008). As Elton points out, Humboldt's idea of a shared staff and student scholarship of research has enormous contemporary relevance.

It is not surprising then that psychology graduates find homes in professions and organisations of many kinds. Businesses seek people with research and analysis skills and who can communicate with passion and commitment, and psychology graduates have business careers up to the highest levels. Connections with marketing, public relations, research and development, human resource management, retail and health service management and sales are clear, but there are also well-worn paths into accountancy and finance where a mix of analysis, communication and numeracy is valued. Psychology graduates also go into teaching, social work, the probation service, local government and the civil service.

## How Does a Psychology Student Become a Professional Psychologist?

As we have seen, the BSc career fallacy leads new students to expect that a first degree in psychology confers immediate entry to a psychology profession. Having discovered that only 20 per cent or so go on to such careers, there is a risk that the student will replace naive optimism with pessimism and feel that the psychology professions are so competitive and oversubscribed, and qualification takes so long, that there is no point aiming for them.

This pessimism is harmful. The harm is that able students with much to offer the psychology professions deny themselves the opportunity of aiming for their first choice. Students from less prominent universities and from widening participation and non-professional backgrounds may be particularly prone to this, as well as those generally lacking in confidence. Students may also fear that universities reflect a class system in which the able and well-healed Oxbridge establishment sweep the professional board while graduates of the (fictional and very low rent) Universities of Poppleton and Uttoxeter (see Laurie Taylor's long-running and highly amusing column in the *Times Higher Education*) are left to flip burgers. While there is no doubt some truth in this, there cannot be a psychology degree in the country without graduates who have successfully entered every one of the psychology professions, and the professions search for the most suitable entrants from a broad range who also reflect the diversity of clients and communities that they serve.

Pessimism may also be unjustified. While highly competitive, the psychology professions may not be as oversubscribed as may be imagined. As students start to focus on life after graduation and think about their careers, many will be aiming elsewhere, to teaching for example or business. The numbers aiming for a psychology profession shrink and may then match the opportunities available better than feared, although this may to some extent be because people rule themselves out for the reasons discussed above. Broadly, strong growth in student numbers is also matched by strong growth in professional careers. The time taken to reach full qualification as a chartered psychologist looks lengthy but it is worth pointing out that this is not excessive for the status and qualification level involved and for the level of expertise and experience required.

Once graduated, subsequent steps vary by specialism but are a mix of apprentice-level work as an assistant psychologist or equivalent, further training, and supervised professional experience. Much or all of this will be paid for or financially supported, including course fees and a bursary or similar to live on. Similarities with early career graduate experiences in business or teaching may not be immediately apparent but they do exist. Both are likely to require apprentice-like junior experience, close supervision with targets to be met, periods of further training and additional qualifications. Full and independent professional status before one's mid- to late-twenties is rare, regardless of specialism, and graduates must accept that from medicine to law to banking, accountancy and the psychology professions, graduate-level professional training and supervision is inevitable and should be welcomed rather than dreaded – lifelong learning is here to stay.

To counter the misconception that the psychology professions are too competitive to be worth aiming for, and to support students from less prominent universities and less advantaged backgrounds, we need to explore what makes a student a credible candidate for a psychology profession. It is certainly not just about getting the best grade. Degree class alone is not a reliable job performance predictor (Barber *et al.* 2005; IRS, 2003) and A-level grade does not necessarily strongly predict either degree class (Huws *et al.* 2006) or job performance. Students need to understand that success at one point in time, perhaps based on hard work and a capacity to absorb facts, although admirable, may not translate into success at another time or in comparison with other students. Later assessments may require more in the way of creativity, or relativist thinking for example, and characteristics that inhibit success at one level may support it at another. The interesting literature on intelligence, personality and academic performance explores this further (e.g. Chamorro-Premuzic & Furnham, 2008; O'Connor & Paunonen, 2007).

Organisations do not necessarily restrict their recruitment only to traditional universities. University attended may reflect academic performance at A-level but as students increasingly attend local universities there are students with great ability and potential at every university. So what are employers looking for and how do they select? There has been a broad shift from job-based to competency-based recruitment and employers now seek graduates with particular competencies, skills or attributes. Competency-based recruitment is viewed as a reliable way to identify graduates with potential who do not just fit a job now, but will be able to grow with an organisation, respond to and lead future change, and give the organisation a competitive advantage. This is not just business speak; organisations in the public sector such as schools and hospitals have targets to meet and are judged on their performance. The competencies sought are often generic and transferable rather than organisation-specific; these can be acquired with development and training in the organisation (IRS, 2003). The Psychology Subject Centre Student Employability Profile (Lantz *et al.*, 2008) lists six categories of competencies including these three:

- Generic competencies:
  - planning and organising
  - influencing

- written communication
- questioning
- listening
- team-working/working with others
- interpersonal sensitivity
- organisational sensitivity
- lifelong learning and development
- Personal capabilities:
  - personal development planning
  - creativity
  - decisiveness
  - initiative
  - adaptability and flexibility
  - achievement orientation
  - tolerance for stress
  - leadership
- Cognitive skills:
  - analysis
  - judgement
  - attention to detail

Many of these relate well to the process of higher education and link to Newman's argument that universities should develop students' critical faculties so that they can see through poor arguments and sloppy reasoning. This is not just about knowing a subject; it is also about the scholarship that develops through studying it. The argument here is that the competencies that make up graduate employability are, to an extent, the flip side of graduate scholarship: the two are alike in many ways. In a similar vein the HEA *Guide No. 3* (2002) lists key competencies sought by employers:

- flexibility, adaptability, coping with and managing change;
- self-motivation and drive;
- analytical ability and decision making;
- communication and interpersonal skills;
- team-working ability and skills;
- organisation, planning and ability to prioritise;
- customer focus and service orientation;
- ability to innovate and instigate change;

- mental and physical resilience;
- leadership ability.

A student with these competencies and qualities, and the ability to offer evidence of them, perhaps by drawing on their activities in the psychology society, a sports club, the student guild and some work experience, will find that graduate opportunities will open up for them.

Can we persuade students of this? The sixth form has perhaps become less of a finishing school aiming at sending well-rounded young people out into the world, and become more like a crammer with the overriding aim of coaching students to get the best grades for university entry. Students seem to bring this focus with them to higher education and behave as if only their grades matter. They have little patience for anything that is not a properly integrated part of their study of psychology, and are reluctant to work for anything that does not have the carrot of a grade attached. If they are studying a psychology degree, psychology is what they expect to study, not study skills, not developing employability, not personal development planning. But as we have seen, although a narrow focus on grade may help a student to get to their first choice of university, in higher education it will be counter-productive. Most psychology students get honours degrees. To be more specific, most get first or second-class honours degrees, in fact about 70 per cent get a second-class honours degree (upper division) – the ubiquitous upper second or 2:1 ('two-one'). Grade therefore frequently fails to distinguish one student from another and is only one factor contributing to employability. As we have suggested above, being able to offer evidence of competencies drawn on a mix of work, especially at a professional placement/internship level, voluntary activity, involvement in student sport, politics or societies, and scholarly activity such as research, is extremely important, usually far more so than category of degree, subject studied or university attended. The key word here though is evidence.

How can students offer evidence of their competencies? A student who has run a student society and worked on placement for IBM for a year will look foolish if he or she is unable use the experience to offer evidence of what they have learned and what competencies they have developed. To be able to use evidence students need to be reflective and self aware, to know how they have developed, what they can do well and what they are learning to do. They need to have thought, for example, about what they have learned on placement about leadership, team work and communication with senior and junior staff and with the public, and about themselves in relation to these competencies. To maximise their academic trajectory, their employability and their personal development, students need to reflect on themselves and their learning. This is sometimes difficult for students; self-awareness and reflection does not necessarily come easily or quickly. Some students defend themselves from it; others seem unable to grasp it at all. Perhaps developing self-awareness and reflection is one of the developmental tasks of late adolescence and early adulthood that come with more sophisticated epistemological reasoning and cognitive development. This topic is dealt with in the next section. However, the point is that it is a misconception that all a student has to do is learn a lot of psychology to get a good grade. Deeper and more reflective learners will ultimately do better. It is also a misconception that a good grade is all that is necessary to get the desired career. Self-awareness and reflection are necessary for both.

So we need to persuade students to take a broader approach to their studies. They need to factor in self-awareness and reflection and to see their personal and competency development as something to actively manage. This is not easy – students may resist anything not directly to do with their subject and course, may not be ready developmentally or may resent intrusion into their personal domain. Personal Development Planning (PDP) may be part of the solution, but simply asking students to keep a PDP portfolio may run up against these problems. How can we integrate this kind of material into a psychology programme?

There may be scope to use students' interest in understanding other people and themselves to turn some of the psychology curriculum towards reflection and self-awareness. It is generally agreed to be important that the first year at university should be different to A-level. Too often it is more of the same but with huge classes and fewer of them. Lecturers must take learning and teaching beyond delivering a verbal and electronic slide summary of key points from a first year textbook and then setting an essay title requiring it to be regurgitated. Universities should seize the option to cast aside the straitjacket of the A-level syllabus, and take heart from Humboldt's suggestion that university scholarship is about joint research into incompletely solved problems. There may be room for a module on the psychology of undergraduate and early adulthood development that could be made personally relevant. It could relate to:

- Erikson and the developmental tasks of adolescence and early adulthood;
- Piaget, Vygotsky and Kohlberg on cognitive development and the development of moral judgement;
- Perry and Baxter-Magolda on epistemological reasoning and cognitive development in undergraduates;

- Biggs, Marton and Säljö, Entwistle and Ramsden and others on meta-learning and approach to study;
- the social psychology of attraction and relationships;
- psychometrics and the measurement and meaning of individual differences and the self;
- investigation of personal interests, preferences and individual differences;
- career development theory;
- personal development planning, preparation for placement and career, the development of competencies and employability.

Embedding PDP, meta-learning and material on reflection and self-awareness in a psychology programme ensures that it is assessed and taken seriously. We know that assessment drives learning (Gibbs & Simpson, 2004) and students will compile a portfolio of their own psychometric measures if it is seen as legitimate applied psychology as well as being personally relevant and interesting. We also know that university challenges students to learn in different ways with less support and that this challenge is important in triggering more sophisticated conceptions of learning and knowledge (Säljö, 1982). It is also clear (Snyder, 1971) that students' sense of their progress at university can strongly affect their sense of their own worth as students. This suggests that teaching about undergraduate and early adulthood development may be useful because it helps to explain and contextualise the challenge of university with sensitivity and support. We want our students to experience university as a profound and life-enhancing experience and leave with a sense of their own worth. A module that offers students information about their development also, in effect, feeds back to them information about their own progress, and we know from the National Student Survey that students would like more, better and more timely feedback. Overall it is odd that in teaching developmental psychology, individual differences and psychometrics we generally do not relate this material explicitly to student experience.

## Teacher's Misconceptions

The chapter began by recognising that we all have misconceptions about psychology because it is such a large and fluid discipline and none of us can cover it all in depth. There may be other misconceptions, however, which are specific to teaching and are about how students learn. The way in which a student sees psychology will be framed by their conceptions of knowledge and how it comes to exist, in other words their epistemological reasoning, or perhaps their cognitive development. We are used to the major changes in thinking and reasoning that take place in middle childhood described by Piaget (as the move from concrete to formal operations), Vygotsky, Bruner and others, but, according to Perry (1970), Baxter Magolda (1992, 1999) and others, there is also cognitive development in later adolescence and early adulthood, the period covered by A-level and undergraduate education. Broadly the conception of knowledge moves from an absolute to a more nuanced and relativist position, eventually with commitment to a reasoned and evidence-based personal position. Initially knowledge may be seen as fixed and absolute, subject only to new discoveries. From this point of view a good teacher and a good textbook lay out the facts and the student's role is to learn them. The textbook especially is reverenced as the ultimate source of knowledge, the ultimate authority.

There are myths about students, staffroom stories of progressive decline in ability, motivation and integrity. There are also myths of the student as superman – as the 'digital native' who has grown up with ITC and can effortlessly multitask despite, or perhaps because of, an attention span of a few seconds. Both are probably untrue or exaggerated and perhaps we judge students too much as if they are fully fledged adults. They are not and they need our specialist educational help and support to manage the transitions that they face. There are transitions from college or sixth form to university, from undergraduate first to second year, from second year to final year or perhaps to a sandwich placement first, and then out of the university. There is much literature on the first of these (for example Tinto, 1975) and much student concern about entering the final year and leaving university. Entering the final year is predictably worrying as most degrees are heavily weighted towards final-year marks which may account for 75 per cent of the degree grade. Surprisingly many of my students claim to have found the transition from first to second year the most difficult as they felt that much more was demanded of them academically.

Students may find it very helpful to have these transitions explained and laid out for them in a sort of road map. There is much that is mysterious to students about undergraduate study and about their own intellectual growth and development. Transition programmes that are explicit about changes and expectations and offer support in meeting them, and a module on the psychology of undergraduate and early adulthood development, such as that outlined above, may help.

# Psychology as a Subject

## *Confusion with clinical work*

The breadth of psychology is a surprise to many new students and differentiating psychology from psychoanalysis, psychotherapy and counselling can be troublesome. Public confusion with psychoanalysis is evident in the still widespread idea that studying psychology means learning how to 'read people's minds'.

Psychoanalysis seems to have penetrated Western culture deeply and its language now permeates society from id, ego and superego to neurosis, fixation, identification and the Oedipus complex. It seems to offer an ability to see behind the mask of self-presentation, a way to reach below the surface to a deeper level of meaning, a hidden truth, a deeper reality. It has been used to explore the mind of the fictional Hamlet, and to guide the marketing of the humble Mars Bar, and it remains an influential perspective in the arts and cultural studies including theatre, literature, anthropology and even classics. Psychoanalysis has survived being written off by psychologists such as Hans Eysenck (1985) but is of limited relevance in academic psychology. Marketing had a psychoanalytic phase in the 1950s and moved on, and research into the effectiveness of psychotherapy tends to broadly favour cognitive behavioural therapy (CBT). Despite its extraordinary influence, and its continued value as a source of insight in clinical practice, psychoanalysis is a cuckoo in the psychology nest. It is vague, intuitive and unvalidated from a strictly positivist standpoint, and has delivered more in the way of cultural analysis than it has as a way to reliably predict and explain human mind and behaviour.

Understanding the historical, social and cultural position of psychoanalysis, let alone its content, is an enormous task for students. It requires a sophisticated and mature understanding of the nature of knowledge to contextualise it. In the absence of this it is too easily traduced in a series of rote-learned descriptions and trite criticisms. Rather than learning snippets of ill-digested theory, students need to understand the aims and perspective of psychoanalysis and how they are different from those of academic psychology.

Confusing academic psychology with counselling and psychotherapy is more easily dealt with by distinguishing it as an undergraduate subject from postgraduate professional training. In misperceiving psychology as counselling and therapy, the aspiring student may underestimate the breadth, rigour and strongly scientific nature of mainstream academic psychology. As we have already observed, psychology is historically the application of science to the understanding and prediction of individual mind and behaviour. The business of psychological therapies (psychotherapy, including counselling as one of many variants) is the use of psychologically grounded interactions to assist people suffering from emotional distress and mental health problems.

Psychology may be a parent discipline of psychotherapy but it is not the only one, the much older discipline of medicine is another, and psychology does not 'own' applications in psychotherapy in the sense that a psychology degree is an essential prerequisite to practise some sort of therapy. The professions of clinical psychology and counselling psychology do belong to psychology under the umbrella of the Health Professions Council but in practice medical specialists such as psychiatrists often work in collaboration with clinical psychologists, nurse therapists and others. Audiologists and many other health professionals may also draw on psychological ideas and practices in their work and there is also a thriving voluntary counselling sector. This is a remarkably complex field and there are many bodies involved. For example the British Association for Counselling and Psychotherapy has a fairly wide brief and a large membership to match. There are also bodies focused on a particular approach, for example the British Psychoanalytical Society which has roots back to 1913 and is a part of the International Psychoanalytical Association and a member of the British Psychoanalytic Council.

Students may have great difficulty in understanding the complexity and overlapping nature of the aims and memberships of organisations in such a complex field. The size of the UK voluntary sector and the depth of interest in psychotherapy mean that the existence of an organisation of some kind does not necessarily mean that well-established career opportunities exist that are open to psychology graduates. Psychology undergraduates should see their university careers service and the British Psychological Society website for advice and information.

The complexities and overlapping nature of organisations and careers in psychotherapy lead on to another misconception: that the professional applications are entirely distinct from each other. Certainly the purposes and contexts may vary, but the underlying concepts, theories and skills remain closely related. Take a secondary school for example. An educational psychologist may be working with children who are experiencing difficulties integrating into the school environment or with social, emotional or academic problems that are interfering with their learning and development. Group and individual interventions may be designed and implemented to overcome these and to improve pupil well-being. The school as a whole may also be experiencing difficulties in structure and leadership and these may manifest themselves in high staff turnover, poor attendance rates, examination results and pupil behaviour and other indicators. An occupational psychologist may be involved, perhaps through a consulting organisation, to improve team work, communication, stress management and leadership and to help improve organisational performance and the well-being of staff and pupils. Some children may also be receiving help from a clinical psychologist, having been referred through a medical practitioner. All three psychologists draw on similar knowledge and skills but apply them in different contexts with different groups of people.

Contexts and client groups differ, but there is much in common, including a commitment to being more than a practitioner. There is widespread acceptance of the importance of research and of the scientist-practitioner model. Commitment to research is the 'scientist' side of this dual model. Taking clinical psychology as an example, it is not only about being an excellent practitioner. Psychologists also need to be able to respond to and to initiate change. Response may be necessary because new clinical problems or possibilities arise. A disorder may become more common, or more widely noticed, the growth in concern at the numbers of people with social anxiety problems for example. Or research may show that it is possible to use CBT as an early intervention in response to a first episode of psychotic disturbance. Both of these are real examples in which psychologists have been involved in the research that has revealed new problems and new possibilities for care and treatment. A scientist-practitioner will also design new treatments and new types of service in response to research findings and to meet local circumstances. For example an established CBT approach may need development to create a local service to reach out to a client group whose needs are not being met. Thus being a scientist requires commitment to keeping up to date with research and being prepared to adapt, design, implement, research and disseminate new treatments and new services. As part of this a scientist-practitioner will be committed to a reflective and evidence-based approach to practice rather than being a blind adherent to one particular way of working, even though there will be much debate about the nature and interpretation of the evidence.

### Maths, statistics and research

New psychology students may underestimate the statistical element in psychology. There is a range of statistical competence in psychology graduates but all will have reached a minimum standard, and there is no escape from a requirement to successfully engage with statistics; competence in research requires nothing less. Some students may fear maths; however, mathematics and statistics are different disciplines and success in statistics requires competent numeracy rather than advanced mathematics. Quite a number of students nonetheless, go weak at the knees when having to deal with any numbers. One problem for students is that they may not realise that they do not have to understand statistics to the same level that is aimed for in mathematics. Psychologists will generally be consumers of the capacity of statistics to extract meaning from quantitative data, and it is a matter of debate how deep an understanding of principles and processes is required. Students may misunderstand the approach to study that is needed for statistics. A clear understanding of basic concepts is required, the logic of probability testing for example, but beyond these concepts there may be a greater emphasis on procedural knowledge rather than conceptual understanding. This may mean a different approach to study, at least initially, to allow the student to carry out basic input procedures and to make some progress in interpreting output. Psychology is a broad discipline, and there are powerful challenges to traditional scientific orthodoxy, as we will see below, so once a threshold level has been reached it is acceptable for wide differences in statistical interest and competence to exist in psychology students.

A consequence of a procedural approach to statistics is that students may not understand what statistical procedures aim to do or that they are based in a particular epistemology or view of how knowledge comes about. A basic distinction is between descriptive statistics that describe and summarise and inferential statistics that calculate the probability of a difference or a relationship occurring by chance. Measures of central tendency and variation can be calculated and also examined visually through exploratory data analysis, vital when correlating data and useful in other circumstances. Descriptive statistics shade into inferential statistics with standard deviation. It is helpful to students to understand that a normal distribution can be used to both describe sales in, for example, a shoe shop, but also calculate the probability of the next customer having feet smaller than size five.

The use of statistics in psychology is specific and a little idiosyncratic. Inferential statistics are inductive (working from the particular to the general) and based in a particular positivist epistemology to enable inferences about populations to be drawn from samples. Students need to know something of the issues here in order to be able to take an evaluative stance later and to be prepared to understand different approaches such as power analysis and effect size.

## *Biological connections*

There are two major areas where biology and psychology overlap and connect. The biology of the brain and nervous system is one and evolutionary psychology, with its potential to offer ultimate causal models of behaviour, is another. Evolutionary theory might suggest that behaviours that preserve the individual and its genes (such as eating, and therefore foraging and hunting, and the related need to compete for territory and 'pecking order' status) and also preserve the species and pass on copies of the individual's genes (reproductive behaviour which may also involve competition for territory and status) are naturally selected for. The differential reproductive potential and input of the two sexes (about 25 children possible for females with the risk and physical consequences of multiple pregnancies versus dozens for males with no physical consequences whatsoever) might arguably lead to competing strategies for maximising reproduction involving greater or lesser investment in offspring. This could contribute to a debate about the extent to which gender can be thought of as a biological rather than a social construct. This kind of conceptual material involving theory, evidence and debate is very much part of psychology students' experience and fits into their expectations of study.

On the other hand, given that mind and consciousness emerge from the activity of the brain and nervous system, and it is useful from a positivist standpoint to break something into its component parts in order to study and understand it, students need to understand the structure and function of the nervous system in some detail. This is more challenging for psychology students. It requires a different kind of learning, less conceptual and more about remembering obscure Latin-based names for specialist parts and functions. Students perhaps need to be told about the nature of this learning in order to be prepared for it. They have to be prepared to learn like medical students and knuckle down to some rote learning. Once they get beyond the difficult terminology, it is rewarding and not necessarily difficult.

## *Psychology as a science*

As we have seen in relation to careers, the concerns of psychology are as old as humanity but the contemporary discipline emerged as the application of science to human mind and experience. There is complexity and challenge in this. Our minds and our social arrangements are sophisticated and highly tuned and cannot be studied in the straightforward way that many natural phenomena can. There are ethical constraints and people respond to attention and interest in ways that inanimate objects generally do not. So psychology students learn to design studies, to collect and analyse data, and to write and critically evaluate research reports in a challenging arena. Psychology is, in the eyes of most psychologists, wholly or largely a science. Its methods, philosophy and approach are based in science both as a discipline and as professional practice, although this is not without challenge.

New students may be attracted by the concerns of psychology; social behaviour, individual differences in temperament and development for example, but may underestimate the importance of science to the whole endeavour. In principle this should not be a problem. Science is a logical system of thought, a philosophy whose application since the enlightenment has been transformative. However 'science' and 'the sciences' are terms that are used loosely and it is easy to sympathise with students who think that science refers to physics, chemistry and biology. They may also understand applied science as relating to, for example, medicine and engineering, but think that they have escaped it in opting for psychology.

This may be particularly so because psychology draws from such a wide range of A-level backgrounds. One university entrant may have studied psychology with media studies, French and English literature; another may have psychology with chemistry, biology and mathematics. Some admissions tutors may, if push comes to shove, prefer the latter candidate (to reassure arts-based applicants, in practice this rarely happens) but in my view one of the joys of psychology is the breadth of expertise and interest of the students studying it. Whatever their background, students will be taught research methodology, usually from a taken-for-granted positivist standpoint and with an experimental focus. Regrettably psychology undergraduates rarely seem to be given much grounding in epistemology or the philosophy of science. Thus their exposure to science is at a technical and procedural level, almost as a catechism of simplified decision rules. A lack of opportunity for debate and reflection, and a failure to contextualise procedures within the history of the discipline and lively current debates over epistemology, can lead students to the next potential misconception.

### Psychology as only *a science, science as* only *a given set of procedures*

Once students have accepted that psychology is a science, they may be prone to the misconception that this is the only way to advance psychological knowledge and that there is no debate about its role and relevance and no choice about its use. Exposure to qualitative methodology and to constructionist epistemology is a breath of fresh air to some but a real challenge to others. This may not happen until the second year and perhaps it is important in the beginning to focus on the traditional core of the discipline, to bring it into sharp relief as a science and to distinguish it from near neighbours such as sociology. But students may see psychology in isolation from social studies and the arts, and find it difficult to grasp that positivism is a matter of debate and development, not an absolute truth.

The obvious solution to this is a bracingly interesting course in critical psychology, social constructionism and qualitative methods. A starting point could be to contextualise the history of psychology within the currents of thought that have shaped it. For example, the classicism of the Enlightenment (represented by objectivity, positivism and materialism) can be contrasted with 19th-century romanticism (represented by subjectivity and intuition). The human or social sciences (sociology, history, philosophy, humanities, and some of psychology) can also be distinguished from the natural sciences (biology, physics, chemistry, and also some of psychology). In the natural sciences, positivism calls for cause-and-effect relationships to be identified and precise laws to be generated allowing for future events to be predicted and explained. Students need to understand that while this is extremely important for natural science, and not unimportant in the social sciences, it does not address all the issues that are of interest to psychologists, or solve all of their problems. Dilthey, arguing from a human science point of view, suggests that while we may seek to explain nature, we should aim to understand people (Makkreel, 1992).

## Psychology in isolation

We will finish by reflecting on a recurring theme: that students may misconceive psychology as a subject in isolation, in a silo. Psychology in reality has fuzzy boundaries and overlaps with pure and applied disciplines in several directions. It is linked and in partnership in research and practice with many other disciplines, professions and currents of thought. This fuzziness is not static; new connections are continually being developed. Students may benefit from understanding the scope and range of psychology as well as its core focus. It may be helpful to task students with finding and exploring fuzzy relationships with other subjects and applications; with physics, history and art as well as biology, business studies and marketing. There are also some long-running themes that could be explored: the relationship of psychology and language can illuminate and illustrate methodology and epistemology in cognitive and social psychology, link back to the medieval concern with rhetoric, to student essay- and report-writing and to the turn to language in cultural and social studies.

## Tackling Misconceptions

Misconceptions would be of little importance if they did not impact on student learning. However, a fair body of research suggests that beliefs influence what individuals notice, learn and forget, and how memories become distorted (Chew, 2006). If current knowledge provides a basis for future learning, then misconceptions could be considered very serious stumbling blocks indeed. Some lecturers may not be aware of misconceptions or think that they need not be explicitly addressed, perhaps thinking that hearing the appropriate lecture or reading a textbook chapter will easily correct them. However, misconceptions are not uncommon even among more advanced psychology students who might be thought to have more developed critical thinking skills. For instance, Higbee and Clay, in a 1998 study of psychology undergraduates, found that about a third believed the common misconception that people use only about 10 per cent of their brain. Research such as this suggests that misconceptions are not easily corrected by routine teaching and study. Winer *et al.* (2002) summarised research into the common belief that individuals' eyes emit rays that reflect off objects allowing them to seen. Their review also found that lectures and readings on sensation and perception were not effective in reducing this misconception and research in other areas of psychology, such as parapsychology (Benassi *et al.*, 1980), found those student misconceptions are resistant to change.

Research endorses various techniques to address student misconceptions. Winer *et al.* (2002) define a process called 'activation' which includes telling students about the misconception, providing accurate information and using meaningful examples to illustrate why misconceptions are incorrect. Chew (2006) makes use of this process with 'ConcepTests' which he has found to be effective in reducing misconceptions in the short term. Originally developed by Mazur (1997), ConcepTests are problems that require students to understand key concepts and include possible answers that illustrate common misconceptions. Chew provides the following as an example of a ConcepTest which he uses to address misconceptions regarding correlation (p.217).

A marriage counsellor studies four different tests designed to predict marital happiness to see which one is best. She administers the four tests to 80 couples who are about to get married. After two years, she measures the marital happiness of the couples and correlates it with each of the four tests with the following results:

Test 1: r = − .73 (correct)
Test 2: r = .62
Test 3: r = .25
Test 4: r = .10

If the therapist wanted to pick the single best test to use in her work, which one should she choose and why?

This question challenges students' perceptions that positive correlations are better than negative ones. Chew (2006) notes however that the effectiveness of using this technique depends upon how it is presented and suggests the following procedure.

- Present the ConcepTest and allow students time to think and come up with what they think is the correct answer.
- Ask students to indicate answers by raising hands (alternatively clicker technology might be used).
- Ask students to discuss their answers with someone sitting nearby who, if possible, answered differently and try to agree on what the answer should be.
- Again ask all students to indicate what they think is the correct answer to determine if any change has occurred.
- Ask students to explain their choices and collectively discuss the right answer.

Winer *et al.* (2002) discuss approaches used by Clement (1993) to combat misconceptions, including fostering cognitive dissonance and using analogies.

   Although techniques to break down misconceptions are available, they are by no means a panacea. Research suggests that many students' misconceptions remain unchanged despite specific interventions, or are corrected in the short term only to re-emerge in the longer term. Kowalski and Taylor (2009) discuss research suggesting that students change misconceptions when they are required to sort through and compare their old beliefs with new information that is inconsistent with what they believe to be true. Change in understanding is likely when students are required to exert effort in evaluating and comparing beliefs; however, some students probably find it easier to disregard, reinterpret or simply reject new information rather than put in the effort to reorganise their existing understanding. They also note some research that suggests that students with lower ability who are less able to engage in metacognitive processes may be less able to understand new information and identify differences between the old and the new. However, their own study found that students of any ability level can change their misconceptions and that critical thinking skills are important to the process.

Research by Cerbin *et al.* (2000) suggests that addressing misconceptions is actually more of a process. They conducted an in-depth study of educational psychology students and suggest that, while lecturers may begin to nudge student misconceptions in a class or over a term, many misconceptions will not be corrected until much later. They suggest that fostering deep understanding should be looked upon as a developmental process that requires restructuring of undergraduates' knowledge across the whole of their experiences. In the light of this research, it seems that while misconceptions abound among psychology students and are resistant to change, a variety of interventions may be effective in addressing them, not the least of which is the fostering of critical thinking skills which is perhaps the hallmark of a psychology degree programme.

## Key Messages

- Undergraduate development and the purpose of university education, especially non-vocational education, may be poorly understood by students, parents and other stakeholders.
- Good reasons for studying psychology as a degree are the pleasure and enjoyment intrinsic to the subject, and the high-level general education that is part of it, encompassing training of the mind and the development of mature judgement, reflection and employability.
- Students need to be aware of and reflective about themselves and their developing competencies in order to maximise their academic trajectory, their employability and their personal development.
- There is much that is mysterious to students about undergraduate study, their own intellectual growth and development, careers and the transition to adulthood. Students may find it helpful to have this mapped out for them to explore,

and a module on the psychology of undergraduate and early adulthood development may be a way to achieve this.

- Common areas of difficulty for new undergraduates are:
  - Differentiation from psychoanalysis, clinical and counselling work.
  - Overlap with the biological sciences.
  - Psychology being essentially a science.
  - Psychology also reaching beyond science and drawing on alternative epistemologies.
  - The parts played by maths in statistics and by statistics in research;
  - Understanding that science in psychology, and research generally, is more than a set of procedures and that epistemologies lie behind methodologies.
  - Understanding that psychology is not a discipline in isolation but is linked and in partnership in research and practice with many other disciplines, professions and currents of thought.
- Misconceptions may not easily be challenged by routine learning and teaching, but specific techniques that foster critical thinking skills and deep understanding may bring about change over time.

## Research Questions

1. How can students be helped to a broader view of undergraduate education and to reflect on themselves and their developing competencies to maximise their academic trajectory, their employability and their personal development?
2. How can the demands for competencies and employability for business and the professions be reconciled both with scholarship and with studying psychology for the pleasure and enjoyment of the subject?
3. How can psychology be presented to new undergraduates to minimise and overcome common areas of difficulty and misconception?

With students and their families making greater financial investment in higher education and graduate employment and employability becoming more important:

- How should undergraduate education be conceptualised and presented to stakeholders?
- What is the future for the non-vocational liberal education university tradition?
- How should the psychology undergraduate structure and curriculum respond?

# References

Barber, L., Hill, D., Hirsch, W. & Tyers, C. (2005). *Fishing for talent in a wider pool: Trends and dilemmas in corporate graduate recruitment.* Institute for Employment Studies Report 421.

Baxter Magolda, M.B. (1992). *Knowing and reasoning in college: Gender related patterns in students' intellectual development.* San Francisco: Jossey-Bass.

Baxter Magolda, M.B. (1999). The evolution of epistemology: Refining contextual knowing at twenty something. *Journal of College Student Development, 40*(4), 333–344.

Benassi, V.A., Singer, B. & Reynolds, C.B. (1980). Occult belief: Seeing is believing. *Journal for the Scientific Study of Religion, 19,* 337–349.

British Psychological Society (BPS) (2007). *So you want to be a psychologist?* Leicester: BPS.

Brown, L.T. (1983). Some more misconceptions about psychology among introductory psychology students. *Teaching of Psychology, 10,* 207–210.

Cerbin, W., Pointer, D., Hatch, T. & Liyoshi, T. (2000). *Problem-based learning in an educational psychology course.* Cited in S.L. Chew, Seldom in doubt but often wrong: Addressing student misconceptions. In D. Dunn and S.L. Chew (Eds.) (2006) *Best practices for teaching introductory psychology.* Mahwah, NJ: Lawrence Erlbaum.

Chamorro-Premuzic, T. & Furnham, A. (2008). Personality, intelligence, approaches to learning and academic performance. *Personality and Individual Differences, 44,* 1596–1603.

Chew, S.L. (2006). Teaching as a problem in applied psychology. In W. Buskist *et al.* (Eds.) *The Teaching of Psychology in Autobiography: Perspectives from Exemplary Psychology Teachers, Vol. 2.* Society for the Teaching of Psychology.

Clement, J. (1993). Using bridging analogies and anchoring intuitions to deal with students' preconceptions in physics. *Journal of Research in Science Teaching, 30,* 1241–1257.

Elton, L. (2008). Collegiality and complexity: Humboldt's relevance to British universities today. *Higher Education Quarterly, 62*(3), 224–236.

Eysenck, H.J. (1985). *Decline and fall of the Freudian empire.* Harmondsworth: Penguin.

Gibbs, G. & Simpson, C. (2004). Conditions under which assessment supports students' learning, *Learning and Teaching in Higher Education, 1,* 3–31.

Higbee, K.L. & Clay, S.L. (1998). College students' beliefs in the ten-percent myth. *The Journal of Psychology, 132,* 469–476.

Higher Education Academy (2002). Guide for Busy Academics No. 3: Using Personal Development Planning to help students gain employment. Retrieved 13 July 2009 from www.heacademy.ac.uk/assets/York/documents/resources/resourcedatabase/guide_for_busy_academics_no3.doc

Huws, N., Reddy, P. & Talcott, J. (2006). Predicting university success in psychology: are subject specific skills important? *Psychology Learning and Teaching, 5,* 35–42.

IRS Employment Review (2003). Competencies in graduate recruitment and selection. *IRS Employment Review, 783,* 44–48.

Johnson, G. (2005, 9 December) Review of G. Graham (2005). The institution of intellectual values: realism and idealism in higher education. *Times Higher Education.* Retrieved on 7 October 2009 from www.timeshighereducation. co.uk/story.asp?storyCode=200290&sectioncode=42

Kowalski, P. & Taylor, A.K. (2009). The effect of refuting misconceptions in the introductory psychology class. *Teaching of Psychology, 36,* 153–159.

Lantz, C., Moysey, L., Dean, L., Tawse, I. & Duncan, A. (2008). *Psychology student employability guide.* York: Higher Education Academy Psychology Network.

Makkreel, R. (1992). *Dilthey: Philosopher of the human studies.* Princeton: Princeton University Press.

Mazur, E. (1997). *Peer instruction: A user's manual.* New Jersey: Prentice Hall.

O'Connor, M.C. & Paunonen, S.V. (2007). Big Five personality predictors of post-secondary academic performance. *Personality and Individual Differences, 43,* 971–990.

Perry, W.G. (1970). *Forms of intellectual and ethical development in the college years.* New York: Holt, Rinehart and Winston.

Säljö, R. (1979). *Learning in the learners' perspective. Some common-sense conceptions.* Department of Education, University of Göteborg.

Säljö, R. (1982). *Learning and understanding.* Göteborg: Acta Universitatis Gothoburgensis.

Snyder, B.R. (1971). *The hidden curriculum.* Cambridge, MA: MIT Press.

Tinto, V. (1975). Dropout from higher education: A theoretical synthesis of recent research. *Review of Educational Research, 45,* 89–125.

Winer, G.A., Cottrell, J.E., Gregg, V., Fournier, J.S. & Bica, L.A. (2002). Fundamentally misunderstanding visual perception: Adults' belief in visual emissions. *American Psychologist, 57,* 417–424.

# Teaching You to Suck Eggs?
## *Using Psychology to Teach Psychology*

### Annie Trapp

I DIDN'T UNDERSTAND IT ... IS THAT BECAUSE I'M A POOR LEARNER ?... OR YOU'RE A POOR TEACHER ..?

This chapter covers the following areas:

- the effect of context and previous experience on teaching and learning;
- the application of psychological knowledge to the design of learning environments;
- examples of psychological principles underlying craft knowledge;
- creating the feedback loop between application and research;
- engaging in the scholarship around psychology education.

## Introduction

It was a salutary moment when, having given a presentation on applying psychological principles to the teaching of psychology, a psychology lecturer asked me for evidence that psychology lecturers were any more effective than other lecturers in teaching their students. Whilst some distant part of my brain considered the challenges in designing a research study that might address this question, I responded in that time-honoured tradition of academics caught in the headlights: 'Mmm, an interesting question,' or 'Indeed, how would we know?' Returning home, I felt disconcerted that I had not been able to respond to the lecturer's challenge more effectively and even disappointed with my discipline that its educators might not stand out from the crowd. After all, as students of psychology and perhaps also in our research we have studied human behaviour including developmental processes, the structures of memory, the ins and outs of group behaviour, the fickleness of decision-making processes and the power of different motivations, all of which have relevance to student learning.

From this anecdote, readers will appreciate that applying psychological perspectives to teaching and learning is a topic to be approached with caution. Nonetheless in the first part of this chapter I will attempt to persuade readers that it is worth exploring the relevance of psychological research, theory and knowledge to teaching and learning.

How we approach teaching will, at the outset, be influenced by our linguistic and cultural background. Whilst in the UK the concept of learning and the concept of teaching stand independently, in many countries there is less of a conceptual distinction between the two words. For example, as discussed by Hudson (2007), the Russian word, *Obuchenie*, 'refers to all the actions of the teacher in engendering cognitive development and growth' in learners (Davydov & Kerr, 1995), in German the word *Unterrichtfach* is best translated as teaching-studying-learning (Kansanen, 1995) as with the Swedish word, *Undervisning*, or the Finnish word, *Opetus*. These words suggest that in some cultural traditions the theoretical background informing the process of teaching and learning is conceptualised as a more closely integrated activity than conceptions of teaching and learning in the UK.

In central and northern Europe there is a strong tradition of Didaktik,[1] the professional science of teachers that focuses on the planned support for learning. Exact definitions are problematic. In essence, it is intended to capture the art of teaching, the process of learning as well as research on teaching in order to achieve an 'educated personality' (Seel, 1999). Hudson (2007) contrasts this approach with the Anglo-American tradition focusing on organisational aspects of curriculum design, behavioural objectives and curriculum evaluation. The strength of the Didaktik approach is that it considers both 'the why and the how' of the relationships between teacher, student and content. The history and divergence of the two approaches has been widely discussed by Kansanen (1995) and Hopmann (2007), and Shulman (1987) identifies linkages between the Didaktik approach and what has become known as the scholarship of teaching and learning, that is, 'the development of knowledge of how to relate specific content in a way that facilitates student learning'.

More variation in approaches to teaching and learning are likely to be accounted for by cultural diversity. Cortazzi (1990) discusses cultures that have a hierarchical view of teaching and learning, positioning teachers as all-knowing with their knowledge being transmitted directly to learners, and those where the relationship between the teacher and students is viewed as more egalitarian. He makes the point that these perceptions will be present in most cultures but with different emphases resulting in different expectations that affect individual presuppositions about learning and teaching. In indigenous populations psychology may be taught within particular ecological, political, historical and cultural contexts (Kim & Park, 2007) and in developing countries limited resources, infrastructure capabilities, access to education and availability of teacher training will influence approaches to teaching and learning (Sánchez-Sosa & Riveros, 2007).

From another perspective we can consider the role of a teacher over time. Traditionally, academic knowledge has passed from the most senior to the most junior in a hierarchical fashion. Times have changed. Widening access to higher education, digital technologies, easier access to information, and the emergence of cross-disciplinary areas are but some of the factors that invite a reconsideration of the skills, knowledge and abilities students already possess and will need in the future and how this learning can best be facilitated.

## Teaching Philosophies

Our values around teaching and learning are likely to be implicit and this is one reason why many training programmes for new lecturers require participants to create a philosophy of teaching statement (Chism, 1998). These statements are intended to encapsulate the new lecturer's views on how learning occurs, how it can be facilitated, what they want students to achieve, how they plan to do it and what goals they have for themselves as a teacher.

Brookfield suggests that the development of a teaching philosophy fufils both a personal purpose: 'a distinctive organising vision – a clear picture of why you are doing what you are doing that you can call up at points of crisis – is crucial to your personal sanity and morale' (p.16); and a pedagogical purpose:

Teaching is about making some kind of dent in the world so that the world is different than it was before you practiced your craft. Knowing clearly what kind of dent you want to make in the world means that you must continually ask yourself the most fundamental evaluative questions of all – What effect am I having on students and on their learning? (Brookfield, 1990, pp.18–19)

Similarly, Goodyear and Allchin (1998) suggest such statements allow lecturers to: 'assess and examine themselves to articulate the goals they wish to achieve in teaching.... A clear vision of a teaching philosophy provides stability, continuity, and long-term guidance.... A well-defined philosophy can help them remain focused on their teaching goals and to appreciate the personal and professional rewards of teaching' (pp.106–107).

These statements can be expressed in a variety of ways, for example as an extended metaphor, a question and answer format, a poem or a worthy essay (though I would not recommend the last). However, the creation of such statements is not unproblematic. Typically these statements include familiar phrases such as 'encourage deep learning', 'driven by student-led approaches', 'focus on enquiry-based learning', 'constructive alignment of assessment practices', 'encouraging active learning' but of course these sound bites make no sense in isolation. Consider the popular phrase 'placing learners at the heart of the learning process'. To my mind this statement can serve to encourage a false dichotomy between teacher-centred and student-centred learning as discussed by Edwards (2001) and worse might imply a shift of responsibility from the teacher to the learner. 'Placing teachers at the heart of the learning process' might provide a more meaningful philosophy. Indeed Laurillard's conversational model of learning (Laurillard, 2002) places responsibility for the design of learning firmly with the teacher. This approach involves the teacher designing reiterative learner–teacher interactions that serve to modify learners' perceptions. In this model it is clearly the teacher's task to consider what is to be learned (in terms of skills, perspectives and approaches) and how those learning goals can be best achieved. 'The challenge for the teacher is to find ways of helping students move from what students know or are capable of doing, and what we want them to understand and have the skill to accomplish' (Laurillard, 2002). Here we have recognition that the student is indeed where the focus of attention should begin and end but the responsibility for facilitating learning remains with the teacher.

Fanghanel (2007), Dunkin (2002), Entwistle and Walker (2002), Hativa and Goodyear (2002) have argued for a greater emphasis on the context for teaching practice rather than a narrow focus on the psychological and cognitive processes involved in teaching and learning. Similarly, Malcolm and Zukas (2001) criticise the psycho-diagnostic approach to understanding learning and claim 'psychological theories are used as tools to inform the ways in which practice takes place; in other words, theory determines practice,' although they later concede that some psychological theories, such as situated cognition and sociocultural psychology, do acknowledge contextual variables.

These arguments for a broader pedagogy that take more account of the context and situatedness of teaching have gained much credence and publications that examine the effects of context on effective learning in higher education abound, for example, Ramsden (1997) and Prosser & Trigwell (2002). Many such publications provide excellent insights and evidence to support the validity of an institutional and contextual approach to understanding the learning process. But, I would argue, we are in danger of creating another false dichotomy, not this time between teaching and learning but between macro (contextual) and micro (process) approaches to designing effective learning environments. Neither approach, by itself, can provide all the answers. There is room not only for both but there is also the potential for useful synergies to be developed through well-constructed research.

Consider, for example, Klafki's (1995) use of Didaktik analysis in identifying questions for teachers to address when designing learning environments:

- What wider or general sense or reality does this content exemplify and open up to the learner? What basic phenomenon or fundamental principle, what law, criterion, problem, method, technique, or attitude can be grasped by dealing with this content as an 'example'?
- What significance does the content in question or the experience, knowledge, ability or skill to be acquired through this topic already have for the learners in this course of study?
- What is the topic's significance for the learners' future?
- How is the content structured (from a pedagogical perspective)?
- What are the special cases, phenomena, situations, experiments, persons, elements of aesthetic experience, in terms of which the structure of the content can become interesting, stimulating, approachable, conceivable or vivid for learners?

Clearly these questions cannot be addressed without acknowledging the embedded relationship between teacher, student and curriculum. Yes, in part contextual factors such as curriculum requirements, resources and institutional strategies will determine solutions but other questions such as how to structure the content of the course to make it interesting, what activities can be used to maximise the potential for learning and consideration of the different pedagogical approaches available can best be answered through the application of psychological knowledge, creativity and skill. With this in mind, the next section focuses on the contribution psychological knowledge can make to the design of learning environments.

## The Application of Psychological Knowledge to the Design of Learning Environments

Laurillard (2002) provides a robust argument for the inefficiency of lectures in meeting the pedagogical needs of individual students but in the majority of institutions they are relied upon as an economical means for teaching large numbers of students. Models of passive learning and knowledge transmission are associated with lectures but this need not be the case. Many of the techniques commonly used to sustain the interest and attention of students in lectures are grounded in psychological concepts and principles. As an example, demonstrating to students the relevance of key ideas in multiple contexts is based on the psychological concept of encoding variability proven to facilitate long-term retention and generalisation of knowledge. In the following table, further examples are provided that illustrate the relationship between craft knowledge used in lectures, the underlying psychological rationale and, importantly, illustrative research. Further examples can be found in Zinkiewicz, Hammond and Trapp (2003) and LLWHC (n.d.).

Adopting some of the approaches identified in Table 4.1 will be appreciated by your students. A survey (NUS, 2008) reported that students found non-interactive lectures an ineffective use of time and that subsequent recall was poor. Their preference was for lectures in which the enthusiasm for the subject was evident, discussion was encouraged and interactive exercises were embedded within the lecture.

Whilst teaching to large groups can provide opportunities for students to engage in mental processes that will facilitate encoding and subsequent retrieval of information, further learning opportunities are available when working with smaller groups. Adopting techniques that allow students to generate inferences, solve problems, articulate newly learned concepts and apply knowledge to different situations will allow students to reach deeper

**Table 4.1**   The application of psychological knowledge to lectures

| Craft knowledge | Psychological principles | Illustrative research |
| --- | --- | --- |
| Tell a good story | Narrative structures are easier to remember than other types of learning materials | Bower & Clark, 1969; Graesser, Olde & Klettke (2002); Haberlandt & Graesser (1985) |
| Present material in a different order from the textbook | Students learn better when they reconstruct the meaningfulness of the material | Bjork (2006) |
| Provide breaks in the lecture. Provide handouts with short tasks included. | Reflection. Assimilation of information. Sustains attention, provides material for reflection. Revising notes reduces the likelihood of forgetting | Von Wright (1992); Baddeley (1999) |
| Present ideas that need to be related close to each other | Contiguity effects | Mayer (2001) |
| Pose questions. Use of personal response systems | Sustains attention. Knowledge retrieval. Less forgetting if students receive useful feedback | Dempster (1997) |
| Get students to do things | The enactment effect | Cohen (1989) |
| Provide opportunities for students to recall, rehearse and explain material introduced in the lecture | The generation effect | Butler & Roediger (2007); McDaniel *et al.* (2007); Ainsworth & Loizou (2003); Chi *et al.* (1994); Magliano *et al.* (1999) |

**Table 4.1**   (*Cont'd*)

| Craft knowledge | Psychological principles | Illustrative research |
|---|---|---|
| Provide tasks to help students retrieve material in different ways | Encoding variability | Maki and Hasher (1975), Moreno & Valdez (2005) |
| Provide lots of examples | Varied examples improve understanding of abstract concepts | Hakel & Halpern (2005) |
| Provide physical activities as an introduction to new concepts | Perceptual-motor grounding | Glenberg & Kaschak (2002) |
| Provide opportunities for discussion | Integrating and synthesising information are beneficial to learning | Bjork (1994); Bransford, Brown & Cocking (2000) |
| Provide opportunities for students to build their own representations | Concept maps. Helps generate semantic relationships | Carnot & Stewart (2006) |
| Provide a box for queries or comments for students to use as they leave the lecture hall | Social anxiety | Russell & Shaw (2009) |
| Revisit material and formative assessments | Spacing effect: distributing practice sessions produces better long-term memory performance | Dempster (1996); Melton (1970); Bahrick *et al.*(1993) |

levels of understanding. Table 4.2 provides some examples of the psychological principles behind the craft knowledge associated with tutorials, seminars and group work. Again this serves as an illustrative example and does not repeat examples listed in Table 4.1. Further examples may be found in Psychology Teaching (HEAPN, 2008) and Bennett, Howe and Truswell (2002), in addition to the references cited in the previous section.

**Table 4.2** The application of psychological knowledge to seminars and group work

| Craft knowledge | Psychological principles | Illustrative research |
|---|---|---|
| Provide opportunities for group work | Situated cognition. Social constructivism. | Halpern (2004) |
| Create opportunities for students to receive expert guidance | Zones of proximal development Scaffolded knowledge and integration of knowledge with prior learning | Vygotsky (1962)<br>Linn & Songer (1993); Linn & Hsi (2000); Slotta & Linn (2000); Linn et al. (2004) |
| Revisit students understanding of previously learned material | Distributed practice facilitates long-term (but not short-term) memory. | Baddeley & Longman (1978); Cull (2000); Cepeda et al. (2006); Simon & Bjork (2001) |
| Make things tough | Challenges can result in better long-term retention and transfer | Bjork (2006) |
| Encourage multiple viewpoints, debates etc. | Creates cognitive disequilibrium, epistemic curiosity and development of cognitive flexibility | Chinn & Brewer (1993); Johnson et al. (1991); Perry (1981) |
| Facilitate structured (rather than unstructured) discussions | Scaffolding | Metcalfe & Kornell (2005); VanLehn et al. (2007) |
| Encourage students to generate their own questions | Construction of knowledge | Rosenshine et al. (1996); Graesser & Person (1994); Craig et al. (2006) |
| Create opportunities for students to teach other students | Construction of knowledge | McKeachie et al. (1986); Davis (1993); Johnson et al. (1991) |

**Table 4.3**  The application of psychological knowledge to assessment

| Craft knowledge | Psychological principles | Illustrative research |
| --- | --- | --- |
| Provide a range of assessment opportunities for students | Sternberg's theory of successful intelligence | Sternberg (2002, 2003, 2005) |
| Use of formative assessment such as pop quizzes | Retrieval improves long term memory | Bjork (1988); Landauer & Bjork (1978); Karpicke & Roediger (2008) |
| Provide opportunities for students to self-regulate their own learning | Students overestimate their level of understanding | Langendyk (2006); Kruger & Dunning (1999) |
| Provision of feedback | The timing of feedback depends on the task | Pahler *et al.* (2005); DiBattista, D. & Gosse, L. (2006) |
| Care in choice of multiple choice questions. Wrong answers can be learned | Encoding specificity | McTighe & O'Connor (2005); Shute (2008); Roediger & Marsh (2005) |
| Provide opportunities for students to test themselves | Retrieval improves long term retention | Chew (2008); Koriat & Bjork (2006) |

When students were asked about their motivations to go to university, nearly a quarter responded that their main reason was 'to stretch me intellectually' or 'to learn critically' (NUS, 2008). The activities identified in Table 4.2 can go a long way towards meeting these expectations by challenging learners to work beyond their comfort zone, to engage in cognitive disequilibrium and to apply their critical thinking skills.

Challenging and stretching students is not in itself sufficient. Students also need to receive feedback on their development and performance, particularly as there is a tendency for some to overestimate their level of understanding (Kruger & Dunning, 1999). This feedback is most likely to be useful to students when attached to formative assessments. Providing a wide range of assessment opportunities that test memory, analytical, creative, and practical skills is supported by Sternberg's theory of successful intelligence (2002) but often ignored in practice. Other psychological principles with reference to research relevant to the design of assessment are illustrated in Table 4.3.

**Table 4.4** The application of psychological knowledge to individual differences

| Craft knowledge | Psychological principles | Illustrative research |
|---|---|---|
| Recognition of individual differences | Psychosocial theories | Robbins *et al.* (2006) |
| Help students adopt effective study practices | Metacognition | Kornell and Bjork (2007) |
| Ensure independent learning is guided or scaffolded | Cognitive load. Working memory | Kirschner *et al.* (2006) |
| Don't 'label' students | Self-efficacy. Deep and shallow learning. Self-fulfilling prophecy | Newstead and Findlay (1997); Prosser & Trigwell (1999) |
| Provide guidance on how to reduce procrastination | Total time hypothesis | Ebbinghaus (1885); Taylor, Pham, Rivkin & Armor (1998) |
| Recognise effects of student expectations, confidence, emotional intelligence and self-efficacy | Social cognitive theory Self-efficacy | Bandura (1986); Zimmerman, Bonner & Kovach (1996); Qualter *et al.* (2007); Qualter *et al.* (2009) |
| Recognise students have different motivations for learning and these may vary during their studies | Motivation. Goal theory | Remedios & Porter (2006); Lieberman & Remedios (2007); Boekaerts (1997) |
| Mutually construct knowledge with students | Student development theory | Baxter Magolda (1992) |

Psychological principles also underpin the design of effective learning environments with respect for individual differences amongst students. These affect a student's approach to learning through, amongst other things, their motivation to learn, their emotive state, their aspirations and expectations and their existing knowledge and assumptions. Table 4.4 illustrates the relationships between craft knowledge, psychological principles and relevant research related to motivation, personality, personal development and metacognitive skills.

This table also has relevance to helping students to develop an understanding of how they learn as research shows that students are often overconfident about their learning (Chew, 2008; Kruger & Dunning, 1999) and adopt ineffectual study strategies (Kornell & Bjork, 2007). Many undergraduate degrees now incorporate some element of study skills within their courses and this provides a perfect opportunity to dispel myths, raise awareness in students about how their own learning is underpinned by well-established psychological principles and how this awareness will help them build appropriate metacognitive strategies to support their studies (Trapp & Hammond, 2008). A recent study suggests that it is not just students that need to increase their understanding around learning processes. Howard-Jones (2009) showed that 43 per cent of trainee teachers disagreed with the statement that 'To learn how to do something, it is necessary to pay attention to it', 34 per cent were not sure if 'Drinking less than 6–8 glasses of water a day can cause the brain to shrink' and 52 per cent agreed 'We only use 10 per cent of our brains.'

It is no coincidence that the tables above capture many of the characteristics of enquiry-based learning including learning as an active process, learning involving discussion with others working on the same problem, an emphasis on conceptual understanding rather than immediate performance, the use of problems or examples that have relevance to students, retrieval as a means to long-term retention of knowledge and provision for metacognitive and reflective opportunities.

## Taking Responsibility for How We Teach

And now, perhaps, we have the reason why psychology lecturers do not stand out from the crowd. Many lecturers across the disciplines already possess the craft knowledge to teach effectively. Some, including some psychology lecturers, do not. Effective teaching can take place without an understanding of psychological principles. However, there are compelling reasons for acquiring it. First, if we wish to improve our performance as lecturers, then having an understanding of the psychological principles that underlie student learning should make it easier for us to design learning environments that will fulfil their purpose. Second, it allows us to undertake research that will help to close the feedback loop between craft knowledge and psychological theory. Third, it allows access to an evidence base that can challenge accepted policies within higher education. Indeed some of the research in the above tables provides evidence that may be regarded as counterintuitive (for example, spaced versus massed practice, or, measures of performance as evidence of long-term learning). Becoming familiar with the current research and literature also allows us integrate emerging theory and research findings emerging from, for example, neuroscience and technology-enabled learning.

This brings us to the final part of the chapter and an invitation to reflect on how we evaluate our own teaching and take up opportunities for contributing to advancing research and scholarship related to psychology education.

Shulman (2000) provides three reasons why we should evaluate the effectiveness of our teaching: policy, pragmatism and professionalism. Research into teaching and learning clearly has the potential to influence policy. Some of the psychological research referenced in this chapter should alert policy makers to the dangers of using performance measures as an index of learning, equating easy learning to efficient learning or underestimating the power of experiential learning and practice. The research challenges many aspects of existing policy and practice but it is in this political arena particularly that contextual variables, such as modularisation, course learning outcomes, staff student ratios and physical learning spaces may be at odds with principles of effective learning. It is this messy world in which we operate that makes it impossible to address broad questions such as 'does, problem-based learning work?' The answer, 'in some situations it does', is unsatisfactory for policy makers.

Establishing an evidence-base for policy makers is difficult to obtain for other reasons that are associated with the publication of research. For example, Slavin (2008) discusses the difficult choice reviewers have in undertaking systematic reviews; setting very high standards and therefore including very few studies or compromising on standards and having much more to say (with appropriate caveats). Slavin also flags up the different values of reviewers in that the issues on which various reviewers choose to compromise and those on which they stand firm vary enormously.

Other issues related to the publication of research are identified by Matlin (2002). First, the paucity of research published in research journals around student learning. Her search in applied cognitive psychology journals from 1996–2000, for example, found only 89 articles relating to undergraduate learning but 64 on eyewitness testimony, even though the latter has everyday relevance to far fewer people. Second, she identifies the separation of publications focusing on psychological research on learning from publications focusing on evaluations of the way we design and teach courses, the first tending to be published in psychological research journals and the latter in journals focusing on teaching psychology. This situation means that, at best, research is slow to inform policy around teaching practice and, at worse is overlooked, resulting in lists of best practices that are not grounded in empirical research (Nummedal *et al.*, 2002).

Pragmatism is the second reason offered by Shulman for engaging in research of our own teaching. This provides a very practical rationale for pursuing the scholarship of teaching and learning. It invites us to ask whether the effort we put into our teaching is worthwhile. This question can be addressed by designing research that addresses one of the following areas identified by Cerbin and Kopp (2004):

- problems of practice such as gaps between the instructor's expectations for student learning and students' performance, including misconceptions and beliefs that prevent students from understanding the subject matter;
- questions about a teaching and learning episode such as an assignment or teaching activity; and
- questions about the introduction of a new teaching practice such as the introduction of problem-based learning.

How we approach research in these areas is likely to be influenced by our own discipline background as this provides us with methodologies with which we are familiar (Huber, 1999). This may not always be the most appropriate way forward as this account from Huber illustrates:

> Bernstein adopted a psychological approach. He started down this path when he realized that his students did not seem to be getting some of the key concepts from his well-polished lectures alone. Hypothesizing that students might do better with more opportunities to interact with the material, Bernstein gave one group of students a live lecture on the topic, gave a videotape of his lecture to a second group of students, and gave an interactive author-ware program on the topic to the rest. When reviewers of the study suggested he needed better control conditions, Bernstein then compared performance among groups reading irrelevant material, groups reading relevant material, groups hearing a live lecture, and groups working on the web. 'This is what you get when you enter into that community,' Bernstein jokes, 'additions of more conditions.'

This example illustrates that it is not always practical to use quantitative methods observing sample sizes and representativeness. In some instances, qualitative and grounded theory approaches may be more appropriate.

If the purpose of the research is to systematically investigate an aspect of one's own teaching, then pedagogical action research as described by Norton (2009) offers a pragmatic way forward. Further approaches including narrative enquiry, case studies, phenomenographic approaches and evaluation research may also be appropriate and the theoretical background for these approaches together with 'how to' guides for conducting research using these approaches are provided in Cousin (2009).

Shulman's third argument for evaluating our teaching and engaging in scholarship is professionalism. As well as professionals within our specific discipline, most of us are also employed as professional educators. This affords opportunities to contribute to the body of research focused on psychology education and to share experiences with other psychology educators. The latter is made considerably easier now that many discipline-based research conferences have a dedicated teaching strand or are willing to accept papers and symposia related to teaching practice.

## Conclusion

In this chapter I have sought to remind readers that the previous experiences and motivations of both lecturers and students will affect the learning process; that psychological knowledge has an important role in the design of learning environments for effective learning; and that as psychologists we should commit to seeking out and building on existing evidence. As with other aspects of our professional roles, it is important to evaluate whether our work is effective. How we approach our teaching will not only impact on student expectations, values and experiences but will also determine our integrity as professional educators.

### Key Messages

- Understand why you teach the way you do.
- Ask yourself to what extent your approach to teaching facilitates learning.
- Recognise that psychological principles of learning underpin much of the craft knowledge of teaching.
- There is a growing evidence-base around understanding teaching and learning processes.
- Encourage debate around teaching practice within your own research community.

## Research Questions

1.  Identify some counterintuitive findings provided by psychological research that relate to teaching practice.
2.  Design a research study related to some aspect of your teaching.
3.  How well do your students understand how they learn?
4.  How do you evaluate yourself as a psychology educator?
5.  What will your students need to know in five years' time?

## Note

1   For readers interested in exploring the Didaktik tradition further, see Klafki (2000).

## References

Ainsworth, S. & Loizou, A.T. (2003). The effects of self explaining when learning with texts or diagrams. *Cognitive Science, 27*, 669–681.

Baddeley. A.D. (1999). *Essentials of human memory*. Hove, UK: Psychology Press.

Baddeley, A.D. & Longman, D.J.A. (1978). The influence of length and frequency of training session on the rate of learning to type. *Ergonomics, 21*(8), 627–635.

Bahrick, H.P., Bahrick, L.E., Bahrick, A.S. & Bahrick, P.E. (1993). Maintenance of foreign language vocabulary and the spacing effect. *Psychological Science, 4*, 316–321.

Bandura, A. (1986). *Social foundations of thought and action*. Englewood Cliffs, NJ: Prentice-Hall.

Baxter Magolda, M. (1992). *Knowing and reasoning in college: Gender-related patterns in students' intellectual development*. San Francisco: Jossey-Bass.

Bennett, C., Howe, C. & Truswell, E. (2002). Small group teaching and learning in psychology. *Report and Evaluation Series 1*. LTSN Psychology: York.

Bjork, R.A. (1988). Retrieval practice and maintenance of knowledge. In M.M. Gruneberg, P.E. Morris & R.N. Sykes (Eds.) *Practical aspects of memory: Current research and issues: Vol. 1* (pp.396–401). New York: Wiley.

Bjork, R.A. (1994). Memory and metamemory considerations in the training of human beings. In J. Metcalfe & A. Simamura (Eds.) *Metacognition: Knowing about knowing* (pp.185–205). Cambridge, MA: MIT Press.

Bjork, R.A. (2006). Making things hard on yourself: Desirable difficulties in theory and practice. *Higher Education Academy Psychology Network Conference Keynote Presentation*. Retrieved May 2009 from www.psychology.heacademy. ac.uk/PLAT2006/assets/presentations/Bjork/RABjorkPLAT2006Keynote.pdf.

Boekaerts, M. (1997). Boosting students' capacity to promote their own learning: A goal theory perspective. *Research Dialogue in Learning and Instruction (Exeter, UK), 1*(1), 13–22.

Bower, G.H. & Clark, M.C. (1969). Narrative stories as mediators for serial learning. *Psychonomic Science, 14*, 181–182.

Bransford, J.D., Brown, A.L. & Cocking, R.R. (Eds.) (2000). *How people learn* (expanded edn). Washington, DC: National Academy Press.

Brookfield, S. (1990). *The skillful teacher.* San Francisco: Jossey-Bass.

Butler, A.C. & Roediger H.L., III (2007). Testing improves long-term retention in a simulated classroom setting. *European Journal of Cognitive Psychology, 19*(4/5), 514–527.

Carnot, M.J. & Stewart, D. (2006). Using concept maps in college level psychology and social work classes. In A.J. Cañas & J.D. Novak (Eds.) *Concept maps: Theory, methodology, technology.* Proceedings of the Second International Conference on Concept Mapping. San José, Costa Rica.

Cepeda, N.J., Pashler, H., Vul, E., Wixted, J.T. & Rohrer, D. (2006). Distributed practice in verbal recall tasks: A review and quantitative synthesis. *Psychological Bulletin, 132*, 354–380.

Cerbin, B. & Kopp, B. (2004). *Classroom inquiry cycle online tutorial home SoTL @ UW-L.* Retrieved May 2009 from www.uwlax.edu/SoTL/tutorial/developingaresearchfocus.htm.

Chew, S.L. (2008). Study more! Study harder! Students' and teachers' faulty beliefs about how people learn. In S.A. Meyers & J.R. Stowell (Eds.) *Essays from e-xcellence in teaching: Vol. 7* (pp.22–25). Retrieved on 30 April 2009 from the Society for the Teaching of Psychology website: http://teachpsych.org/resources/e-books/eit2007 /eit2007.php

Chi, M.T.H., de Leeuw, N., Chiu, M. & LaVancher, C. (1994). Eliciting self-explanations improves understanding. *Cognitive Science, 18*, 439–477.

Chinn, C. & Brewer, W. (1993). The role of anomalous data in knowledge acquisition: A theoretical framework and implications for science instruction. *Review of Educational Research, 63*, 1–49.

Chism, N.V.N. (1998). Developing a philosophy of teaching statement. *Essays on Teaching Excellence, 9*(3), 1–2. Professional and Organizational Development Network in Higher Education.

Cohen, R.L. (1989). Memory for action events: The power of enactment. *Educational Psychology Review, 1*(1), 57–80.

Cortazzi, M. (1990). Cultural and educational expectations in the language classroom. In B. Harrison (Ed.) *Culture and the language classroom* (pp.54–65). Hong Kong: Modern English Publications and the British Council.

Cousin, G. (2009). Researching learning in higher education. New York: Routledge.

Craig, S.D., Sullins, J., Witherspoon, A. & Gholson, B. (2006). The deep-level reasoning effect: The role of dialogue and deep-level-reasoning questions during vicarious learning. *Cognition and Instruction, 24*, 565–591.

Cull, W.L. (2000). Untangling the benefits of multiple study opportunities and repeated testing for cured recall. *Applied Cognitive Psychology, 14,* 215–235.

Davis, B.G. (1993). *Tools for teaching.* San Francisco: Jossey-Bass.

Davydov, V. V. & Kerr, S.T. (1995). The influence of L. S. Vygotsky on education theory, research and practice. *Educational Researcher 24*(3), 12–21.

Dempster, F.N. (1996). Distributing and managing the conditions of encoding and practice. In R. Bjork & E. Bjork (Eds.) *Memory* (pp.317–344). New York: Academic Press.

Dempster, F.N. (1997). Distributing and managing the conditions of encoding and practice. Retrieved on 26 February 2009 from http://aerj.aera.net at University of York. *Applying Psychological Theories* 165.

DiBattista, D. & Gosse, L. (2006). Test anxiety and the Immediate Feedback Assessment Technique. *Journal of Experimental Education, 74,* 311–327.

Dunkin, M.J. (2002). Novice and award-winning teachers' concepts and beliefs about teaching in higher education. In N. Hative & P. Goodyear (Eds.) *Teacher thinking, beliefs and knowledge in higher education* (pp.41–57). Netherlands: Kluwer Academic Publishers.

Ebbinghaus, H. (1885). Uber das Gedachtnis. Leipzig: Dunker. [H. Ruyer & C.E. Bussenius, Trans. (1913), *Memory.* New York: Columbia University.]

Edwards, R. (2001). Meeting individual learner needs: Power, subject, subjection. In C. Paechter, M. Preedy, D. Scott & J. Soler (Eds.) *Knowledge, power and learning.* London: Sage.

Entwistle, N. & Walker, P. (2002). Strategic alertness and expanded awareness within sophisticated conceptions of teaching. In N. Hativa, & P. Goodyear (Eds.) *Teacher thinking, beliefs and knowledge in higher education* (pp.15–39). Dordrecht: Kluwer Academic Publishers.

Fanghanel, J. (2007). Investigating university lecturers' pedagogical constructs in the working context. City University, London. *Report for Higher Education Academy.* Retrieved May 2009 from www.heacademy.ac.uk/assets/York/documents/ourwork/research/fanghanel.pdf

Glenberg, A.M., & Kaschak, M. (2002). Grounding language in action. *Psychonomic Bulletin & Review, 9,* 558–565.

Goodyear, G.E. & Allchin, D. (1998). Statement of teaching philosophy. *To Improve the Academy 17,* 103–22.

Graesser, A.C. & Person, N.K. (1994). Question asking during tutoring. *American Educational Research Journal, 31,* 104–137.

Graesser, A.C., Olde, B. & Klettke, B. (2002). How does the mind construct and represent stories? In M.C. Green, J. J. Strange & T.C. Brock (Eds.) *Narrative impact: Social and cognitive foundations* (pp.231–263). Mahwah, NJ: Lawrence Erlbaum Associates.

Haberlandt, K. & Graesser, A.C. (1985). Component processes in text comprehension and some of their interactions. *Journal of Experimental Psychology: General, 114,* 357–374.

Hakel, M. & Halpern, D.F. (2005). How far can transfer go? Making transfer happen across physical, temporal, and conceptual space. In J. Mestre (Ed.) *Transfer of learning: From a modern multidisciplinary perspective* (pp.357–370). Greenwich, CT: Information Age Publishing.

Halpern, D.F. (2004). Creating cooperative learning environments. In B. Perlman, L.I. McCann & S.H. McFadden (Eds.) *Lessons learned: Practical advice for the teaching of psychology, Vol. 2* (pp.165–173). Washington, DC: Association for Psychological Science.

Hativa, N. & Goodyear, P.M. (2002). Conceptualisation of teachers' thinking, beliefs and knowledge about teaching and learning in higher education. In N. Hativa and P.M. Goodyear (Eds.), *Teacher thinking, beliefs and knowledge in higher education* (pp.335–359). Dordrecht: Kluwer Academic Publishers.

HEAPN (Higher Education Academy Psychology Network) (2008). Psychology Teaching: Working with small groups. Higher Education Academy Psychology Network. Retrieved on 7 October 2009 from www.psychology.heacademy.ac. uk/docs/pdf/p20080208_Teaching_Psychology_small_groups.pdf

Hopmann, S. (2007). Restrained teaching: The common core of Didaktik. *European Educational Research Journal, 6*(2), 109–124.

Howard-Jones, P.A. (2009). *Introducing neuroeducational research: Neuroscience, education and the brain from contexts to practice.* Abingdon: Routledge.

Huber, M.T. (1999). *Disciplinary styles in the scholarship of teaching: Reflections on the Carnegie Academy for the Scholarship of Teaching and Learning.* A paper presented at the 7th International Improving Student Learning Symposium Improving Student Learning through the Disciplines. 6–8 September 1999, University of York, UK. Retrieved May 2009 from www.carnegiefoundation. org/pub/sub.asp?key=452&subkey=609.

Hudson, B. (2007). Comparing different traditions of teaching and learning: What can we learn about teaching and learning? *European Educational Research Journal, 6*(2), 135–146.

Johnson, D.W., Johnson, R.T. & Smith, K.A. (1991). *Active learning: Cooperation in the college classroom.* Edina, MN: InteractionBook.

Kansanen, P. (1995). The Deutsche *Didaktik* and the American Research on Teaching. In P. Kansanen (Ed.) *Discussions on some educational issues VI* (pp.97–118). Research Report 145. Department of Teacher Education, University of Helsinki. (ED394958).

Karpicke, J.D. & Roediger, H.L. (2008). The critical importance of retrieval for learning. *Science, 319*, 966–968.

Kim, U. & Park, Y.S. (2007). Development of indigenous psychologies: Understanding people in a global context. In M. Stevens & U. Gielen (Eds.) *Toward a global psychology: Theory, research, intervention, and pedagogy.* New Jersey: Lawrence Erlbaum Associates.

Kirschner, P.A., Sweller, J. & Clark, R.E. (2006). Why minimal guidance during instruction does not work: An analysis of the failure of constructivist, discovery, problem-based, experiential, and inquiry-based teaching. *Educational Psychologist, 41,* 75–86.

Klafki, W. (1995). Didaktische Analyse als Kern der Unterrichtsvorbereitung [Didactic analysis as the core of preparation of instruction]. *Journal of Curriculum Studies*, 27(1), 13–30 (Jan.–Feb.)

Klafki, W. (2000). Didaktik analysis as the core of preparation of instruction. In I. Westbury, S. Hopmann & K. Riquarts (Eds) *Teaching as a reflective practice: The German Didaktik tradition* (pp.15–40). Mahwah: Lawrence Erlbaum Associates.

Koriat, A. & Bjork, R.A. (2006). Illusions of competence during study can be remedied by manipulations that enhance learners' sensitivity to retrieval conditions at test. *Memory and Cognition, 34,* 959–972.

Kornell, N. & Bjork, R.A. (2007). The promise and perils of self-regulated study. *Psychonomic Bulletin & Review, 14,* 219–224.

Kruger, J. & Dunning, D. (1999). Unskilled and unaware of it: How difficulties in recognizing one's own incompetence lead to inflated self-assessments. *Journal of Personality & Social Psychology, 77,* 1121–1134.

Landauer, T.K. & Bjork, R.A. (1978). Optimum rehearsal patterns and name learning. In M.M. Gruneberg, P.E. Morris & R.N. Sykes (Eds.) *Practical aspects of memory* (pp. 625–632). New York: Academic Press.

Langendyk, V. (2006). Not knowing that they do not know: Self-assessment accuracy of third-year medical students. *Medical Education, 40,* 173–179.

Laurillard, D. (2002). *Rethinking university teaching* (2nd edn). London: RoutledgeFalmer.

Lieberman, D.A. & Remedios, R. (2007). Do undergraduates' motivations for study change as they progress through their degrees? *British Journal of Educational Psychology, 77,* 379–395.

Linn, M.C. & Hsi, S. (2000). *Computers, teachers, peers: Science learning partners.* Mahwah, NJ: Lawrence Erlbaum Associates.

Linn, M.C. & Songer, N.B.(1993). How do students make sense of science? In *Merill-Palmer Quarterly*, 39, 47–73.

Linn, M.C., Eylon, B.S. & Davis, E.A. (2004). The knowledge integration perspective on learning. In M.C. Linn, E.A. Davis & P. Bell (Eds.) *Internet environments for science education* (pp.29–46). Mahwah, NJ: Lawrence Erlbaum Associates.

LLCWH (Centre for Lifelong Learning at Work and Home) (n.d.). *25 principles of learning.* University of Memphis. Retrieved May 2009 from www.psyc.memphis.edu/learning/whatweknow/index.shtml

Magliano, J., Trabasso, T. & Graesser, A.C. (1999). Strategic processing during comprehension. *Journal of Educational Psychology, 91,* 615–629.

Maki, R.H. & Hasher, L. (1975). Encoding variability: A role in immediate and long-term memory? *American Journal of Psychology*, 88, 217–231.

Malcolm J. & Zukas, M. (2001). Bridging pedagogic gaps: conceptual discontinuities in higher education. *Teaching in Higher Education*, 6(1), 33–42.

Matlin, M.W. (2002). Cognitive psychology and college-level pedagogy: Two siblings who rarely communicate. In D. Halpern & M. Hakel (Eds.) *New directions in teaching and learning: Using the principles of cognitive psychology as a pedagogy for higher education* (pp.87–103). San Francisco: Jossey-Bass.

Mayer, R.E. (2001). *Multimedia learning*. New York: Cambridge University Press.

McDaniel, M.A., Anderson, J. L., Derbish, M.H. & Morrisette, N. (2007). Testing the testing effect in the classroom. *European Journal of Cognitive Psychology*, 19, 494–513.

McKeachie, W.J., Pintrich, P.R., Lin, Y. & Smith, D. (1986). *Teaching and learning in the college classroom: A review of the research literature*. Ann Arbor: National Center for Research to Improve Postsecondary Teaching and Learning, University of Michigan.

McTighe, J. & O'Connor, K. (2005). Seven practices for effective learning. *Educational Leadership*, 63, 10–17.

Melton, A.W. (1970). The situation with respect to the spacing of repetitions and memory. *Journal of Verbal Learning and Verbal Behavior*, 9, 596–606.

Metcalfe, J. & Kornell, N. (2005). A region or proximal of learning model of study time allocation. *Journal of Memory and Language*, 52, 463–477.

Moreno, R. & Valdez, A. (2005). Cognitive load and learning effects of having students organize pictures and words in multimedia environments: The role of student interactivity and feedback. *Educational Technology Research and Development*, 53, 35–45.

Newstead, S.E. & Findlay, K. (1997). Some problems with using examination performance as a measure of teaching ability. *Psychology Teaching Review*, 6, 14–21.

Norton, L.S. (2009). Action research in teaching and learning: A practical guide to conducting pedagogical research in universities. Abingdon: Routledge.

Nummedal, S.G., Benson, J.B. & Chew, S.L. (2002). Disciplinary styles in the scholarship of teaching and learning: A view from psychology. In M.T. Huber & S. Morreale (Eds.) *Disciplinary styles in the scholarship of teaching and learning: A conversation*. Washington, DC: American Association for Higher Education.

NUS (National Union of Students) (2008). NUS student experience report. Retrieved on 30 April 2009 from www.nus.org.uk/PageFiles/4017/NUS_StudentExperienceReport.pdf

Pahler, H., Cepeda, J.T., Wixted, J.T. & Rohrer, D. (2005). When does feedback facilitate learning of words? *Journal of Experimental Psychology: Learning, Memory & Cognition*, 31, 3–8.

Perry, W.G., Jr. (1981). Cognitive and ethical growth: The making of meaning. In A.W. Chickering and associates, *The modern American college* (pp.76–116). San Francisco: Jossey-Bass.

Prosser, M. & Trigwell, K. (1999). *Understanding learning and teaching: The experience in higher education*. Malabar, FA: Open University Press.

Qualter, P., Whiteley, H.E. & Gardner, K.J. (2007). Emotional intelligence: Review of the literature and implications for practice. *Pastoral Care in Education, 25*(1), 11–20.

Qualter, P., Whiteley, H.E., Morley, A.M., Dudiak, H. & Anderson, J. (2009). The role of Emotional Intelligence in the decision to persist with academic studies in HE post-compulsory education. *Post-Compulsory Education, 14*(3), 219–231.

Ramsden, P. (1997). The context of learning in academic departments. In F. Marton, D. Hounsell & N. Entwistle (Eds.) *The experience of learning* (pp.198–216). Edinburgh: Scottish Academic Press.

Remedios, R. & Porter, L.J. (2006). The effects of deadlines and goal orientation on intrinsic motivation. *Psychology of Education Review, 30*(1), 24–38.

Robbins, S.B., Allen, J., Casillas, A., Peterson, C.H. & Le, H. (2006). Unraveling the different effects of motivational and skills, social, and self-management measures from traditional predictors of college outcomes. *Journal of Educational Psychology, 98*, 598–616.

Roediger, H.L. III & Marsh, E.J. (2005). The positive and negative consequences of multiple-choice testing. *Journal of Experimental Psychology: Learning, Memory, and Cognition, 31,* 1155–1159.

Rosenshine, B., Meister, C. & Chapman, S. (1996). Teaching students to generate questions: A review of the intervention studies. *Review of Educational Research, 66*, 181–221.

Russell, G. & Shaw, S. (2009). A study to investigate the prevalence of social anxiety in a sample of higher education students in the United Kingdom. *Journal of Mental Health, 18*(3), 198–206.

Sánchez-Sosa, J. & Riveros, A. (2007). Theory, research, and practice in psychology in the developing (majority) world. In M. Stevens & U. Gielen (Eds.) *Toward a global psychology: Theory, research, intervention, and pedagogy*. New Jersey: Lawrence Erlbaum Associates.

Seel, H. (1999). 'Allgemeine Didaktik' (General didactics) and 'Fachdidaktik' (Subject didactics). In B. Hudson, F. Buchberger, P. Kansanen & H. Seel (Eds.) *Didaktik/Fachdidaktik teaching profession?* (pp. 85–93). Umea, Sweden: TNTEE Publications. Retrieved May 2009 from http://tntee.umu.se/subnetworks/subnetwork_e/archive/seel_eng.pdf

Shulman, L. (1987). Knowledge and teaching: Foundations of the new reform. *Harvard Educational Review, 57*(1), 1–22.

Shulman, L. (2000). From Minsk to Pinsk: Why a scholarship of teaching and learning? *The Journal of Scholarship of Teaching and Learning, 1*(1), 48–53.

Shute, V. (2008). Focus on formative feedback. *Review of Educational Research, 78*(1), 153–189.

Simon, D. & Bjork, R. (2001). Metacognition in motor learning. *Journal of Experimental Psychology: Learning, Memory and Cognition, 27*, 907–912.

Slavin, R.E. (2008). Response to comments: Evidence-based reform in education: Which evidence counts? *Educational Researcher, 37*(1), 47–50.

Slotta, J.D. & Linn, M.C. (2000). The knowledge integration environment: Helping students use the internet effectively. In M.J. Jacobson & R. Kozma (Eds.) *Learning the sciences of the 21st century* (pp.193–226). Hillsdale, NJ: LEA.

Sternberg, R.J. (2002). Beyond *g:* The theory of successful intelligence. In R.J. Sternberg & E.L. Grigorenko (Eds.) *The general factor of intelligence: How general is it?* (pp.447–479). Mahwah, NJ: Lawrence Erlbaum.

Sternberg, R.J. (2003). Construct validity of the theory of successful intelligence. In R.J. Sternberg, J. Lautrey & T.I. Lubart (Eds.) *Models of intelligence: International perspectives* (pp.55–77). Washington, DC: American Psychological Association.

Sternberg, R.J. (2005). The theory of successful intelligence. *Interamerican Journal of Psychology, 39*(2), 189–202.

Sternberg, R. (2008). Applying psychological theories to educational practice. *American Educational Research Journal, 45*, 150–165. Retrieved May 2009 from http://aer.sagepub.com/cgi/content/abstract/45/1/150.

Sternberg, R.J. & Grigorenko, E.L. (2000). *Teaching for successful intelligence.* Arlington Heights, IL: Skylight.

Taylor, S.E., Pham, L.B., Rivkin, I.D. & Armor, D.A. (1998). Harnessing the imagination: Mental simulation, self-regulation, and coping. *American Psychologist, 53*, 429–439.

Trapp, A.L. & Hammond, N.V. (2008). *Study skills for psychology students.* In G. Davey (Ed.) *Complete psychology.* London: Hodder Arnold.

VanLehn, K., Graesser, A.C., Jackson, G.T., Jordan, P., Olney, A. & Rose, C.P. (2007). When are tutorial dialogues more effective than reading? *Cognitive Science, 31*, 3–62.

Von Wright, J. (1992). Reflections on reflection. *Learning and Instruction, 2*(1), 59–68.

Vygotsky, L.S. (1962).*Thought and language.* New York: Wiley.

Zimmerman, B.J., Bonner, S. & Kovach, R. (1996). *Developing self-regulated learners: Beyond achievement to self-efficacy (psychology in the classroom).* Washington. American Psychological Association.

Zinkiewicz, L., Hammond, N. & Trapp, A. (2003). Applying psychology disciplinary knowledge to psychology learning and teaching. York: LTSN Psychology. Retrieved on 30 April 2009 from www.psychology.heacademy.ac.uk/docs/pdf/p20030321_r2p.pdf

# 5

# Bravery and Creativity through the Curriculum

## Douglas A. Bernstein and Dominic Upton

IN SURE ONLY TWO STUDENTS FELL ASLEEP LAST TIME I USED THIS LECTURE . . .

This chapter covers the following areas:

- establishing an authoritative student-centred teaching curriculum;
- the value of classroom demonstrations for promoting active learning and critical thinking;
- the use of psychological science in developing and implementing assessments;
- the creation of 'desirable difficulties' for students;
- the fact that authoritative student-centred learning can take place within any subject, class or teaching medium.

When the time comes to start planning your next, or your first, series of lectures (whether this be called a course, a module or programme), there is an understandable temptation to teach it the same way you taught it the last time, or to teach it as it was taught to you. If the course has gone well in the past, or if you enjoyed the course when you took it, why mess with success, especially when so many other things in your professional and personal life are competing for your time and attention? The answer is, of course, that you don't have to. Every year for decades, for generations, thousands of psychology lecturers in higher education have offered thousands of courses that are just fine as they are. No students are harmed, though they might be bored, some students may learn something, and no major problems or complaints result. However, if you have – or would like to develop – an orientation to teaching that goes beyond doing the minimum, if you have a desire to teach in a way that inspires and intrigues your students, and that challenges them (and you) to go beyond minimum requirements, you will find this chapter useful. In it, you are invited to consider taking an authoritative, student-centred approach to psychology curriculum development in which success is defined as helping students to understand and long remember class material, to enhance their critical thinking skills, and to foster their ability to engage in active, independent learning.

Taking this approach will require more than minimal effort from you and extraordinary effort from your students. It is an approach that some of your students might not appreciate, especially not at first, but it is one to which they will acclimatise and adjust, and maybe even enjoy. Even if not immediately, many and perhaps most students will thank you later, either explicitly or implicitly. Sometimes they will thank you verbally and sometimes even in writing. Some years after he took an introductory psychology honours course taught by one of us (DB) at a large university in the USA, a high-achieving but previously under-challenged single honours psychology student wrote a note that read, in part:

> When I took your intro psych course, I hated you and I hated the way you made us work like dogs. But by the end, even though I only got a B, I felt proud because this was a major accomplishment. It was the first time I realized that I have what it takes to do just about anything I set my mind to. Now that I have nearly completed medical school, I realize how valuable your course and your teaching methods were. I am sorry I was such a pain in the ass.

Similarly, another student taking an introductory psychology course on a dietetics degree programme e-mailed to the other one of us (DU): 'I appreciate the value of your teaching and the subject matter now.' When it was pointed out to the student that this wasn't the message conveyed at the time of teaching, the ex-student responded: 'It takes time to appreciate the value; it didn't come in the module, but it has certainly come in later on my course and definitely in my professional practice: I now know how to learn.'

By now you are probably wondering what kind of torture is going to be recommended that you inflict on your students, but never fear. Our suggestions are not radical ones. It is just that they may violate some of the assumptions and expectations that you, and certainly your students, might have about the curriculum in higher education. Three main factors to consider in curriculum development are initially discussed. Subsequently, some advice and practical suggestions are provided for organising your courses in ways that research, and long experience, indicates can maximise students' learning, as well as improve their key academic skills, all the while making the teaching enterprise a little more stimulating for you.

## Three Guiding Factors in Curriculum Planning

The three main things to consider when planning your curriculum are (a) what you want your students to learn; (b) who your students will be; and (c) how you are going to teach them.

### *What do you want students to learn?*

Only general advice about this question can be offered, because its answer will depend on what you will be teaching, and at what level. Perhaps you will be in charge of a basic introduction to psychology, research methods, neuropsychology, or personality theories. Maybe you will be teaching advanced material in quantitative methods or biological psychology. The content of your teaching may be constrained by a list of topics prescribed by your academic unit or by the accreditation requirements, or you might have complete freedom in selecting what to teach. It is most likely, however, that there will be some flexibility in both the content and the delivery. At one end of the scale you may have to deliver within the confines of the British Psychological Society (BPS) curriculum to a large group of psychology students in their first two years at university (i.e. material contained within the QAA benchmark statements). On the other end of the spectrum you may be delivering a specialist final-year module on a specialised area of psychology, related to your research, to a small group (this is not to say that your research area is unpopular!) of final-year students, or even master's level students. Whatever the case, you will no doubt want your course to reflect the current state of psychological science as well as the latest directions in theory and research in the domain to be covered. So while you may be guided by tradition and/or the content outlines used by others or directed by external bodies, you have to ensure that there is still creativity in your material and content and that you are not overly constrained by external commitments.

It is also important that you include abundant examples of how the material in your course is linked to theories and research in other scientific domains, both within and outside of psychology. To take just a few familiar examples, neuroscience research on neurotransmitters has informed the development and use of psychoactive drugs for the treatment of mental disorders. Research on object perception, such as the impact of expectancy, is linked to research on person perception, including research on cognitive and biological bases of interpersonal attraction and intergroup prejudice. Furthermore, psychologists' research on cognitive biases in decision making has had a considerable impact in fields such as medicine and economics. These and dozens of other interesting and often unexpected linkages can enliven lectures and serve as the basis for some of the active, independent learning assignments described later.

The same goes for applications: the results of research in psychological science are constantly being applied in many areas of everyday life, from testing centres and psychotherapy offices to equipment design studios, medical facilities, factories, offices and courtrooms, to name a few. Your students probably know something about the more clinical applications, but they may well be in the dark about the rest (Klatzky, in press). So take advantage of your opportunity to highlight these applications, not only to emphasise the value of research in psychological science, but also to set the stage for assignments in which students can engage in further explorations of the applications you mentioned, and to seek out others that you didn't.

Finally, in constructing your reading list, choose a mixture of the classic and the recent, and focus on the bibliography that appears at the end of each book or article. Think about and point out to your students the value of those bibliography items as initial guides to further independent study and to shaping the content of written assignments and/or classroom presentations.

### Who will your students be?

The answer to this question will surely have an impact on the development of your course. If you are going to be teaching a small group of master's level students in a seminar room, the level of discourse, the kinds of assignments you set, the readings you select, the amount of time devoted to presentations by students and the difficulty of the assessments you choose are all likely to be at a 'high' level, requiring a more questioning, synthesising and evaluative framework from the students. Similarly, if you are teaching introductory material in an amphitheatre full of first-year students, you will not be able to assume nearly as much prior knowledge, and you will have to adjust all these variables. That adjustment reflects common sense, but it is a mistake to go too far in the downward direction when teaching larger groups of students and/or less advanced students. Teaching these kinds of students may mean that you have to teach differently, but it does not necessarily require a 'dumbing down' of the course.

This point is stressed because, as described later, it is easier than you might think to create meaningful discussions, small-group exercises, and many other kinds of active learning experiences at every level of study, in large classes, and even online. Even though the range of student ability and motivation is likely to be wider in larger classes, you don't have to adopt an academic version of the convoy principle by teaching at the pace or level that would be ideal for the slowest students.

Remember the student comments quoted earlier. To us, the messages were that in classes large or small, live or online, students should not just be *taught* things; they should be challenged to *learn* things, and in the process to stretch themselves to explore the limits of their ability. So instead of planning a course that allows students to remain in their educational comfort zone, consider a plan that will push them beyond it. Consider helping them to discover what they are capable of doing in an educational setting, instead of letting them do what they have always done.

In other words, think about who your students will be, and what they already know, but don't create a self-fulfilling prophecy by assuming that your students' weaknesses force you to make radical adjustments in your teaching methods, course requirements, or outcome expectations. There is even less justification for making such adjustments on the basis of individual students' self-serving requests or self-identified characteristics. For one thing, fairness demands that all students be required to meet the same standards. Although it is obviously necessary (and a legal requirement) to alter assessment procedures or other aspects of a course for students with documented physical or cognitive disabilities, it seems to us that always kowtowing to individual students' perceived learning styles or assessment preferences is inappropriate and counter-productive. It can better promote these students' success, in higher education and in professional and personal life, by asserting that to survive, thrive and prosper, they will often have to adjust to the needs and demands of the world, which at the moment happens to include the requirements of our courses. Neither we, as lecturers, nor our students will ever find out how much more they can accomplish unless required to try.

### How are you going to teach?

Making reasoned decisions about which teaching methods to use in your course requires thinking about the roles that you and your students play in the higher education enterprise. Who is supposed to do what, and why? There are several well-known answers to this question.

Some lecturers in higher education see themselves mainly as repositories of facts and experience and that their role is to show up at fixed times and places to deliver lectures that transmit their knowledge and wisdom to students whose role is to sit quietly and, like sponges, absorb it. In this *teacher-centred* model, the tutor or lecturer is an active information dispenser, a '*sage on the stage*' (King, 1993) – or if teaching online – perhaps a '*star from afar*', while students are cast as passive recipients. Images of mid-air refuelling operations or influenza inoculations come to mind in that this model requires students to do no more than be in the right place at the right time to get what they need.

Other lecturers see themselves as facilitators of learning rather than as dispensers of knowledge. The lecturers' role in various *student-centred* models is not passive but, compared to the teacher-centred model, is less active, or active in a different way. In the more extreme versions of these models, lecturers mainly set the stage, create the context, provide the advice and guidance and supply the opportunity for students to learn for themselves. So the tutor provides a course outline, an assessment plan, and a list of readings and other assignments, but those assignments are likely to focus mainly on individual or group projects and activities through which students learn what they need to learn to write a required assignment, gather and analyse research data, engage in work based learning, or the like. Lecture or seminar time may be devoted largely or entirely to some combination of student presentations of their out-of-class work, to collaborative problem-solving projects, formal or informal debates and discussions about readings and tutor-led activities which require all students' active participation. Much as the client-centred therapist tries to create conditions in which clients can solve their own problems, the student-centred lecturer creates conditions in which students occupy an unusually active role.

The lecturer, acting as a '*guide on the side*' (King, 1993), may seldom if ever deliver a formal lecture (Rimer, 2009). Depending on individual lecturers' preferences, there can be an endless variety of student-centred course formats, each featuring different blends of student and lecturer activity and responsibility. From the students' point of view, though, all of them offer a learning environment which is a lot like joining a gym. They have access to a complete array of exercise facilities, as well as to the help, advice, and supervision of fitness experts, and the company and support of other members with similar goals. Everything they need to succeed is available seven days a week, maybe 24 hours a day, and though the least fit among them may initially need more help, the results they achieve will depend almost entirely on whether, how, and how diligently each person takes advantage of what the gym has to offer.[1] But the relationship between customer and personal trainer is not quite the same as that between lecturer and student.

One respondent in a report by Lomas (2007) put it this way: 'I pay my council tax for certain services but all I have to do is put my dustbin bags out once a week. Higher education is a *partnership* between lecturers and students. Students are not buying a product or a service; they are investing time in a *joint* venture' (p.40, our emphasis added).

There is considerable controversy over the relative value of these teaching models and their various subtypes. The controversy continues largely because there is far too little research in applied settings to provide empirical guidance to lecturers – especially those new to higher education – about which model to choose (Daniel & Poole, 2009). Accordingly, most tutors end up basing their instructional model partly on what their own best (or worst) lecturers did or didn't do, and partly on what they think about students as people. Do I want to be like Professor X or Lecturer Y? How was it done when I was at university? Are students adult enough, and responsible enough, to take charge of their own learning, or do they need to be spoon-fed, pushed and monitored? Will the right and responsibility to learn on their own help them to flourish or just invite them to loaf? Will they ever make anything of themselves if lecturers are not there to be sure they do what is good for them?

Questions like these remind us of a similar controversy relating to the value of various parenting styles. Research in developmental psychology suggests that, in Western cultures at least, the parenting style most closely associated with adaptive social, emotional, and moral development, and the fullest expression of children's intellectual capabilities, is the one described as *authoritative* (Eisenberg *et al.*, 2006; Parke & Buriel, 2006; Paulussen-Hoogeboom *et al.*, 2008; Thompson, 2006). In contrast to parents who are *permissive* (i.e. affectionate, but exerting little or no control or discipline), *uninvolved* (i.e. disinterested in their children's lives), or *authoritarian* (i.e. harsh, autocratic, punitive), authoritative parents tend to be firm but understanding, to make demands and impose discipline, but in a reasonable way and in an atmosphere of caring in which there can be give-and-take discussion of why rules are important and must be followed (Baumrind, 1971; Maccoby & Martin, 1983).

In higher education, there are tutor-centred lecturers who, like uninvolved parents, see no need to do more than provide students with the basics: they come to their lecture theatres at the appointed hours, deliver their lectures, set reading and writing assignments, mark examinations and dispense marks. For these individuals, curriculum planning involves little more than distributing or posting the same requirements they always use; they may or may not update their lectures and examinations. As in the case of authoritarian parents, these tutors offer students little or no room for discussion or argument. Rules are rules, deadlines are deadlines, and there are no exceptions. High achievement is expected, and rewarded with good grades, but not nurtured through personal contact or encouraging words. Weakness or failure is ignored, other than to punish it with a low mark. These lecturers tend to be annoyed by (and may ignore) students' requests for help, and are unlikely to go out of their way to offer help to those whose slow progress indicates that they might be struggling.

At the other extreme are lecturers who, like permissive parents, are deeply involved in facilitating the learning process, perhaps too much so, and they fear the possibility of doing anything that might over-stress students or stifle their personal and academic growth. Some of these lecturers want to teach a particular body of material, but they tend to 'spoon-feed' it through slow and careful lectures, supported by study sheets, practice tests, rewards for completing reading assignments, and all sorts of other student support aids designed to make it virtually impossible for anyone to fail. Other, more extreme advocates of permissive teaching allow students to learn what they want to learn in the way they want to learn it.

These lecturers may allow students to influence the content of the course and they may offer a menu of assessment options from which individual students may choose. These tutors set requirements and deadlines, but are flexible about enforcing them. They sometimes make special arrangements with, and allowances for, individual students on a case-by-case basis. They are eager to help students succeed, even if it means lowering standards for success, such as by offering certain individuals 'extra credit' opportunities.

They reach out to students whom they feel might need assistance, and spend countless hours working with those who ask for help. They see students' *efforts* to succeed as being at least as deserving of reward as the *outcome* of those efforts, as manifested in assessment results. This approach may be partly responsible for the strong sense of entitlement that many students bring with them to higher education (Lomas, 2007). One recent study of university students found that about 40 per cent of them believe that they deserve a grade of B simply for coming to class or doing assigned readings (Roosevelt, 2009).

Between these extremes there are lecturers and tutors who, like authoritative parents, take the role of firm but fair disciplinarians. They care about their teaching and their students, but they reward outcome, not effort. These lecturers are willing to help, but not to the point of creating dependency in their students or allowing themselves to be exploited. They reward academic success with personal support as well as high grades, and though they listen to students' requests for special consideration, they are unwilling to make special deals. They think carefully about their rules and standards, announce them in advance and then enforce them consistently.

Daniel (2009) has described the difference between permissive and authoritative teaching in higher education as defining the difference between school *teachers* and university lecturers. Lecturers, he says, expect a lot from their students, expect them to do considerable independent learning, and hold them responsible for their successes or their failures. In contrast, school teachers tend to expect less, to focus on and worry about students' potential weaknesses and problems (sometimes becoming 'codependent enablers' of those problems) and, while giving students credit when they succeed, tend to blame themselves when students fail.

There is not much research on the parallel between parenting styles and teaching styles (Aitkin *et al.*, 1981; Paulson *et al.*, 1998; Pellerin, 2004; Wentzel, 2002) and what there is does not come from higher education. However, it does support the view that common social learning principles are operating in both parenting and teaching. Further, the results of this research are consistent with the view that an authoritative teaching style that incorporates the active learning elements found in student-centred approaches is the one most likely to bring out the best in students. Experience, and the results of other research cited later, suggest to us that this authoritative, student-centred model offers the best chance for promoting long-term retention of *what* students learn, as well as fostering independent effort and critical thinking *while* they learn it.

# A Plan for Authoritative Student-Centred Teaching

As with parenting, no single version of a particular teaching model is always the best, and that distinction is not claimed for authoritative, student-centred teaching. Indeed, you may disagree with the assessment of this approach simply because you have found another that works best for you. If so, you can stop reading now. However, if you are at least interested in the possibility of implementing the authoritative, student-centred teaching approach outlined, let's consider how you can go about doing so.

## *Follow the basic principles of effective teaching*

The first step is simply to be sure some basic principles of effective teaching are being followed. Many psychology staff are not familiar with these principles, simply because they began their careers in higher education after years of apprenticeship to expert mentors in research and scholarship, but with little or no formal preparation for their teaching role (e.g. Buskist *et al.*, 2002). They were forced to rely on their wits and their guts, along with informal advice, the examples set by their own lecturers and whatever readings they ran across about how to teach. However, with increasing recognition of the importance of teaching in higher education, a number of courses have been developed for individuals new to teaching. Furthermore, there is an expectation on most new lecturers that there will be some form of professional training in teaching and learning. These are based on the UK Professional Standards Framework, launched in February 2006. However, the question of whether these standards have been taken up enthusiastically across all sectors of higher education and whether this has resulted in a demonstrable change in lecturer behaviour is still unresolved.

The most authoritarian or uninvolved lecturers among us don't necessarily see the previous state of affairs (i.e. no control, no training in teaching, no support) as all that bad. Having survived their own teaching trial by fire, they are content to let academic Darwinism run its course. Unfortunately, when it comes to teaching, it is not just the fittest who survive. And many of the less fit lecturers in psychology lecture theatres in higher education today got to be the way they are because, having little information about the teaching process, they got off to a bad start, had bad experiences, developed considerable anxiety about teaching and thus became less and less interested in teaching, let alone in trying to teach better (Bernstein, 1983). The results of this process can be harmful to these lecturers' professional development, not to mention their personal lives. Worse, it can foster ineffective teaching that not only impairs the quality of their students' education but creates negative role models for future generations of lecturers (Bernstein, 2006).

To assure that the trajectory of your own teaching effectiveness will be more positive, you are urged to adopt the following principles, all of which are consistent with an authoritative, student-centred approach to teaching (Chickering & Gamson, 1987):

*1 Encourage student–staff contact*    Frequent and fruitful contact between students and staff inside and outside the classroom is important for establishing and maintaining students' motivation and involvement in the learning process. When students know that their lecturer cares about their progress, they are more likely to persist at learning tasks, even when the tasks are difficult. Further, the experience of getting to know at least a few lecturers as individuals can enhance students' intellectual and emotional commitment to learning.

*2 Encourage cooperation among students*    Like effective work in other realms, effective learning can be enhanced when students are allowed to collaborate, at least part of the time, rather than labouring in isolation. Though it is obviously important to evaluate the performance of individuals for the purpose of giving marks, collaborative learning offers the advantage of helping students develop social responsibility while interacting with others whose ideas and thoughts expand their own thinking and deepen their own understanding (Halpern & Hakel, 2003; Huber & Morreale, 2002).

*3 Encourage active learning*    Learning is not a spectator sport. Students learn, retain and understand more course material when they actively engage it – by talking about it, writing about it, questioning it, debating it, applying it and relating it to what they already know – rather than sitting passively as information washes over them in lectures, videos or other pre-packaged formats (Bonwell & Eison, 1991; Gardner, Heward & Grossi, 1994; Horwitz & Christie, 2000; Kellum, Carr & Dozier, 2001). As noted more than a century ago by the then-president of Harvard University: 'A mind must work to grow' (Eliot, 1869, quoted in Bok, 2006, p.123).

*4 Give prompt feedback*    In order to focus their efforts to learn, to profit from mistakes, and to draw satisfaction from progress, students need feedback about what they know and what they don't know (e.g. Butler &

Roediger, 2008; Ory, 2003; Roediger & Karpicke, 2006). This feedback should be quick enough and frequent enough to guide students' efforts; it can take the form of pre-tests on course material as well as all sorts of quizzes, examinations, papers, projects and other assignments that help students reflect on how far they have come in accomplishing their learning goals and how far they still have to go. Indeed frequent assessment of knowledge, including through the use of student response technology (Electronic Voting Systems (EVS), 'zappers' or 'clickers') in the classroom, can help solidify students' knowledge (e.g. Bjork & Linn, 2006; Kelly, 2009) while also giving *you* feedback on the impact of your teaching.

5 *Emphasise 'time on task'*    There is no substitute for paying attention and devoting time to the task of learning (e.g. Halpern & Hakel, 2003; Peterson, 2006). Lecturers can play a vital role in promoting adequate 'time on task' by focusing most of every class session on the material to be learned, while avoiding the trivial or irrelevant. There is a place for fun in learning, but if they are to succeed, students need to learn to use time wisely, in class and elsewhere, including by adopting effective study and time-management skills. Having these skills is a vital aid to learning, especially for those students whose backgrounds or academic preparation are weakest. You don't have to coddle students, but be ready to help them develop their time management and study skills by referring them to relevant campus resources and readings (e.g. Pauk & Owens, 2008).

6 *Communicate high expectations*    As already mentioned, if you expect a lot from your students, you are more likely to get it. A lecturer's high expectations can maximise the performance of all students – from the brightest and most motivated to those who are less well-prepared or initially less eager to exert themselves. When students experience their lecturer's high expectations as realistic, even if challenging, their expectations of themselves tend to rise accordingly.

7 *Be organised and prepared*    The organisation and planning that goes into your curriculum help determine what students will learn, and how easily they will learn it. Presenting a well-planned and well-organised programme on Day 1 also tells students that you care about your teaching, and about them. The perception of a lecturer as caring, in turn, is associated with higher student ratings of lecturer performance (Levy & Peters, 2002).

8 *Communicate enthusiasm*    Effective, and highly rated, lecturers also tend to communicate their enthusiasm, even love, for psychology, and for

teaching. There are many ways to get this message across. Lively lectures, fascinating demonstrations and other dramatic classroom activities will certainly convey enthusiasm for the teaching enterprise, but so do high-quality, carefully chosen multimedia presentations, innovative assignments and projects, challenging exams, and even fair and well-conceived grading systems. When students sense their lecturer's authentic passion for psychology, the effect can be contagious.

*9 Be fair and ethical* Fairness and the highest ethical standards – in presenting material, in dealing with students, and in evaluating them – is fundamental to effective, high-quality teaching (Forsyth, 2003). A related goal is to ensure that students deal fairly with one another in the classroom. Students thrive in learning situations where the lecturer's integrity, and their confidence in that integrity, governs all aspects of the course. High ethical standards should be evident in lectures that make all students feel welcome, in even-handed marking, in unbiased consideration of students' requests and in the avoidance of even the appearance of impropriety in faculty–student relationships. Discrimination, bias, or abuse of power has no place in teaching.

There is only space to outline the basic principles of effective teaching so, especially if you are a new lecturer, there are other books on the basics of teaching in higher education, and of teaching psychology in particular (e.g. Buskist & Davis, 2006; Forsyth, 2003; Goss-Lucas & Bernstein, 2005; Gurung & Schwartz, 2009; Fry *et al.*, 2009).

### Establish clear lecturer and student roles and rules

The cornerstone of authoritative, student-centred teaching is treating students as responsible adults. This means giving them clear information about your course, your teaching philosophy and rules, what you will be offering, and an outline of their rights and obligations. It also means keeping your end of the bargain and holding students responsible for keeping theirs.

Establishing your role as an authoritative lecturer begins on the first day of the academic year, when you distribute your module guide or lecture programme outline. At the outset you might describe this relatively brief document as a key contract between you and your students and talk about it on that first day as a way to introduce and illustrate your teaching goals. For example, if one of your goals is to promote students' ability to engage in independent learning, critical thinking or team work in problem-solving, highlight the fact that there will be relatively little traditional lecturing. Let them know that in order to fully participate in the discussions, group work, and other classroom activities that will take up the bulk of your time together it is important that they complete the readings for each session before that session, and that they should review the readings afterward. This would be in contrast to the permissive lecturer who would be inclined to implement a wide variety of strategies designed to repeatedly remind students to complete assigned readings, and who might even award points for doing so. Authoritative lecturers prepare the assignments, explain their importance and let the chips fall where they may.

Students will be particularly interested in how their performance will be assessed and marked (often to the exclusion of more important information), so be sure to describe, and give the students a chance to ask questions about, the number and types of summative (and, of course, formative) assignments there will be and how final marks will be determined. Give this information in a friendly and matter-of-fact manner, with no apologies. If you make it clear through your demeanour that the course is planned as it is for good reasons, and you state those reasons, your students will accept your authority and will not be as likely to try to negotiate with you (Roosevelt, 2009). Experienced lecturers will tell you that, like a parent's sons or daughters, a lecturer's students want and like structure in their curriculum. Many will want that structure to come from the tutor, not from aggressive peers who suffer from an inflated sense of entitlement (Scholl-Buckwald, 1985).

Be honest with your students about the amount of work that will be required in your lecture programme. Assure them that students at their level can accomplish it all, but don't underplay the effort that will be necessary to succeed. Outline whether you intend to spend lecture time giving lectures or creating more active and collaborative learning experiences; let your students know that there will not be enough time to address all the concepts, theories, applications, and other information that you expect them to learn. Spell out the implications of this fact, to wit: the students will be responsible for doing a lot of learning on their own and will be expected to display that learning on your assessment instruments.

If your marking system rewards outcome rather than effort, be explicit about this because some students in higher education are amazingly effort-oriented. One university student summed it up this way:

> If you put in all the effort you have and get a C, what is the point? If someone goes to every class and reads every chapter in the book and does everything

the lecturer asks of them and more, then they should be getting an A like their effort deserves. If your maximum effort can only be average in a lecturer's mind, then something is wrong. (Roosevelt, 2009, p.A15)

Something is wrong, indeed, and it can be argued, what's wrong is that this person's lecturers had probably supported, or at least failed to correct, an inaccurate and immature view of what matters in assessing students' performance.

Spend some time on the first day, too, reviewing any other rules and expectations listed in your course outline, such as whether attendance matters to you, whether you want students to raise a hand and be recognised before speaking, whether eating or drinking in lecture is permitted, and the like. The course outline should also include the rules that will govern *your* behaviour (hence, it is a true contract). For example, you can ask students not to start packing up their things before the end of a lecture, but you will have a better chance of getting compliance if you have pledged not to extend a class session past its scheduled ending time. In short, the more explicit your written rules are, the less trouble you will have with rule violations, and with applying previously announced penalties (see Figure 5.1). Don't assume that students will already know these rules. For some students, rules that seem intuitively obvious to you may be utterly new to them – especially to those who have been in permissive learning environments.

Most of your students will rise to the challenge you set for them (Timpson & Bendel-Simso, 1996), but for those who can't, or don't wish to, handle the workload then they should be supported in gracefully exiting with their credits and any intermediate awards that are available. There are many such students, and though the question of how to counsel them is far beyond the scope of this chapter, we need to recognise that not all people entering higher education will have found their calling; some may wish to explore other avenues and may be just as happy and successful, or possibly more so, without completing their university studies (just look at Bill Gates).

### *Plan active learning experiences*

Most of us know that passively listening to lectures, even well-presented ones, can get boring after a while (see Johnson *et al.*, 1998 for a review of work on lectures). Hence as mentioned earlier, it is suggested that you supplement your lectures with lots of opportunities for *active learning*, which means that students (a) do something other than watching and listening;

APPLICATION FOR A PSYCHOLOGY ••• MAKE-UP EXAMINATION_____ SEMESTER, 2001•

Professor _____

After completing the information requested below and obtaining the necessary signature, please give, or fax (•••—••••), this form to your instructor. Once we have verified the accuracy of the information you have provided, and confirmed that your reason for requesting a make-up exam is acceptable, an alternate exam date, time, and place will be arranged. All make-up exams will take place after the regular exam.

Important note: Unless you are requesting a make-up exam because of a last-minute illness or emergency, this form must be turned in at least 7 days before the date of the regularly scheduled exam. If you miss this deadline you will not be eligible for a make-up exam.

Please provide the following information:

I, _____ certify that I am unable to take the Psychology ••• exam scheduled for _____, 2001• because [Please be clear and specific when describing your reason and be sure to obtain a confirming signature]:

_____
_____
_____
_____
_____

Your name: _____
Your signature: _____
Your student ID#FF _____
Your phone number: _____
Your e-mail address: _____

Confirmed by (please print name): _____
Signature: _____
Position or relationship to student: _____
Telephone number: _____
E-mail address:_____

**Figure 5.1**   An excuse-documentation form

We have used this form to help students establish the legitimacy of their request to take an exam at other than the regularly scheduled time and place. You can create versions of this form for dealing with other student requests relating to any academic situation.

(b) work on skill development rather than just trying to absorb information; and (c) are required to engage in higher-order thinking about course material (e.g. 'what does it mean?' rather than just 'what am I supposed to remember?') (Bonwell & Eison, 1991).

You can promote active learning in an endless number of ways. For example, you can assign small-group problem-solving tasks; set up classroom debates; ask students to write and discuss 'one-minute essays' about particular topics (e.g. 'what do you think Milgram's obedience studies say about human beings?'); let students use EVS (or even low-tech 'thumbs up' or 'thumbs down' signals) to indicate agreement or disagreement with lecture content or a debatable point (e.g. that 'stress is a meaningless concept') or to respond to quick multiple-choice questions based on the main point of the previous 15 minutes of your lecture (Heward, 1997; Kelly, 2009).

Students enjoy active learning experiences, and they show special interest in courses that incorporate them (Moran, 2000; Murray, 2000; Rimer, 2009). Active learning methods help students to go beyond memorising isolated facts, to think more deeply about course material, to consider how new material relates to what they already know and to apply what they have learned to new and different situations. This kind of more elaborate thinking about course material also makes it easier for students to remember that material. Studies of pupils in school settings and students at universities and colleges have all found that active learning methods are followed by better test performance and greater class participation as compared with passive instructional techniques (e.g. Chu, 1994; Brelsford, 1993; Kellum, Carr, & Dozier, 2001; Meyers & Jones, 1993; Schmidt *et al.*, 2009; Upton, 2006).

Some active learning techniques, such as the 'one-minute essay', are quick and easy, while others, such as debates or collaborative learning projects, are more time-consuming and take more effort to organise and carry off successfully. Many, such as small-group critiques of a research article, lend themselves nicely to the classroom setting, while others, such as finding new applications of psychological science, or new linkages between seemingly unrelated subfields, are ideal out-of-class assignments. Often, the in-class and out-of-class activities can be related, such as when groups of students learn about research methods by conducting surveys, observations, or other projects outside of class, and then offer in-class presentations of their work. These presentations are not only wonderful opportunities for active and collaborative learning, but they also help students – some of whom will become the next generation of lecturers – to begin honing their classroom teaching skills (Bernstein, 2006).

Of course, active learning does not have to be traditional or paper based. For the past few years there has been a growing recognition of the role of computers and other technology for learning and teaching and, specifically, in promoting active learning (e.g. Barak & Rafeli, 2004; Barak *et al.*, 2006; Upton, 2006; Upton & Cooper, 2006) through the use of wireless laptops, voting 'clickers' or EVS and other appropriate technology.

Promoting active learning from afar – through online connections – is increasing throughout higher education (both within the UK and worldwide). In such settings, traditional face-to-face lectures, seminars and tutorials are replaced by interaction with some combination of alternative media such as hypertext, multimedia objects and programmes, streaming video, or directed and moderated online discussions. However, it is no longer sufficient to merely provide distance learning students with a set of lecture notes or published material (Kinney, 2001). The online material should encourage interaction and engagement, for example through multimedia presentations, searching and responding to discussion points, online discussions (whether synchronous or not) and having instant feedback through online MCQs. All of these options can promote active learning, but the role of lecturers is an enhanced one – they have to be in command, not only of their subject matter and appropriate pedagogical approaches, but also of the technology.

If promoting active learning is a new idea for you (whether in the classroom or via distance learning), the advice is to start slowly, with short, easy methods and move on to more elaborate ones as you gain experience and confidence with this approach. Detailed instructions for promoting active learning can be found in the instructor's resource manuals that accompany most major psychology textbooks, and in a number of activities handbooks (e.g. Benjamin *et al.*, 1999; see chapter 12 in this book for a list of appropriate resources).

Remember, though, that the authoritative, student-centred approach does not require the abandonment of traditional lectures. Indeed, the approach does not even prescribe the strength of the mixture of active learning and more traditional teaching techniques. Though some lecturers have dropped the lecture format altogether (Roosevelt, 2009), it is far more common to see active learning experiences being used to add flavour and spice to lectures. The preference is to create variety and a change of pace – for our students and ourselves – so that every class session features segments of varying length in which students become participants, not spectators. In accordance with the famous 20-minute rule (i.e. named for the period during which students can typically remain focused on a lecture), it is suggested that lectures be organised so that each 20-minute segment is separated from the next by a period of active learning, such as conducting an engaging demonstration, providing an opportunity to answer a question or express an opinion (EVS makes such options easy to arrange), or devoting a few minutes to small-group or individual work on some problem or task. During these active learning segments, the tutor may take the lead, or may simply move around the classroom, answering questions, making comments and the like, before reconvening the whole group for the next lecture segment. It is also recommended that there be breaks within the lecture programme/module/course. Obviously a three-year degree programme that is merely lecture-focused should not be encouraged nor a three-year degree programme that requires just engagement with online activities. There have to be breaks, there has to be variety and there has to be engagement and activity.

### *Exploit the potential of demonstrations to promote active learning and critical thinking*

Like lectures, classroom demonstrations have long been a part of traditional classroom teaching. They offer a way to illustrate a wide variety of psychological concepts, principles and phenomena. A video of young children passing or failing a conservation task can help make Piaget's stages of cognitive development come alive for students, just as a taped interview with a patient can give bipolar disorder a human voice. But although demonstrations can be vivid and dramatic, they do not automatically promote active learning. Many demonstrations, such as those just mentioned, are fascinating but, because they leave students in the role of passive observers, might not be as memorable as they could be.

With some creative adjustments, however, almost any demonstration can become an opportunity for students to engage in active learning as well as critical thinking. Indeed, of all the active learning activities presented here, demonstrations are among the easiest and most enjoyable – for students and their lecturers. Consider again that taped interview with an individual with mental health problems. Instead of simply telling students that they are about to hear someone who has been diagnosed as bipolar, you could ask them to play the role of diagnosticians, and to decide on the basis of their reading assignments and a handout of DSM-IV or ICD-10 disorder categories which diagnosis they think the patient should receive, and why.

At the end of the tape, you can ask the class to vote on a diagnosis and, in the following discussion, students can describe the specific behaviours that led to their decision. This option is virtually guaranteed to produce deeper cognitive processing of the interview content, more elaborate consideration of what it conveyed and an evidence-based discussion of which aspects of the patient's behaviour met which diagnostic criteria. Furthermore, all of these activities can be undertaken equally well online as in a classroom.

You could also demonstrate the power of compliance norms by asking a student to make a funny face or take off a shoe. But it would be so much more memorable, and so much more personally meaningful, to *all* the students if you asked everyone to stand, turn in a circle, jump up and down, or carry out some other pointless activity. This version of the demonstration gives everyone a personal experience with compliance and makes it impossible for anyone to think 'I wouldn't have done that'. This is the type of activity that is only possible in a classroom setting! However, creative minds will probably discover and implement such online activities to demonstrate practically all psychological principles taught on an undergraduate degree.

Other demonstrations can be of particular value in explicitly targeting the development of critical thinking skills, especially in relation to scientific research methods. Rather than merely lecturing about those methods, and the logic underlying them, you can ask students to use those methods and that logic in analysing and drawing conclusions about a demonstration. Suppose, for example, you were to perform – or show a video of – an impressive magic trick involving apparent mind-reading, clairvoyance, or some other psychic phenomenon. If you wish to integrate classroom and online activities, there are a number of videos of such 'psychic' tricks on YouTube. Students can be directed to the site to review the video and propose explanations for the alleged psychic phenomenon. When discussing the video (either in the lecture theatre on online) some students will accept the demonstration as a genuine psychic event but, no matter their reaction, they will have been placed in the position of a scientist who has seen a phenomenon in need of explanation. You can then use this as a basis for the task you set for the class, to analyse what they saw using scientific methods and logic, and generate plausible rival hypotheses about how the trick was done. They can be assigned to work on this task alone or in groups, in class or in time for the next one, and to report on their findings, hypotheses and conclusions in writing or orally (again either in the classroom or online). A useful framework for working on the task is the following set of questions for critical thinking (Bernstein *et al.*, 2008):

- What am I being asked to believe or accept (e.g. a claim of psychic power or an assertion by a researcher about the cause of some phenomenon)?
- What evidence is available to support the assertion (e.g. a case study, a correlational study, a survey, an experiment, etc.)?
- Are there alternative ways of interpreting the evidence (e.g. perhaps the phenomenon or observed relationship was influenced by factors other than those asserted as important)?
- What additional evidence would help to evaluate the alternatives (e.g. new data from a new study redesigned to be better able to eliminate plausible rival hypotheses)?
- What conclusions are most reasonable, given all the evidence?

These questions, which are essentially a distillation of the logical reasoning of scientists in any field, can be applied to other demonstrations as well. For example, after demonstrating opponent processes in vision, you can ask students to use the questions to consider your assertion that opponent colour afterimages (i.e. seeing red after staring at green) occur because of processes in the eye, whereas opponent movement illusions (i.e. seeing upward motion after staring at downward motion) occur because of processes in the visual cortex. With some careful and critical thinking, the students should realise that they can design a simple study in which they look at the original colour or movement display with only one eye, then close that eye, open the other one, and see if the afterimage appears.[2]

In short, it is suggested that you not only take every opportunity to spice up lectures or the delivery of material with demonstrations, but that you choose demonstrations in which students can be active participants instead of passive observers – or revise normally passive demonstrations to make them more engaging.

### *Apply the psychology of learning to student assessment*

The authoritative, student-centred approach that is advocated can be employed not only in teaching, but in assessing student progress and achievement. Indeed, certain assessment practices can serve to support the instructional aspects of the approach. Specifically, one can apply what psychological scientists have discovered about the learning process in choosing and scheduling assessment methods. The goal is not only to acquire valid information about students' knowledge, but also to enhance the students' ability to retain course material. This is important because students all too often store course information only as long as necessary in order to earn a good mark. The fact that most students forget most of what they hear or read in a course within a few weeks or months (e.g. Rickard *et al.*, 1988) is consistent with the results of laboratory research on human learning and memory in general (Anderson, 2000). Students' *performance* on course evaluations does not necessarily reflect long-term *retention*, which is what most lecturers think of as *learning*. There is probably no way to prevent this forgetting process, but research in cognitive psychology suggests that certain study and evaluation procedures might help students to retain course information longer (e.g. Bjork, 1999; Bjork & Linn, 2006). In this text there is only space to offer only a few quick examples; for more information on applying the psychology of learning in your classroom, consult other sources (e.g. Halpern & Hakel, 2003).

## Massed vs. distributed practice

Long-term retention is improved when students engage in numerous study sessions (distributed practice) rather than when they 'cram' during a single session on the night before a quiz or exam (massed practice). With this in mind, consider giving enough exams and quizzes that students will be reading and studying more or less continuously. You can also promote distributed practice by including a few unannounced quizzes. Some more permissive colleagues do not give these 'pop' quizzes for fear of creating a stressful classroom atmosphere, but the benefits outweigh the potential costs. Further, there are ways to minimise the stress problem while allowing students to reap the benefits of the steady reading and studying, and regular class attendance, which pop quizzes encourage. For example, it might be possible that 'pop' quizzes can be part of the summative assessment process associated with the module or course. In one case, the instructor gave six unannounced quizzes throughout the term, and allowed students to use the sum of their scores on these quizzes to replace their lowest exam score (Bayly & Spiker, 2003). This arrangement motivated students to do well on pop quizzes, and to view them as opportunities to compensate for a poor exam performance.

## Desirable difficulties

Long-term retention of course material can be improved by creating 'desirable difficulties' (Bjork & Linn, 2006). For example, learning is aided not only by opportunities to repeatedly retrieve, re-store, and again retrieve the same information, but especially when the student is asked to retrieve information in a random fashion, not in the same order in which material was originally presented (e.g. Bjork, 1999). In fact, it can be argued that random retrieval forces students to learn to access information without the help of cues provided by the order in which questions are asked. So consider giving exams and quizzes that require students to retrieve information about past as well as current course material, and present the items in random order.

### Rapid feedback

Learning is enhanced when students receive prompt and constructive feedback that helps them to identify and correct mistakes (Chickering & Gamson, 1987; Ory, 2003). If many days, or even weeks, pass between taking a test and receiving feedback on it, an important learning opportunity will have been missed.

## Some Final Thoughts

In this chapter, a framework for the design of your course or module curriculum has been presented. There has been encouragement to think about curriculum development in a way that might help you to break with the past and the traditional perspective and adopt an approach that is more dynamic and student focused. Taking the authoritative student-centred approach will require some effort – from you and your students – but the rewards will be rich and long lasting. It was argued, too, that the model presented is appropriate for any area of psychology, for any level or type of student, for any setting.

Here are some important points that you should take away from this chapter:

- consider the *who* (are your students), the *what* (do you want them to learn) and the *how* (you teach them);
- use practical examples;
- students need to learn things, not be taught things;
- teaching is a joint venture between you and your students but you each have your own separate roles;
- authoritative, student-centred teaching can promote learning;
- accept that measures of success vary among students;

- student performance is enhanced by active engagement, whether this be classroom or online based;
- consider your assessment methods – what do you want your students to learn, which may differ from what you ask them to recall;
- create desirable difficulties and provide rapid feedback;
- don't just listen to us, learn for yourself.

Two of the key components to success in teaching are the use of practical examples and demonstrating the value of psychology in everyday life. We have tried to follow our own advice in this chapter by providing examples, guides and tips on how you can use an authoritative student-centred framework in your own practice. However, these are not presented as rigid rules to be followed to the letter, but as ingredients in a recipe for greater success and enjoyment in teaching. Just as it is expected that students learn a lot for themselves, it is appreciated that you, too, will discover the appropriate amount of each teaching ingredient and how they can best be blended for you, your subject and your students. Consequently, you are encouraged not only to try the methods presented here, but also to explore other new and innovative methods that you encounter in further reading and in discussions with colleagues. Hopefully, the new methods you decide to try will take you into new realms of teaching experience, and we wish you success and satisfaction as you explore them!

## Key Messages

- When planning your curriculum you need to consider: What you want your students to learn, who your students are, and how you are going to teach them.
- Take time to plan your curriculum so as to maximise your students' learning experience.
- Identify at the outset clear lecturer and student roles and responsibilities.
- Involve your students in active learning.
- Establishing a student-centred teaching curriculum can take place in any teaching setting in any topic with any group.

## Research Questions

1. How do the key principles of authoritative student centred teaching vary according to individual differences?
2. How can e-learning enhance authoritative student-centred teaching?

3. How can you enhance authoritative student-centred teaching in your subject?
4. How can you enhance *your* teaching practice, teaching practice in general?
5. What desirable difficulties can be introduced into your class?

## Notes

1 This analogy was suggested by an anonymous participant at the 2009 National Institute on the Teaching of Psychology. We thank her for her insight, and we are sorry that we cannot give her personal credit.
2 Because the opponent motion process does indeed occur in the brain, switching eyes will not destroy the afterimage. However, the opponent color process occurs in the eye, so looking at a white screen with an eye that has not seen the original colour will result in no afterimage.

## References

Aitkin, M., Anderson, D. & Hintz, J. (1981). Statistical modeling of data on teaching styles. *Journal of the Royal Statistical Society, 144*, 419–461.

Anderson, J.R. (2000). *Cognitive psychology and its implications* (5th edn). New York: Worth.

Barak, M. & Rafeli, S. (2004). Online question-posing and peer assessment as means for web-based knowledge sharing. *International Journal of Human-Computer Studies, 61*(1), 84–103.

Barak, M., Lipson, A. & Lerman, S. (2006). Wireless laptops as means for promoting active learning in large lecture halls. *Journal of Research on Technology in Education, 38*, 245–263.

Baumrind, D. (1971). Current patterns of parental authority. *Developmental Psychology Monographs, 4*(1, part 2).

Bayly, M. & Spiker, M. (2003, January). *The much maligned pop quiz: How to improve its image and simultaneously benefit the student.* Paper presented at the 25th National Institute on the Teaching of Psychology, St. Petersburg Beach, Florida, USA.

Benjamin, L., Nodine, B., Ernst, R. & Blair Broeker, C. (Eds.) (1999). *Activities handbook for the teaching of psychology: Vol. 4.* Washington, DC: The American Psychological Association.

Bernstein, D.A. (1983). Dealing with teaching anxiety. *Journal of the National Association of Colleges and Teachers of Agriculture, 27*, 4–7.

Bernstein, D.A. (2006). A vertical model for the development of teaching skills. Presentation at the Annual Meeting of the Association of Heads of Departments of Psychology, Atlanta, Georgia, November 17.

Bernstein, D.A., Penner, L.A., Clarke-Stewart, A. & Roy, E.J. (2008). *Psychology* (8th edn). Boston: Houghton Mifflin Company.

Bjork, R.A. (1999). Assessing our own competence: Heuristics and illusions. In D. Gopher & A. Koriat (Eds.) *Attention and performance XVII. Cognitive regulation of performance: Interaction of theory and application* (pp.435–459). Cambridge: MIT Press.

Bjork, R.A. & Linn, M.C. (2006). The science of learning and the learning of science: Introducing desirable difficulties. *APS Observer, 19.* Retrieved 12 February 2009 from www.psychologicalscience.org/observer/getArticle.cfm?id=1952

Bok, D.C. (2006). *Our underachieving colleges: A candid look at how much students learn and why they should be learning more.* Princeton, NJ: Princeton University Press.

Bonwell, C. & Eison, J. (1991). Active learning: Creating excitement in the classroom. *ASHE-ERIC Higher Education Report No. 1.* Washington, DC: The George Washington University School of Education and Human Development.

Brelsford, J.W. (1993). Physics education in a virtual environment. *Proceedings of the 37th Annual Meeting of the Human Factors and Ergonomics Society.* Santa Monica, CA: Human Factors.

Buskist, W. & Davis, S.F. (2006). *Handbook of the teaching of psychology.* Oxford: Blackwell.

Buskist, W., Tears, R., Davis, S.F. & Rodrigue, K.M. (2002). The teaching of psychology course: Prevalence and content. *Teaching of Psychology, 29,* 140–142.

Butler, A.C. & Roediger, H.L. (2008). Feedback enhances the positive effects and reduces the negative effects of multiple-choice testing. *Memory & Cognition, 36,* 604–616.

Chickering, A. & Gamson, Z. (1987). Seven principles for good practice in undergraduate education. *American Association for Higher Education Bulletin, 39,* 3–7.

Chu, J. (1994). Active learning in epidemiology and biostatistics. *Teaching and Learning in Medicine, 6,* 191–193.

Daniel, D.B. (2009, January 6). When helping hurts: Teaching as codependency. Paper presented at the 31st annual National Institute on the Teaching of Psychology, St. Petersburg Beach, Florida.

Daniel, D.B. & Poole, D.A. (2009). Learning for life: An ecological approach to pedagogical research. *Perspectives on Psychological Science, 4,* 91–96.

Eisenberg, N., Fabes, R.A. & Spinrad, T.L. (2006). Prosocial development. In W. Damon & R.M. Lerner (Series Eds.) & N. Eisenberg (Vol. Ed.) *Handbook of child psychology* (6th edn): *Vol. 3, Social, emotional, and personality development* (pp.646–718). New York: Wiley.

Forsyth, D.R. (2003). *The professor's guide to teaching: Psychological principles and practices.* Washington, DC: American Psychological Association.

Fry, H., Ketteridge, S. & Marshall, S. (2009). *A handbook for teaching and learning in higher education* (3rd edn). London: Taylor and Francis.

Gardner, R., Heward, W.L. & Grossi, T.A. (1994). Effects of response cards on student participation and academic achievement: A systematic replication with inner-city students during whole-class science instruction. *Journal of Applied Behavior Analysis, 27*, 63–71.

Goss-Lucas, S. & Bernstein, D.A. (2005). *Teaching psychology: A step by step guide.* Mahwah, NJ: Lawrence Erlbaum.

Gurung, R.A.R. & Schwartz, B.M. (2009). *Optimising teaching and learning.* Hoboken, NJ: Wiley-Blackwell.

Halpern, D.F. & Hakel, M.D. (2003, July/August). Applying the science of learning to the university and beyond: Teaching for long-term retention and transfer. *Change*, 36–41.

Heward, W.L. (1997). Four validated instructional strategies. *Behavior and Social Issues, 7*, 43–51.

Horwitz, P. & Christie, M.A. (2000). Computer-based manipulatives for teaching scientific reasoning: An example. In M.J. Jacobson & R.B. Kozuma (Eds.) *Innovations in science and mathematics education: Advanced designs for technologies of learning* (pp.163–191). Mahwah, NJ: Erlbaum.

Huber, M. & Morreale, S. (2002). Situating the scholarship of teaching and learning: A cross-disciplinary conversation. In M. Huber & S. Morreale (Eds.) *Introduction to disciplinary styles in the scholarship of teaching and learning: Exploring common ground.* Menlo Park, CA: Carnegie Foundation for the Advancement of Teaching.

Johnson, D.W., Johnson, R.T. & Smith, K.A. (1998). *Active learning: Cooperation in the college classroom.* Edina, MN: Interaction Book Company.

Kellum, K.K., Carr, J.E. & Dozier, C.L. (2001). Response-card instruction and student learning in a college classroom. *Teaching of Psychology, 28*, 101–104.

Kelly, K.G. (2009). Student response systems ('clickers') in the psychology classroom: A beginner's guide. Society for the Teaching of Psychology Office of Teaching Resources in Psychology. Retrieved on 22 February 2009 from http://teachpsych.org/otrp/resources/kelly09.pdf

King, A. (1993). From sage on the stage to guide on the side. *College Teaching, 41*, 30–35.

Kinney, N.E. (2001). A guide to design and testing in online psychology courses. *Psychology Learning and Teaching, 1*, 16–20.

Klatzky, R.L. (in press). Giving psychological science away: The role of applications courses. *Perspectives on Psychological Science.*

Levy, G. & Peters, W. (2002). Undergraduates' views of best college courses. *Teaching of Psychology, 29*(1), 46–48.

Lomas, L. (2007). Are students customers? Perceptions of academic staff. *Quality in Higher Education, 13*(1), 31–44.

Maccoby, E.E., & Martin, J.A. (1983). Socialization in the context of the family: Parent–child interaction. In E. M. Hetherington (Ed.), P. H. Mussen (Series Ed.), *Handbook of child psychology: Vol. 4: Socialization, personality, and social development* (pp.1–101). New York: Wiley.

Meyers, C. & Jones, T.B. (1993). *Promoting active learning: Strategies for the college classroom.* San Francisco: Jossey-Bass.

Moran, D.R. (2000, June). *Is active learning for me?* Poster presented at APS Preconvention Teaching Institute, Denver.

Murray, B. (2000). Learning from real life. *APA Monitor, 31,* 72–73.

Ory, J. (2003). The final exam. *American Psychological Society Observer, 16,* 23–24, 34–35.

Parke, R.D., & Buriel, R. (2006). Child development and the family. In W. Damon & R.M. Lerner (Series Eds.) & N. Eisenberg (Vol. Ed.) *Handbook of child psychology* (6th edn), *Vol. 3: Social, emotional, and personality development* (pp. 429–504). New York: Wiley.

Pauk, W. & Owens, R.J.Q. (2008). *How to study in college* (9th edn). Belmont, CA: Wadsworth.

Paulson, S.E., Marchant, G.J. & Rothlisberg, B.A. (1998). Early adolescents' perceptions of patterns of parenting, teaching, and school atmosphere. *The Journal of Early Adolescence, 18,* 5–26.

Paulussen-Hoogeboom, M.C., Stams, G.J.J.M., Hermanns, J.M.A., Peetsma, T.T.D. & van den Wittenboer, G.L.H. (2008). Parenting style as a mediator between children's negative emotionality and problematic behavior in early childhood. *Journal of Genetic Psychology, 169,* 209–226.

Pellerin, L.A. (2004). Applying Baumrind's parenting typology to high schools: Toward a middle-range theory of authoritative socialization. *Social Science Research, 34,* 283–303.

Peterson, C. (2006). *A primer in positive psychology.* New York: Oxford University Press.

Rickard, H.C., Rogers, R., Ellis, N.R. & Beidleman, W.B. (1988). Some retention, but not enough. *Teaching of Psychology, 15,* 151–153.

Rimer, S. (2009, January 13). At M.I.T., large lectures are going the way of the blackboard. *The New York Times,* p.A12.

Roediger, H.L. & Karpicke, J.D. (2006). The power of testing memory: Basic research and implications for educational practice. *Perspectives on Psychological Science, 1,* 181–210.

Roosevelt, M. (2009, February 18). Student expectations seen as causing grade disputes. *The New York Times,* p. A15.

Schmidt, H.G., Cohen-Schotanus, J. & Arends, L.R. (2009). Impact of problem-based, active learning on graduation rates for 10 generations of Dutch medical students. *Medical Education, 43,* 211–218.

Scholl-Buckwald, S. (1985). The first meeting of the class. In J. Katz (Ed.) *Teaching as though students mattered: New directions for teaching and learning* (pp.13–21). San Francisco: Jossey-Bass.

Thompson, R.A. (2006). The development of the person: Social understanding, relationships, self, conscience. In W. Damon & R.M. Lerner (Series Eds.) & N. Eisenberg (Vol. Ed.) *Handbook of child psychology: Vol. 3. Social, emotional, and personality development* (6th edn). New York: Wiley.

Timpson, W.M. & Bendel-Simso, P. (1996). *Concepts and choices for teaching: Meeting the challenges in higher education.* Madison, WI: Magna Publications.

Upton, D. (2006). Online learning in speech and language therapy: Student performance and attitudes. *Education for Health, 19*, 22–31.

Upton, D. & Cooper C.D. (2006). Developing an on-line health psychology module. *Innovations in Education and Teaching International, 43*(3), 233–245.

Wentzel, K.R. (2002). Are effective teachers like good parents? Teaching styles and student adjustment in early adolescence. *Child Development, 73*, 287–301.

# 6

# Non-Sadistical Methods for Teaching Statistics

## Andy P. Field

IVE BEEN TOLD SOME OF YOU HAVE AN UNREASONABLE FEAR OF STATISTICS... SO IVE KEPT THE MATHS TO THE BARE MINIMUM...

This chapter covers the following areas:

- the unique challenges that face us when teaching statistics to psychologists (such as maths anxiety and a lack of student motivation);
- the Quality Assurance Agency's (QAA) and British Psychological Society's (BPS) guidelines for curriculum content and how these fit with more general principles of providing students with statistical literacy to take into the real world;
- the challenges facing us when teaching statistics, including student characteristics, large-group teaching, reducing anxiety, increasing motivation, the use of computers and textbook choice;

- a debate about the general approaches (such as using humour) and specific classroom techniques for reducing anxiety and increasing student motivation that might gel with your personal delivery style.

*Statistics are like bikinis. What they reveal is suggestive, but what they conceal is vital.* (Aaron Levenstein)

The aim of this chapter is to overview some of the unique challenges that face us when teaching statistics to psychologists, and to use the available evidence to suggest ways to overcome these challenges.

Statistics is an important topic. First it underpins the entire psychology curriculum at all levels of education. Psychology is a scientific discipline; you simply cannot learn psychology without understanding the philosophy of science and the statistical techniques that underpin that philosophy. This fact is acknowledged by the The Quality Assurance Agency for Higher Education (QAA) in the UK who, in consultation with the British Psychological Society (BPS), have published benchmark statements that define broadly the content and quality expectations of undergraduate degree programmes in psychology (The Quality Assurance Agency for Higher Education, 2007). In the QAA report, research methods are identified as a core knowledge area within psychology, but they also permeate five of the six defining principles for psychology and are core to the vast majority of both the transferable and subject-specific skills that students acquire through their psychology degree. Table 6.1 is a summary of the QAA-identified psychology-degree related defining principles, and transferable and specific skills that contain a direct or implied connection to research methods and statistics. This table should convince you that statistics and research methods are the very essence of a psychology degree.

A second thing to consider is the increasing importance of statistical literacy in society as a whole. My favourite definition of statistical literacy is 'People's ability to interpret and critically evaluate statistical information and data-based arguments appearing in diverse media channels, and their ability to discuss their opinions regarding such statistical information' (Gal, 2000) because it embodies the range of sources of statistical information that the average person has to negotiate in everyday life. People are bombarded with 'facts and figures' from politicians, newspaper journalists, TV and radio news, as well as in the workplace and advertisements. In his wonderful popular science book, *Bad Science*, Ben Goldacre (2008) reviews some high-profile

**Table 6.1** Table showing the QAA-identified defining principles, general and subject-specific skills for undergraduate psychology programmes in the UK that embody research methods and statistics (based on information from The Quality Assurance Agency for Higher Education, 2007)

| Defining principles | General skills | Specific skills |
|---|---|---|
| 1. Aim to produce a scientific understanding of the mind, brain, behaviour and experience, and of the complex interactions between these | Communicate effectively. Effective communication involves developing a cogent argument supported by relevant evidence and being sensitive to the needs and expectations of an audience | Apply multiple perspectives to psychological issues, recognising that psychology involves a range of research methods, theories, evidence and applications |
| 2. Present multiple perspectives in a way that fosters critical evaluation | Comprehend and use data effectively. This is accomplished through the significant core of research training in a psychology degree that acquaints graduates with understanding, analysing and presenting complex datasets | Integrate ideas and findings across the multiple perspectives in psychology and recognise distinctive psychological approaches to relevant issues |
| 3. Develop an understanding of the role of empirical evidence in the creation and constraint of theory, and also in how theory guides the collection and interpretation of empirical data | Problem-solve and reason scientifically. The research process, enables graduates to identify and pose research questions, to consider alternative approaches to their solutions and to evaluate outcomes | Carry out empirical studies involving a variety of methods of data collection, including experiments, observation, psychometric tests, questionnaires, interviews and field studies |
| 4. Include the acquisition and knowledge of a range of research skills and methods for investigating experience and behaviour, culminating in an ability to conduct research independently | Make critical judgements and evaluations. The need to take different perspectives on issues and problems, and to evaluate them in a critical and sceptical manner to arrive at supported conclusions.... The | Carry out an extensive piece of independent empirical research … demonstrating the ability to reason about the data and present the findings effectively; discussing findings in terms |

| No. | | | |
|---|---|---|---|
| | | importance of looking for similarities and general principles to increase the power of the analysis is also stressed | of previous research; evaluating methodologies and analyses employed |
| 5. | Develop knowledge, leading to an ability to appreciate and critically evaluate theory, research findings and applications | Use effectively personal planning and project management skills… In particular, psychology degrees culminate in the completion of an independent, empirical inquiry where a pragmatic approach to a time-limited project is required | Employ evidence-based reasoning and examine practical, theoretical and ethical issues associated with the use of different methodologies, paradigms and methods of analysis in psychology |
| 6. | | Handle primary source material critically | Generate and explore hypotheses and research questions |
| 7. | | Be computer literate. Psychology students … will display, at the very least, skill in the use of word processing, databases and statistical software packages | Identify and evaluate general patterns in behaviour, psychological functioning and experience |
| 8. | | | Analyse data using both quantitative and qualitative methods |
| 9. | | | Present and evaluate research findings |
| 10. | | | Use a variety of psychological tools, including specialist software, laboratory equipment and psychometric instruments |

examples of journalists misreporting scientific findings (for example, the MMR scandal in the UK) and companies making claims based on 'science' about their products (e.g. homeopathic remedies), both of which have a huge societal impact. The importance of being able to evaluate critically the statistical and scientific information in the world should not be underestimated. Society is becoming increasingly driven by the scientific model yet the media are rarely equipped to present science critically or accurately. As such, the very least we can do is to provide our psychology students with the transferable skills necessary to evaluate scientific evidence for themselves (Rumsey, 2002).

This chapter reviews some basic principals in teaching statistics to psychologists. I begin by reviewing the nature of the problem before looking at some general issues in deciding what to teach on your course. I then move on to explore how statistics should be taught by looking at both specific (e.g. the challenges of large-group teaching, textbook choice) and some general issues (e.g. student characteristics, the use of humour and gimmicks to increase motivation and reduce anxiety). The chapter ends with a brief overview of the main points.

## 666 – Numbers Are the Beast: What's So Hard about Teaching Statistics?

*If I had only one day left to live, I would live it in my statistics class: it would seem so much longer.*

As this classic joke suggests, psychology students hate statistics. The very mention of 'statistics' can invoke spontaneous states of coma, frustration or just plain terror in the typical psychology student. Ask anyone who teaches statistics to undergraduate psychologists and they will regale you with tales of students who are anxious, bored, unmotivated and constantly wondering why they are being tortured with statistics when they hoped to spend three years analysing their friends on a leather couch. As such, engaging students in statistics is not only essential for their survival in our pseudo-scientific media world; it is, I would argue, the greatest challenge in teaching psychology. If can make your students love their statistics course, then you have the teaching equivalent of turning faeces into gold.

According to Conners *et al.* (1998), there are four main problems in teaching statistics to undergraduate psychologists: statistics anxiety, motivation, performance extremes (it is difficult to pitch the level of the material because students tend to be either brilliant or hopeless at statistics), and making learning last. Arguably the latter two of these problems will be eased by addressing motivation and anxiety. There is a long-held assumption that a major obstacle in teaching statistics is that students suffer anxiety and lack of motivation about statistics courses. Statistics anxiety has been seen as 'one of the most significant barriers that instructors encounter while teaching statistics' (Bessant, 1992, p.143) and students are believed to display 'considerable fear of anything with the slightest quantitative flavor to it' (Blalock, 1987, p.164).

Data supporting this assumption of anxiety is hard to unearth. One recent study suggests that 25.1 per cent of sociology students reported being 'very anxious' and 32.8 per cent 'anxious' about taking a statistics course (DeCesare, 2007). Another cites values of 2/3 to 4/5 of graduate students experiencing uncomfortable levels of statistics anxiety (Onwuegbuzie & Wilson, 2003). Significantly more women than men report being anxious, and lower expected course grades predicted higher levels of reported anxiety (DeCesare, 2007). Although this research shows that the majority of students are anxious about statistics, it is not the case that they all are.

Statistics anxiety typically has a detrimental effect on course performance. Positive attitudes to statistics have been found to enhance performance on introductory statistics courses (Elmore & Vasu, 1980) whereas statistics anxiety causally decreases performance (Benson, 1989; Onwuegbuzie & Wilson, 2003). Statistics anxiety affects a student's ability to understand research articles, to analyse and to interpret statistical data, and it reduces memory efficiency when trying to understand and to learn new statistical material (Onwuegbuzie & Wilson, 2003). Blalock (1987) suggested that overcoming fears should be a primary goal in teaching statistics.

Students often perceive statistics as unconnected to their degree topic, which leads them to believe that it is unimportant (Paxton, 2006). This perception could be exacerbated if the link to research methods is not directly made in core psychology courses (see below). Also, many students enter their psychology degree programme unaware that data analysis is part and parcel of the scientific model to which psychology aspires. These factors reduce student motivation. Student motivation is also, of course, closely linked to statistics anxiety: anxiety reduces student's self-efficacy, which reduces their achievement expectancies, and makes them likely to give up when confronted with challenging material (Paxton, 2006).

In the wider context this anxiety and reduced motivation might prevent some very gifted students from pursuing careers in psychology because they feel that a lack of confidence with statistics might prevent them from doing their job effectively or lead colleagues to perceive them as 'stupid'. Although the obvious examples are research or academic posts, a great many psychology careers make use of the fundamental research skills that are the backbone of the society's core undergraduate curriculum. It will also prevent many students from acquiring the transferable and discipline-specific skills identified by the QAA. As I have alluded to before, it will also mean that some students leave their degrees ill equipped to evaluate the statistical information and data-based arguments with which they are bombarded in everyday life.

Giving psychology students basic statistical literacy skills is harder than ever because the foundations upon which we can build are being eroded. Undergraduate psychology students' core mathematical skills are on the decline: a study that took measures of calculation, algebraic reasoning, graphical interpretation, proportionality and ratio, probability and sampling, and estimation (Mulhern & Wylie, 2004) showed, broadly speaking, that a 1984 cohort outperformed a 1992 cohort on some measures, and the 1992 cohort outperformed a 2002 cohort on all measures. In the United States, too, the National Assessment of Adult Literacy (NAAL) report on quantitative literacy (which can be summed up as the ability to use numbers in printed materials for interpretation or calculation) claimed that only 13 per cent of adults were proficient, 33 per cent were intermediate, 33 per cent basic and 22 per cent below basic (Hulsizer & Woolf, 2009). If students have any insight into their abilities, then they will be less confident and, consequently, more anxious about statistics courses than in the past. It is increasingly important, therefore, to strive to engage students in statistical material in a way that decreases anxiety and increases motivation. In this chapter I will, in due course, look at methods for reducing fear and increasing student motivation and engagement.

## What Should We Teach?

The QAA benchmarks and BPS curriculum for the graduate basis for registration in the UK provide a broad framework within which to develop your own curriculum. The QAA identifies the core statistical outcome for students as learning 'the nature and appropriate statistical analysis of data'. In terms of skills, Table 6.1 summarises in detail the research methods-related skills expected of a graduate psychology student in the UK. The QAA summarises these skills by suggesting that a student should as a bare minimum be able to 'reason scientifically and demonstrate the relationship between theory and evidence; reason statistically and demonstrate competence in a range of statistical methods; initiate, design, conduct and report an empirically based research project under appropriate supervision' but typically they should 'reason scientifically, understand the role of evidence and make critical judgements about arguments in psychology; pose, operationalise and critique research questions; demonstrate substantial competence in research skills through practical activities; reason statistically and use a range of statistical methods with confidence; and competently initiate, design, conduct and report an empirically based research project under appropriate supervision.'

## What skills do we want students to acquire?

In terms of the specific content that might lead to these goals, there is a reasonable amount of consistency across degree programmes (for example, I doubt you would find a psychology degree that did not cover *t*-tests, ANOVA and regression). It would not be appropriate for me, even if I had the space, to attempt to prescribe a curriculum of 'necessary' statistical procedures that should be covered. Instead, I will use this section to consider some general issues in curriculum design.

In designing your course it is worth considering not just the hoops that the BPS (or any other accrediting body for that matter) might expect you to jump through, but also what you want to achieve. Accepting the basic point that we should attempt to make students statistically literate as a transferable skill (Rumsey, 2002), regardless of whether they can perform a MANOVA or whatever test, then we might think about the core skills required to understand and critique statements such as 'A study of thousands of men found that eating 10 or more servings of tomato sauce or tomatoes a week reduced prostate cancer risk by 45 per cent' (http://news.bbc.co.uk/1/hi/health/4896026.stm). In a thought-provoking paper, Utts sums up the problem elegantly: 'What good is it to know how to carry out a *t*-test if a student cannot read a newspaper article and determine that hypothesis testing has been misused?' (Utts, 2003, p.78).

Utts (2003) suggests seven core statistical ideas that could be described as 'useful life skills'. These are:

- when causal relationships can and cannot be inferred, including the difference between observational studies and randomised experiments;
- the difference between statistical significance and practical importance, especially when using large sample sizes;

- the difference between finding 'no effect' and finding no statistically significant effect, especially when sample sizes are small;
- sources of bias in surveys and experiments, such as poor wording of questions, volunteer response and socially desirable answers;
- the idea that coincidences and seemingly very improbable events are not uncommon because there are so many possibilities (to use a classic example, although most people would consider it an unbelievable coincidence/unlikely event to find two people in a group of 30 that share the same birthday, the probability is actually .7, which is fairly high);
- 'confusion of the inverse' in which a conditional probability in one direction is confused with the conditional probability in the other direction (for example, the prosecutor's fallacy);[1]
- understanding that variability is natural, and that 'normal' is not the same as 'average' (for example, the average male height in the UK is 175 cm; although a man of 190 cm is, therefore, well above average, his height is within the normal range of male heights).

Although it is clearly desirable to teach these skills within a psychology context, if we are to provide students with transferable skills, then we might consider whether we can use real-world examples to teach these skills. This could have the benefit of making the class more interesting (see my subsequent section on exterminating boredom), and also helping students to apply knowledge beyond the psychological realm. For example, most students use mobile phones, and might be interested in media headlines reporting that mobile phone use causes brain tumours (e.g. 'Mobile phones "can give you brain tumours"' in the *Daily Telegraph* on 7 September 2008). By inspecting the data from such a study (e.g. Lönn *et al.*, 2005), and responses to that study (e.g. the 'Letters to the Editor' about the Lönn *et al.* study, which point out several flaws), students can learn about the inherent subjectivity of research and data analysis as well as practise applying their own critical skills to real research/data (that hopefully interest them). Some useful examples of statistics-related media faux pas can be found at Chance News (see the weblink in Online Resources below).

### Throwing out the recipe book

It is very easy to forget aims such as these when designing statistics courses in favour of a focus on doing tests and 'recipe book' style teaching. For example, despite widespread criticism of null hypothesis significance testing (NHST)[2]

(Miles & Field, 2007), most students end their degrees unaware of these criticisms. In fact, many students finish their degrees armed with a great many misconceptions about hypothesis testing. Let's take, for example, the *p*-value, a concept so fundamental to psychological statistics that you might reasonably expect students to at least understand what it represents. Haller and Kraus (2002) carried out a study in which they presented participants with six statements relating to a scenario in which a *p* = .01 had been found, and were asked which of the statements were true. In fact all statements were false but reflected common misconceptions about NHST. They found that all students asked this question said that at least one of the statements was correct. However, the students really should not be blamed for their ignorance because the same study showed that 80 per cent of the lecturers and professors who taught statistics also endorsed at least one of the statements. However, even though only one in every five methods lecturers knew the correct answer, they still fared better than their research-active colleagues who did not teach statistics, 90 per cent of whom thought at least one of the statements was correct.

Over 10 years ago the Board of Scientific Affairs (BSA) of the American Psychological Association (APA) convened a committee called the Task Force on Statistical Inference (TFSI) whose charge was 'to elucidate some of the controversial issues surrounding applications of statistics including significance testing and its alternatives; alternative underlying models and data transformation; and newer methods made possible by powerful computers.' The eventual report produced by the chair of this committee was published in *American Psychologist* (Wilkinson, 1999) and suggests (amongst other things) that 'It is hard to imagine a situation in which a dichotomous accept–reject decision is better than reporting an actual *p* value or, better still, a confidence interval. Never use the unfortunate expression "accept the null hypothesis". Always provide some effect size estimate when reporting a *p* value' and

Always present effect sizes for primary outcomes. If the units of measurement are meaningful on a practical level (e.g. number of cigarettes smoked per day), then we usually prefer an unstandardized measure (regression coefficient or mean difference) to a standardized measure (*r* or *d*). It helps to add brief comments that place these effect sizes in a practical and theoretical context. (p.599)

These guidelines fit with two of Utts's (2003) core statistical ideas (the need to understand the effect of sample size, the difference between statistical significance and practical importance, the difference between finding 'no effect' and finding no statistically significant effect). It seems to me then that to fulfil the aims of providing real-world statistical literacy and also discipline-specific statistical literacy, we should strive to place a greater emphasis on inspecting data, quantifying effects (with confidence intervals and effect sizes) and the inherent subjectivity of data interpretation and uncertainty within results. Rather than teaching rule-based acceptance/rejection of hypotheses, we should encourage students to treat data analysis rather like solving a crime in which evidence (all of which has some uncertainty attached to it) is accumulated. Once the evidence stacks up sufficiently in favour of one interpretation, then we go with it, but acknowledge that there is still some uncertainty involved.

## *Which test should I use?*

Recipe-book teaching encourages students to follow rules, and one rule that seems to be encouraged is that for every situation there is one, and only one, *correct* statistical test to apply. Failure to apply this *correct* test will at best result in failing your degree and at worst find you burning in the fires of hell while Satan pastes your body with cream cheese before setting loose his hell-gerbils to feast upon you. I have often imagined a world in which every student asking me 'Which test I should use?' has to first give me £1. In this world, I am the proud owner of a very expensive shiny new drum kit.

When faced with the question of 'which test should I use?' my stock response is 'you should probably use a general linear model'. It will come as no surprise to anyone reading this chapter that most statistical procedures used in psychology (e.g. the *t*-test, ANOVA, regression, chi-square, loglinear analysis, logistic regression, mixed model ANOVA, hierarchical linear models, factor analysis, discriminant function analysis) are based on the principles of the linear model (Cohen, 1968; Field, 2009b). It makes sense (to me at least) to teach the general linear model (GLM) first; once students have an understanding of this, most other tests can be explained as variations on this basic theme. In my textbook *Discovering Statistics using SPSS*, and my course I take this approach. Readers are first introduced to the only equation that they need to know:

$$\text{outcome}_i = (\text{model}) + \text{error}_i$$

The word 'model' in this equation can then be replaced with 'the mean', then a simple linear model ($b_0 + b_1 X_1$) or more complex one ($b_0 + b_1 X_1 + b_2 X_2 \ldots$). As such, you begin by showing that the mean is a model, that there is error attached to that model, that this error can be measured (sums of squares and the standard deviation) to tell us something useful about the fit of the model to the data. These ideas can then be extended to regression and all that changes is the complexity of what replaces 'model' in the equation. Assessing a regression model for error and the use of sums and squares to measure fit are directly analogous to when the model is the mean; as such, you are reinforcing existing knowledge but in a new context. The *t*-test and ANOVA can then be introduced as special cases of the linear model. If students have absorbed what they have previously learnt then ANOVA simply becomes a specific application of knowledge that they already have – it need not be perceived as a new and completely different topic. ANOVA can easily be extended to ANCOVA within a GLM context and so on. The key thing is that students are introduced to concepts (models, fit, sums of squares, etc.) relevant to every topic and that are, therefore, reinforced throughout the course. The emphasis is on building specific knowledge around a core of concepts that underpin the GLM. The advantages (in my opinion) of this approach are:

- there is a gradual building of knowledge upon a core of foundation concepts that are reinforced in each session;
- it emphasises the conceptual similarities between statistical tests rather than creating apparent differences between them;
- it makes complex topics such as ANCOVA and hierarchical linear models relatively easy to understand because students already possess a core scaffold of knowledge on which to hang more advanced concepts. For example, if ANOVA is explained as GLM, then it is a simple matter to show students that you merely extend the linear model to include a continuous predictor (the covariate).

One final point is that, regardless of what you teach, it is important not to think of statistics as a lone course. Students often struggle to see the relevance of data analysis to psychology. To this end, data gathering exercises and analysis should be incorporated into the other core QAA topics (e.g. cognitive psychology, developmental psychology, etc.). There is evidence that teaching research methods within 'non-methods' classes improves students' quantitative reasoning (Bridges *et al.*, 1998). In addition, incorporating data analysis into other core courses reinforces what is learnt in statistics classes and provides an opportunity for students to actively generalise their knowledge beyond the specific examples used to teach them.

# How to Teach Statistics

There are thousands of resources available for teaching statistics, whether they be web pages containing PowerPoint slides, instructional flash movies, songs, jokes, cartoons, class activities, handouts (see the end of this chapter), textbooks, or research articles and books with pedagogic advice. A chapter is too small a space to do justice to the enormous effort that a great many people have put into helping others to teach statistics (and students to learn it). All I can do is to try to assimilate some of the evidence on what is good practice interspersed with my own intuitions about what works. I will attempt to look at how statistics should be taught to psychologists by looking first at two general topics: individual characteristics of students, and how humour can be a useful tool in teaching. These themes should be borne in mind as I look at more specific issues such as how to deal with large-group teaching, the use of computers in statistics teaching and, finally, how to choose a textbook. In all sections I will return to my earlier theme of how to keep students motivated and to reduce their anxiety.

Although I will do my best to help you along your way, it is worth mentioning three other resources. First, an article by Becker (1996) which summarises the literature (up to that point) on teaching statistics. She found that about 33 per cent of studies looked at computer use in statistics teaching, 14 per cent evaluated teaching materials, and about 53 per cent looked at teaching approaches. Her article is a very useful point from which to discover articles that explore these topics. Second, a great deal of the research into teaching statistics appears in *The Journal of Statistics Education*, a free online journal, and for research specific to psychology try *Teaching of Psychology*. Last, but certainly not least, is an excellent book *A Guide to Teaching Statistics* (Hulsizer & Woolf, 2009), which takes a much more detailed journey through the teaching of statistics than I can here. I recommend this book to both new and experienced statistics teachers.

## *Student characteristics*

Several personality variables are important in predicting success on and attitudes towards statistics courses. We have seen already, for example, that statistics anxiety causally decreases performance (Benson, 1989; Onwuegbuzie & Wilson, 2003). Attitudes to quantitative concepts, perception of mathematical ability, state anxiety, basic mathematical achievement, expectations of grade outcome, gender, previous performance in a maths class and the number of previous maths classes all significantly predicted success on an introductory statistics course (Feinberg & Halperin, 1978). In this study, men perceived themselves as better at maths and did better on the course. Course performance is also predicted by positive attitudes to statistics, confidence and motivation to learn (Schutz *et al.*, 1998). In a meta-analysis of gender differences in applied statistics achievement, it appeared that males outperform females when the outcome was exams or mathematical problem-solving, but when the outcome was grades, females outperformed males (Schram, 1996).

This very brief review of some of the student characteristics that might affect course performance reinforces my general point that motivation and anxiety are key barriers to learning: students who have negative attitudes to mathematics and statistics, or who lack confidence or motivation, typically do worse. Although gender differences exist, they appear to depend on what the outcome measure is; however, females do seem to have lower expectations of their performance and mathematical abilities and have more negative attitudes towards quantitative concepts (Feinberg & Halperin, 1978). Given the large female-to-male ratio on psychology courses, this highlights the absolute necessity to create a supportive learning environment and to foster positive attitudes and expectations about the course. We will now look at some ways that such attitudes might be encouraged.

## *Humour and teaching statistics*

In the classroom, 'humour' can take the form of jokes, cartoons or even songs. For a comprehensive summary of resources refer to Lesser and Pearl (2008), and a database of examples go to the Consortium for the Advancement of Undergraduate Statistics Education (CAUSE) website. My teaching and writing has always incorporated a 'humorous and self-deprecating style' (to quote my publishers) which has contributed to my winning teaching awards from both my university and the BPS, and a book award for *Discovering Statistics Using SPSS* in 2007. This style is just the way I am, not some master stroke of genius on my part. However, I have recently been thinking about the merits and problems with using humour in the statistics classroom. I recently wrote a review of whether humour was a useful tool in reducing statistics anxiety and increasing student motivation (Field, 2009a), and there are other excellent reviews of the use of humour and fun resources for statistics teaching (Friedman *et al.*, 2002; Lesser & Pearl, 2008). I'll summarise the main points here.

Humour in teaching is difficult to study because one person's hilarious joke is another person's tumbleweed rolling across the lecture theatre. Consequently, there is only a small literature on the subject. If you ask students, then research suggests that 96.6 per cent report that they would want an 'ideal' teacher to use humour often or occasionally (Epting *et al.*, 2004) and student evaluations of teachers' effectiveness and appeal are positive related to their use of humour (Bryant, *et al.*, 1980). Does this make humour effective as an educational tool for reducing anxiety and improving learning?

Certainly, conventional wisdom suggests that humour in public speaking is a good thing, and that the information gained by an audience is enhanced by humour because it increases attention. However, when comparing humorous and non-humorous speeches, there is conflicting evidence about whether humour improves information retention (Gruner, 1967). One study that specifically evaluated a statistics course that used humorous cartoons as a means to reduce statistics anxiety showed that not only did students perceive the cartoons as having reduced their anxiety, but scores on the maths anxiety rating scale significantly diminished from pre- to post-course (Schacht & Stewart, 1990). However, there was no control condition in which cartoons were not used so it is unclear whether the use of cartoons was the causal agent in reducing anxiety.

In terms of assisting learning, there are some studies (although not all specific to statistics teaching) suggesting that humour can be a useful tool in facilitating learning. A study on children manipulated televised educational programmes so that they contained clips of humorous programmes (such as *The Muppet Show*) or non-humorous inserts placed such that they didn't interrupt an educational point. Results showed that children learnt more from educational films containing humorous inserts compared to films containing non-humorous inserts or no inserts (Zillmann *et al.*, 1980). The authors concluded that the humorous inserts increased learning by improving attention. These humorous inserts where fairly randomly interspersed within the educational content and were unrelated to the material to be learned. Garner (2006) compared undergraduate evaluations of three 40-minute lecture videos on statistics research methods with or without humour inserts. Students shown the humour videos gave significantly higher ratings to the lesson, how well it communicated information and the quality of the lecturer. Students exposed to the humour conditions also recalled significantly more information on the topic. Berk and Nanda (2006) found that humorous directions given to students had a significant (and practically important) effect on student attitudes towards content and anxiety in statistics courses and showed moderate correlations with overall achievement. Kaplan and Pascoe (1977) systematically manipulated whether humour in a lecture was related to the topic being taught (concept-related humour), was unrelated humour, or was a mix of the two. Compared to lectures with no humour, concepts presented humorously were not better remembered immediately after the lecture, but were at 6-week follow up. This suggests that humour can be a useful tool in making learning last (one of the four obstacles mentioned earlier). However, the effect that humour had was concept-specific; unlike in Zillman *et al.*'s study, humour did not improve overall learning – it improved only recall of the specific concepts that were described using humour. One strategic approach to teaching statistics might, therefore, be to use humour selectively when explaining particularly difficult constructs. In line with this suggestion, Lesser and Pearl (2008) suggest that fun should not be perceived as frivolous and unrelated to the course (a piece of advice I would personally do well to attend to more than I do). They suggest asking yourself five questions:

- What is the fun item or artefact (e.g. a particular comic strip)?
- What is the course goal or statistical concept you would associate with the item?
- Where would you use the item (e.g. in class or on a website)?
- What would you do/say/ask in class before using the fun item to 'set it up'?
- What would you do/say/ask in class after using the fun item?

Songs can be a very useful tool for reinforcing statistical material (Lesser, 2001; Lesser & Pearl, 2008; VanVoorhis, 2002). The CAUSE website lists an astonishing 50 songs composed by various people about statistics (including such delights as 'Give Stats a Chance' sung to the tune of 'Give Peace a Chance', and 'I Got You Bayes' sung along to the famous Sonny and Cher song of almost the same name). I find songs a useful way to break up lectures, and have a few of my own contributions to the world of statistical music. One example is 'The Transformation Song' which is sung to the tune of Britney Spears's 'Hit Me Baby One More Time':

> My Distribution is killing me
> Why can't it be shaped normally? [Normally]
> My K-S test is significant; it is a Sign … to
> Transform my data one more time

VanVoorhis (2002) compared GPA-matched groups of psychology statistics students who either read three definitions or sang jingle versions. The singing group performed significantly better on short-answer test items. Performance was significantly correlated with student's self-rating of their familiarity with the jingle.

The potential benefits of using humour in the classroom are that it enhances communication, reduces student anxiety, 'humanises' the lecturer (making them seem more approachable), improves recall of information, makes the course more interesting, fosters openness in the teaching environment and increases student participation and attention (see Field, 2009a; Friedman *et al.*, 2002; Lesser & Pearl, 2008, for reviews). However, it is not without pitfalls too. The research supporting humour as a teaching tool has, by necessity, been fairly limited. There are numerous styles of humour, and the extent to which humour can be a useful tool probably depends on the extent to which the teacher's personality lends itself to being funny. Bryant *et al.* (1980) categorised the humour characteristics of lecturers and found interesting gender differences. Humour was overall associated with effectiveness in male tutors but not female tutors. For male tutors, funny stories were better than jokes, riddles or puns. Spontaneous humour was found to be more effective than prepared humour, humour related to the topic being taught was better than unrelated humour, hostile/aggressive humour and nonsense humour correlated with effectiveness but sexual humour did not. Effectiveness was correlated with humour that involved characters other than the tutor or students. For female tutors the use of puns had a *detrimental* relationship with effectiveness. No other humour characteristics correlated with effectiveness for female tutors. The authors suggest that these gender differences may stem from students' gender stereotypes of appropriate behaviour in the classroom; 30 years on from this study these stereotypes have (on the whole) changed for the better and in a more contemporary setting we might find very different results.

Another potential danger with using humorous examples is that you stray too far from the topic that you teach. One way to bring some humour into the lecture theatre while staying 'on topic' is to find examples of real research that address important theoretical questions, but that are tested in an unusual way and can feed into not only amusing comments but also lively discussions about methods and research design. My textbook (Field, 2009b) is littered with such examples. One such study by Miller *et al.* (2007) used lap dancers as an ingenious method of testing an important evolutionary theory that the 'oestrus' phase (during which females are more sexually receptive and attractive) has been uniquely lost in human females.

Miller and his colleagues reasoned that if the 'hidden oestrus' theory is incorrect then men should find women most attractive during the fertile phase of their menstrual cycle compared to the pre-fertile (menstrual) and post-fertile (luteal) phase. To measure how attractive men found women in an ecologically valid way, they measured the tips received by lap dancers during different phases of their cycle. This piece of research addresses an important scientific study, is probably intrinsically interesting to a great many psychology students (who are predominantly female), may tie in with what they learn about evolutionary psychology, but also opens up many avenues for jokes (mine usually involve the conversation that might have happened in an imaginary meeting between Miller and his funding body when he told them he needed the money to meet lap dancers).

A final point worth considering stems back to my comment that one person's funny is another person's tumbleweed (or worse still, offensive comment). In fact, my advocation of the aforementioned lap dancing study in my review of using humour in statistics teaching (Field, 2009a) provoked some letters to the editor accusing me of all sorts of things. Similarly, my textbook has been banned at a Tehran book fair and refused adoption at some colleges in more conservative parts of the US because of the 'lively' content. What this shows more than anything is that opinions differ and you need to be sensitive to your audience (chapter 2 on student issues has a discussion of student diversity that is pertinent here). Although it does not matter if your textbook gets banned, it does matter if you offend one of your students with a careless joke. As liberal-minded academics, the risks may be low, but it is important that you generate an environment in which students feel able to talk to you if they feel uncomfortable with what you have said or the examples that you choose.

## The Challenges of Large-Group Teaching: Gimmicks

In chapter 2, the topic of large-group teaching was raised. Large-group teaching (actually, any size group teaching) is particularly problematic in statistics courses because of student anxiety and (lack of) motivation. Keeping the students interested is an enormous challenge. A second challenge is making these sessions interactive when students are so anxious about the subject. In this section I look at some of gimmicks that people have used to keep students interested in statistics. One obvious way to reduce anxiety and increase motivation is to make the sessions lively, interactive and funny (see the previous section on humour). Having written probably more than I should on why smutty and self-deprecating jokes should routinely be made in statistics classes, I intend to focus now on some specific classroom techniques that people have used to keep students interested and involved.

One technique I have used to encouraging class participation (which is good for active learning) is chocolate. Early on in the course I reward responses to questions (whether right or wrong) with chocolates. This seems to have the effect of making a generally friendlier environment, but also reinforces active participation. It is also a good opportunity to show that I am not the kind of person who ridicules incorrect answers but does praise attempts at the correct answer. I have also found chocolate a useful tool when explaining partitioning variance (in, for example, regression and ANOVA). In one such demonstration, three students volunteer (who do not have a chocolate allergy and are willing to eat chocolate in front of 250 of their peers) to participate. Each is given a label representing a variable in the data example. A chocolate bar is then produced representing the variance in the outcome variable. The first student/variable is asked how many chunks of the chocolate they would like to eat. They will respond (i.e. 4 chunks) and that amount of chocolate is broken off and they eat it. The next variable/student is then asked how much they want. They are also asked whether they would like the first student to vomit up the chocolate so that they can eat that or whether they would prefer some fresh chocolate from the bar. When they ask for fresh chocolate, then this can be used to illustrate 'unique variance' and the idea of a semi-partial correlation: a predictor in regression should not explain variance that another variable already explains (i.e. it should not want chocolate that has already been eaten), but should explain unique variance (i.e. eat a fresh bit of chocolate). By comparing how much chocolate each student/variable eats we can also demonstrate the notion that different predictors explain different amounts of variance in regression.

Speaking of chocolate, others have reported techniques that use chocolate too. Dyck and Gee (1998) used M&Ms to illustrate the concept of a sampling distribution. Briefly, each student was given a packet of M&Ms that they opened. The class decided on a colour (e.g. blue) and each student counted the number of sweets they had of that colour. They could then eat the sweets. Five students were randomly sampled and reported the number of blue sweets that they had. The mean was then computed. A further five students then reported their data and the mean was again computed. Further samples were taken and eventually a frequency of sample means created. The population mean was also computed by collecting the values from all students. This neat demonstration illustrated that the sampling distribution mean is an approximation of the population mean, that the sampling distribution variance is smaller than that of the population, and that the shape of the sampling distribution is approximately normal. Self-report data and a quiz suggested that this demonstration was fun for students but that they also learnt from it.

Using data from students has been advocated by others too (Schacht & Stewart, 1992). In their demonstration students were given two vignettes describing a crime during which police interview a youth. In one vignette the youth behaves disrespectfully but respectfully in the other. Students read only one of the two vignettes and then rate the punishment that they would deliver to the youth on a Likert scale. Data from the class are collected on the board, descriptive statistics computed (and possibly a *t*-test). In addition, Schacht and Stewart advocate using cartoons as a stimulus from which to get students to generate research questions and then classroom data. For example they are shown a cartoon in which a cat stands by a sign that reads 'Cat shower' but instead of a shower head there is a large tongue. From this students generate a hypothesis (such as 'how many licks does a cat need to clean itself?') and then students generate estimates. These lively classroom activities get students thinking about the research process as well as keeping their attention. However, if you are getting students to generate their own research question and data, it is worth having some limits on what question they ask based on the student group (for example, collating data about sexual preferences or activities might make some students feel very awkward or embarrassed).

One technique that I use a lot is lively examples, which I try to base around popular youth culture and bizarre research. My lectures and materials (Field, 2009b; Field & Miles, in press) are strewn (not literally) with dead bodies, ejaculating quail, bug-eating celebrities, black metal bands and men with eels up their anus. I am not alone. Dolinsky (1998) reports using datasets provided with SPSS that showed whether people had watched an X-rated movie. Students predicted the number of people and were surprised to find how low the real value was compared to their estimate. The crosstabs procedure was then used to break down the data to show that the high rates that they predicted matched the rates in young males (this drove the student's expectations), but that the rates were extremely low in older people and females (hence the low overall rate of positive responses). Morgan (2001) reports a demonstration using 50 real obituaries from local newspapers that students code for age, gender, the number of children and so on. These data are then used to illustrate important issues such as real data are messy (not all obituaries have the necessary information to code, for example, the number of surviving children), outliers matter (a child death will skew the mean age of death), real questions can be answered (do men really die younger than women?), and correlation does not mean causation (for example, a positive correlation between the age of death and the number of children does not mean that having more children makes you live longer). Using these data, students can actively generate other hypotheses. Morgan rightly cautions that students need to be warned about the content of the session (they may have had a recent bereavement) and suggests that a useful precaution might be to use newspapers from a different area. This reiterates an important general point that I mentioned in the previous section, which is that it is important to find your own voice and be sensitive to the group that you teach. Talking about men with eels up their anus suits my delivery style, and I teach in a very liberal part of the UK, but these unusual examples make my book less well received in more conservative parts of the world.

## Calculations or Computers?

With the advent of user-friendly and versatile statistical packages such as SPSS, Minitab, Systat, SAS and R, there is probably less need than ever to teach statistical tests 'by hand'. Whereas in the past courses would have been based on teaching the underlying mathematics of tests, nowadays a greater emphasis can be placed upon conceptual understanding while leaving computers to crunch the numbers. In fact, psychology departments use computers in about 70 per cent of introductory statistics courses (Bartz & Sabolik, 2001). Textbooks also routinely integrate theory and computer application with varying emphasis on theory (see the next section). Some authors have actively urged teachers to move away from computational formulae and towards definitional formulae which tell the student something about what the statistic means conceptually (Guttmannova *et al.*, 2005). Others similarly stress that less emphasis should be placed on calculations and more on interpretation and conducting statistical studies (Utts, 2003).

Personally, I find some calculations (such as sums of squares, and $F$-ratio) useful because the computations give such a good conceptual flavour of what the statistics represent (Guttmannova *et al.*, 2005); however, I rely heavily on conceptual understanding, interpretation and doing the tests on SPSS more than number crunching. I agree with some good points made by Hulsizer and Woolf (2009) who suggest that too much hand calculation can hinder learning because (a) it is not what students would do when conducting real research; (b) they can become too focused on 'getting the right answer' at the expense of understanding what the test is doing/showing; and (c) hand calculations do little to reduce maths anxiety. However, some students seem to like them: when asked, 43.8 per cent said that they preferred hand calculations, with the majority claiming that learning by computers was 'cheating' (Maltby, 2001). Of course, by using computers we are also developing some important transferable skills in computer literacy (Raymondo & Garrett, 1998), computer-based data analysis and spreadsheet use.

Computers can be useful in other ways than just running statistical tests. Emond (1982) describes a computer simulation in which values of the slope and intercept in regression are changed to show students what effect it has on the model. In addition, animated diagrams that illustrate statistical concepts (e.g. the method of least squares) can improve students' retention of these ideas (Wender & Muehlboeck, 2003). Interactive statistical programs such as Estimating Statistics (ESTAT) which is designed to illustrate concepts such as the mean and standard deviation appear also to be popular with students (Britt *et al.*, 2002).

## Which Textbook?

Textbooks that teach statistics to psychologists typically integrate theory with computer applications. They vary in their emphasis on theory or application. In this section, the textbooks I mention represent a pseudo-random sample of the many available. I have not read every textbook that there is to read and, therefore, those that I mention are ones that I like and happen to know about. Authors of books not cited should not take offence; there are simply too many good books to mention. There are books that focus mainly on theory and add the computer application of these methods as addenda to this theory; these books vary from the introductory (e.g. Coolican, 2009; Howitt & Cramer, 2008; Langdridge & Hagger-Johnson, 2009; Miles & Banyard, 2007; Wright & London, 2009a) to the more advanced (e.g. Howell, 2006; Tabachnick & Fidell, 2007). Other books take a different approach and use the power of computers to teach at a more conceptual level and to avoid (to a lesser or greater degree) the mathematics behind the tests (e.g. Brace *et al.*, 2009; Dalgaard, 2008; Dancey & Reidy, 2008; Kinnear & Gray, 2008; Pallant, 2007; Verzani, 2004; Wright & London, 2009b). Some other books are a sort of hybrid between these two extremes in which the fairly substantial statistical theory is integrated with practical examples based on computer software that are used to reinforce the conceptual understanding of the theory (e.g. Crawley, 2007; Field, 2009b; Field & Miles, in press).

Many textbooks aim to reduce student anxiety about statistics by emphasising the application of statistics at the expense of equations, whereas others, such as my own, are rather heavier on theory but attempt to use humorous examples and a flippant writing style to keep students motivated and fear-free. On the plus side, chapters from humorous textbooks are rated by students as more enjoyable (Klein *et al.*, 1982). However, the same study seemed to suggest that humorous book chapters did not significantly improve learning, interest, persuasiveness and the desire to read more. Damn. Furthermore, the credibility of the author was inversely related to the amount of humour used. Best not to take anything I say too seriously then.

In choosing a textbook it is important to find one that fits your style and teaching ethos (as well as covering the content that you wish to cover, obviously). Hulsizer and Woolf (2009) suggest that the choice of textbook should be based on:

- conceptual orientation (do you want to emphasise computation or conceptual understanding?);
- level of difficulty (interestingly, they recommend relying on your own assessment and not that of the author);
- chapter topics and organisation (for example, if you favour my approach of teaching everything in terms of a GLM, then you would want a book that introduces the GLM early on and then explains things like ANOVA using this framework);
- core formulae and vocabulary (this is related to the previous point in that if you want ANOVA taught as a GLM then the formulae in the book will be somewhat different to if you wanted to teach it as a stand-alone test); and
- type and quality of datasets and examples.

After you have carefully considered these five criteria, I think you will find that my books are the best (Field, 2009b; Field & Miles, in press).

## Conclusions

This chapter has been the briefest of journeys through some of the issues we face when teaching statistics and some of the techniques that we can use to overcome these hurdles. The two major obstacles we face are students' lack of motivation and anxiety about the courses. Overcoming these barriers is half of the battle in providing students with a solid grounding in statistical methods for psychological research. In this chapter I have tried to look at some general principles that we should adopt in constructing our curriculum and in particular urging you to think about what skills will be useful not just for psychological research but in life after university. In terms of getting students to engage with the subject, I have reviewed individual characteristics that need to be considered, before looking at whether humour is a useful tool in motivating students and reducing anxiety. From there, I addressed some specific issues such as how much to incorporate computers within your teaching, how interactive classroom techniques can help students to be more active in their learning, and how you might choose a textbook. There are a great many other issues to consider that simply cannot be covered in one chapter but I hope I have at least inspired you to think more about how you deliver statistics and to go and find out more for yourself.

## Key Messages

- Teaching statistics offers unique challenges because students may be more anxious and less motivated than for other subjects.
- In curriculum design we should not only consider how statistics will be used within psychology research but endow students with skills that will help them to interpret data in the real world (such as news reports of research).
- We should consider teaching statistical tests around the core concepts that underlie the general linear model.
- Humour and lively examples can be a useful tool in reducing anxiety and increasing motivation, but be sensitive to your student group when considering what material is acceptable.
- It is possible to engage students in large groups by using interactive data-collecting sessions, thinking up demonstrations in which students participate and using inducements to encourage students to answer questions.

## Research Questions

1. Does using humour and lively examples in statistics teaching enhance student learning or merely entertain?
2. Do 'gimmicks' and activities involving student participation in large-group teaching enhance student understanding of statistical concepts?

3. Does structuring teaching around core concepts of the general linear model help reduce confusion over 'which test' to use to analyse data?
4. Does teaching general transferable data-interpretation skills help students to apply statistical methods to psychological data?
5. Do hand calculations improve student understanding of statistical concepts or hinder them from understanding how to apply and interpret statistical procedures?

## Notes

1   Imagine that there has been a murder. The police have a DNA sample from the murderer, and test people in the country until they get a DNA match ($D$). This happens, and the DNA matches you. The chances that you did not commit the homicide ($H$) are one in a million. The prosecutor suggests that the probability of your not being the murderer ($H$), given the DNA match ($D$ – the data), is one in a million. The prosecutor's fallacy is that their one in a million is not the probability of $H$ given $D$, it is the probability of $D$ (getting a DNA match) given $H$ – that the person who matched the DNA is not the murderer. In other words they have assumed that the conditional probability of $H$ given $D$ is the same as the conditional probability of $D$ given $H$. But they are not. Given that there are (about) 60 million people in the UK, there are probably about 60 people who match the DNA who did not do the murder and you are just unlucky enough to be one of them. The probability that you are not the murderer is not 1 in 1,000,000, but is close to 59/60 or about 0.98 (see Miles & Field, 2007).
2   A favourite quote of mine is 'The almost universal reliance on merely refuting the null hypothesis is a terrible mistake, is basically unsound, poor scientific strategy, and one of the worst things that ever happened in the history of psychology' (Meehl, 1978, p.817).

## Further Reading

Hulsizer, M.R. & Woolf, L.M. (2009). *A guide to teaching statistics: Innovations and best practices*. Chichester, UK: Wiley-Blackwell.

## Online Resources

Andy P. Field's website (www.statisticshell.com/). This contains free handouts for a range of statistical techniques.

Chance News (http://chance.dartmouth.edu/chancewiki/index.php/Main_Page). A useful source for interesting examples of media bloopers involving probability, maths and statistics.

Consortium for the Advancement of Undergraduate Statistics Education (www.causeweb.org/). A collection of wide-ranging resources including fun statistics-related songs, cartoons, poems, jokes, and videos (I kid you not).

David C. Howell's website (www.uvm.edu/~dhowell/StatPages/StatHomePage.html). Some useful materials.

David Kenney's website (http://davidakenny.net/kenny.htm). A wide range of instructional tutorials.

Discovering Statistics Using SPSS (www.uk.sagepub.com/field3e/default.htm). Support materials include PowerPoints slides, instructional flash moves, flash-card glossaries, MCQs, self-test questions, answers to tasks in the textbook and study skills.

Higher Education Academy Psychology Network resources page (www.psychology.heacademy.ac.uk/html/resources.asp) a searchable database of statistics links.

StatNotes (http://faculty.chass.ncsu.edu/garson/PA765/statnote.htm). A wide range of extremely good tutorials on (typically more advanced) statistical techniques.

# References

Bartz, A.E. & Sabolik, M.A. (2001). Computer and software use in teaching the beginning statistics course. *Teaching of Psychology, 28*(2), 147–149.

Becker, B.J. (1996). A look at the literature (and other resources) on teaching statistics. *Journal of Educational and Behavioral Statistics, 21*(1), 71–90.

Benson, J. (1989). Structural components of statistical test anxiety in adults: An exploratory model. *Journal of Experimental Education, 57,* 247–261.

Berk, R.A. & Nanda, J.P. (2006). A randomized trial of humor effects on test anxiety and test performance. *HUMOR: International Journal of Humor Research, 19*(4), 425–454.

Bessant, K.C. (1992). Instructional design and the development of statistical literacy. *Teaching Sociology, 20,* 143–149.

Blalock, H.M. (1987). Some general goals in teaching statistics. *Teaching Sociology, 15*(2), 164–172.

Brace, N., Kemp, R. & Snelgar, R. (2009). *SPSS for Psychologists* (4th edn). Basingstoke: Palgrave Macmillan.

Bridges, G.S., Pershing, J.L., Gillmore, G.M. & Bates, K.A. (1998). Teaching quantitative research methods: A quasi-experimental analysis. *Teaching Sociology, 26*(1), 14–28.

Britt, M.A., Sellinger, J. & Stillerman, L.M. (2002). A review of ESTAT: An innovative program for teaching statistics. *Teaching of Psychology, 29*(1), 73–75.

Bryant, J., Crane, J.S., Comisky, P.W. & Zillmann, D. (1980). Relationship between college-teachers use of humor in the classroom and students evaluations of their teachers. *Journal of Educational Psychology, 72*(4), 511–519.

Cohen, J. (1968). Multiple regression as a general data-analytic system. *Psychological Bulletin, 70*(6), 426–443.

Conners, F.A., McCown, S.M. & Roskos-Ewoldson, B. (1998). Unique challenges in teaching undergraduates statistics. *Teaching of Psychology, 25*(1), 40–42.

Coolican, H. (2009). *Research methods and statistics in psychology* (5th edn). Hodder Arnold.

Crawley, M.J. (2007). *The R book*. Chichester: Wiley-Blackwell.

Dalgaard, P. (2008). *Introductory statistics with R* (2nd edn). New York: Springer.

Dancey, C. & Reidy, J. (2008). *Statistics without maths for psychology: Using SPSS for Windows*. Harlow: Prentice Hall.

DeCesare, M. (2007). 'Statistics anxiety' among sociology majors: A first diagnosis and some treatment options. *Teaching Sociology, 35*(4), 360–367.

Dolinsky, B. (1998). An active learning approach to teaching statistics. *Teaching of Psychology, 28*(1), 55–56.

Dyck, J.L. & Gee, N.R. (1998). A sweet way to teach students about the sampling distribution of the mean. *Teaching of Psychology, 25*(3), 192–195.

Elmore, P.B. & Vasu, E.S. (1980). Relationship between selected variables and statistics achievement – building a theoretical model. *Journal of Educational Psychology, 72*(4), 457–467.

Emond, W.J. (1982). Some benefits of micro-computers in teaching statistics. *Computers & Education, 6*(1), 51–54.

Epting, L.K., Zinn, T.E., Buskist, C. & Buskist, W. (2004). Student perspectives on the distinction between ideal and typical teachers. *Teaching of Psychology, 31*(3), 181–183.

Feinberg, L.B. & Halperin, S. (1978). Affective and cognitive correlates of course performance in introductory statistics. *Journal of Experimental Education, 46*(4), 11–18.

Field, A.P. (2009a). Can humour make students love statistics? *The Psychologist, 22*(3), 210–213.

Field, A.P. (2009b). *Discovering statistics using SPSS: And sex and drugs and rock 'n' roll* (3rd edn). London: Sage.

Field, A.P. & Miles, J.N.V. (in press). *Discovering statistics using SAS: And sex and drugs and rock 'n' roll*. London: Sage.

Friedman, H.H., Friedman, L.W. & Amoo, T. (2002). Using humor in the introductory statistics course. *Journal of Statistics Education, 10*(3). Retrieved on 18 February 2009 from www.amstat.org/publications/jse/v2010n2003/friedman.html.

Gal, I. (Ed.). (2000). *Adult numeracy development: Theory, research, practice*. Cresskill, NJ: Hampton Press.

Garner, R.L. (2006). Humor in pedagogy: How ha-ha can lead to aha! *College Teaching, 54*(1), 177–180.

Goldacre, B. (2008). *Bad science.* London: HarperPerennial.

Gruner, C.R. (1967). Effect of humor on speaker ethos and audience information gain. *Journal of Communication, 17*(3), 228–233.

Guttmannova, K., Shields, A.L. & Caruso, J.C. (2005). Promoting conceptual understanding of statistics: Definitional versus computational formulas. *Teaching of Psychology, 32*(4), 251–253.

Haller, H. & Kraus, S. (2002). Misinterpretations of significance: A problem students share with their teachers? *MPR-Online, 7*(1), 1–20.

Howell, D.C. (2006). *Statistical methods for psychology* (6th edn). Belmont, CA: Thomson.

Howitt, D. & Cramer, D. (2008). *Introduction to research methods in psychology.* Harlow: Prentice Hall.

Hulsizer, M.R. & Woolf, L.M. (2009). *A guide to teaching statistics: innovations and best practices.* Chichester, UK: Wiley-Blackwell.

Kaplan, R.M. & Pascoe, G.C. (1977). Humorous lectures and humorous examples – some effects upon comprehension and retention. *Journal of Educational Psychology, 69*(1), 61–65.

Kinnear, P.R. & Gray, C.D. (2008). *SPSS 16 Made Simple.* Hove: Psychology Press.

Klein, D.M., Bryant, J. & Zillmann, D. (1982). Relationship between humor in introductory textbooks and students evaluations of the texts appeal and effectiveness. *Psychological Reports, 50*(1), 235–241.

Langdridge, D. & Hagger-Johnson, G. (2009). *Introduction to research methods and data analysis in psychology.* Harlow: Prentice Hall.

Lesser, L.M. (2001). Musical means: Using songs in teaching statistics. *Teaching Statistics, 23*(3), 81–85.

Lesser, L.M. & Pearl, D.K. (2008). Functional fun in statistics teaching: Resources, research and recommendations. *Journal of Statistics Education 16*(3), Retrieved on 22 June 2009 from www.amstat.org/publications/jse/v2016n2003/lesser.html.

Lönn, S., Ahlbom, A., Hall, P., Feychting, M. & Swedish Interphone Study Group (2005). Long-term mobile phone use and brain tumor risk. *American Journal of Epidemiology, 161*(6), 526–535.

Maltby, J. (2001). Learning statistics by computer software is cheating. *Journal of Computer Assisted Learning, 17*(3), 329–330.

Meehl, P.E. (1978). Theoretical risks and tabular asterisks: Sir Karl, Sir Ronald, and the slow progress of soft psychology. *Journal of Consulting and Clinical Psychology, 46*, 806–834.

Miles, J.N.V. & Banyard, P. (2007). *Understanding and using statistics in psychology: A practical introduction.* London: Sage.

Miles, J.N.V. & Field, A.P. (2007). Perspectives on significance testing. *The Irish Journal of Psychology, 28*(1–2), 13–26.

Miller, G., Tybur, J.M. & Jordan, B.D. (2007). Ovulatory cycle effects on tip earnings by lap dancers: Economic evidence for human estrus? *Evolution and Human Behavior, 28*, 375–381.

Morgan, B.L. (2001). Statistically lively uses for obituaries. *Teaching of Psychology, 28*(1), 56–58.

Mulhern, G. & Wylie, J. (2004). Changing levels of numeracy and other core mathematical skills among psychology undergraduates between 1992 and 2002. *British Journal of Psychology, 95*, 355–370.

Onwuegbuzie, A.J. & Wilson, V.A. (2003). Statistics anxiety: Nature, etiology, antecedents, effects, and treatments – a comprehensive review of the literature. *Teaching in Higher Education, 8*(2), 195–209.

Pallant, J. (2007). *SPSS survival manual* (3rd edn). Open University Press.

Paxton, P. (2006). Dollars and sense: Convincing students that they can learn and want to learn statistics. *Teaching Sociology, 34*(1), 65–70.

Quality Assurance Agency for Higher Education, The (2007). *Psychology*. Retrieved on 23 June 2009 from www.qaa.ac.uk/academicinfrastructure/benchmark/statements/Psychology07.pdf

Raymondo, J.C. & Garrett, J.R. (1998). Assessing the introduction of a computer laboratory experience into a behavioral science statistics course. *Teaching Sociology, 26*(1), 29–37.

Rumsey, D.J. (2002). Statistical literacy as a goal for introductory statistics courses. *Journal of Statistics Education, 10*(3). Retrieved on 23 June 2009 from www.amstat.org/publications/jse/v2010n2003/rumsey2002.html.

Schacht, S.P. & Stewart, B.J. (1990). What's funny about statistics – a technique for reducing student anxiety. *Teaching Sociology, 18*(1), 52–56.

Schacht, S.P. & Stewart, B.J. (1992). Interactive user-friendly gimmicks for teaching statistics. *Teaching Sociology, 20*(4), 329–332.

Schram, C.M. (1996). A meta-analysis of gender differences in applied statistics achievement. *Journal of Educational and Behavioral Statistics, 21*(1), 55–70.

Schutz, P.A., Drogosz, L.M., White, V.E. & DiStefano, C. (1998). Prior knowledge, attitude, and strategy use in an introduction to statistics course. *Learning and Individual Differences, 10*(4), 291–308.

Tabachnick, B.G. & Fidell, L.S. (2007). *Using multivariate statistics* (5th edn). Boston: Allyn & Bacon.

Utts, J. (2003). What educated citizens should know about statistics and probability. *The American Statistician, 57*(2), 74–79.

VanVoorhis, C.R.W. (2002). Stat jingles: To sing or not to sing. *Teaching of Psychology, 29*(3), 249–250.

Verzani, J. (2004). *Using R for introductory statistics*. Boca Raton, FL: Chapman & Hall.

Wender, K.F. & Muehlboeck, J.S. (2003). Animated diagrams in teaching statistics. *Behavior Research Methods Instruments & Computers, 35*(2), 255–258.

Wilkinson, L. (1999). Statistical methods in psychology journals: Guidelines and explanations. *American Psychologist, 54*(8), 594–604.

Wright, D.B. & London, K. (2009a). *First (and second) steps in statistics*. London: Sage.

Wright, D.B. & London, K. (2009b). *Modern regression techniques using R: A practical guide*. London: Sage.

Zillmann, D., Williams, B.R., Bryant, J., Boynton, K.R., & Wolf, M.A. (1980). Acquisition of information from educational-television programs as a function of differently paced humorous inserts. *Journal of Educational Psychology, 72*(2), 170–180.

# 7

# Where Angels Fear to Tread
## *The Undergraduate Research Project*

Mark Forshaw and Susan Hansen

I LIKE IT WHEN PSYCHOLOGISTS STUDY MY FORAGING BEHAVIOUR... I'M NOT SO KEEN WHEN THEY LOOK AT HOW I ATTRACT A MATE ... A GIRL LIKES TO KEEP A FEW SECRETS ......

*Teachers open the door, but you must enter by yourself.* (Chinese proverb)

This chapter covers the following areas:

- issues in person and resource management attached to project supervision;
- debates around qualitative and quantitative research within the framework of student projects;
- staff development in supervision;
- the place of the research project in the undergraduate curriculum and its importance in the student's career;
- issues around assessment of undergraduate research work.

The undergraduate, final-year research project in psychology (commonly but erroneously called a 'dissertation' by some) is a unique piece of assessment in the canon of undergraduate life for a number of reasons. The first is that it is so substantial, often accounting for a third or so of the final degree classification. A great deal rests on the project. Secondly, it is the only time in the vast majority of degrees where the style of 'teaching' differs markedly from the usual 'chalk and talk', in that this is a genuine instance of supervision, and, we would argue, coaching, and the development of an important social dyad. Thirdly, it is different from other assessments in that it tests a different set of skills from conventional essays and examinations. Finally, it represents an interesting challenge to markers, in that no two projects are the same but must be, in some way, judged according to common criteria. These assessment criteria must be specific enough to be clearly appropriate marking criteria for psychology projects, but generic enough to account for the considerable diversity in projects, from qualitative to quantitative, from social to biological, from cognitive to constructionist, from developmental to neurological. In short, the project is tough for the student, and tough for the tutor. It encapsulates the skills of planning, desk research, critical analysis, social engagement, ethics, time management, and, in short, is 'graduateness' in microcosm.

It is surprising, then, that Forshaw's (2004) volume was the first textbook directly specifically at undergraduate psychology project students (a few others appearing on the market since). Before that, only books on generic research, or research in the social sciences, existed. There is still, at the time of writing, no known volume dedicated to supporting lecturers in supervising undergraduate research projects, and this chapter represents the first, modest steps in that direction. If one wishes to regard psychology as a modular activity, reflecting the structure of most university courses in the UK and internationally, then one sees a plethora of writings on other aspects. Textbooks on cognitive psychology or biological psychology abound, for example. These often include activities to support lecturers in their work. However, we still have only generic works on research supervision aimed at the supervisor themselves. Good though some of these are, there is a gap in the market.

To some degree, this might highlight a mode of thinking that has dominated our world for some time; it might be the case that we assume that all lecturers, by virtue of their training in research, are able to supervise effectively. This might be true, but it also could be a dangerous assumption. No matter the level of skill, anyone can benefit from some introspection, and from the suggestions and reflections of others. Some of the greatest researchers make the worst supervisors, and some of the least research-active individuals in departments are excellent supervisors, and each could learn from the other.

## Supervisory Skills

When we engage in peer observation of teaching, as we all should on a regular basis, we direct this mostly at observation of lectures, seminars and workshops. It simply does not occur to the majority of lecturers to consider inviting a colleague to observe and comment on an undergraduate research supervision meeting. This seems somewhat perverse given the relative importance of the research project in the overall scheme of things. If we observe a single lecture given by a colleague, we see, typically, one tenth, or even a twentieth where modules also have weekly seminars, of a module which constitutes around one fifteenth or so of a student's final classification. However, by observing a supervision session, one could be party to a tenth of the entire supervisory activity of a module worth up to a third of the degree. A tenth of a third is much, much greater than a twentieth of a fifteenth. In fact, it is greater by a factor of ten. Of course, this overlooks the contributions of study time or independent 'directed learning', but nevertheless reveals an important bias in our thinking and practice.

Of course, by observing the dyad in action, we disturb the balance somewhat, but that also applies to entire lectures or workshops, but no one suggests we should avoid peer observations or external quality assessments because of that. More difficult is setting out criteria on which to judge good supervisory meetings. However, this need not be a particular challenge.

We have come to understand and expect that we are judged according to our ability to communicate in relation to a set of learning outcomes. The average lecture is intended to be a particular journey upon tracks laid down at the outset. These tracks are the learning outcomes for the specific lecture or other teaching component. Supervisory meetings can work similarly. There is more scope for deviation, because the consultation is more reciprocal in nature, but it should still be guided by learning outcomes, which could even be articulated in such a way as to be 'standing items' running from meeting to meeting. In addition to that, there are other criteria, such as successful communication, including answering the student's questions, and terminating the meeting effectively and efficiently, leaving the student with a 'to-do' list. It is not difficult to imagine a pro forma quality assurance checklist that would be suitable for a research supervision session and useful for peer observation. It is equally conceivable that our colleagues who are counsellors, for example, can contribute considerably to our understanding of what constitutes a good and a bad research supervision session.

If we were to ask academics what makes a good research supervisor, we might be surprised by the diversity of answers. Firstly, we should make clear that research supervision in general is not the same thing as research supervision at the higher levels. There are commonalities, of course; the differences in level are probably highly significant. By the time one is supervising a PhD candidate, various 'filters' have been put in place, each of which is an assay of the candidate's research capabilities. Fewer filters apply in the case of the final-year undergraduate, who has merely had to pass, minimally, a handful of research assignments, some of which may have been group efforts. To express it frankly, what makes the undergraduate research project unique is that it is often an attempt to conduct proper research, but with inadequate resources. These include, sometimes, the human resource of an ill-equipped student who simply is not naturally disposed to research, lacking skill, motivation, or both, and physical resources. How often are we forced to accept that a student project would have been so much better had we been able to support it better with time, equipment, and so on. Simply, the undergraduate project is an exercise in cutting one's cloth according to one's means. Skimping, saving and rationing are the order of the day. This implies that practical considerations are just as important as the academic ones. It is precisely that task of balancing economic practicalities with the need to oversee and conduct worthwhile research that is what we are not overtly trained in. We rely on common sense and astute judgement, and hope that we possess both in good measure.

## Supervision and Coaching

We must always reflect, therefore, on what makes the research project different from other teaching elements. A crucial aspect of this is the nature of the dyad inherent in the dedicated, one-to-one, highly specific teaching that occurs in the research consultation that is so at odds with the group dynamics that dominates, necessarily, the lecture theatre or the workshop. Central to the research supervision process, and almost entirely missing from the lecture environment, is what we can easily refer to as *coaching*. In the research environment, the supervisor is a coach. Coaching has been defined in a myriad of ways inappropriate to enter into here, but at the heart of the activity is a set of shared goals that are a result of the development of the individual. In a nutshell, it is helping someone to help themselves (Cope, 2004). The student starts with a seed of an idea, and the supervisor points out the best soil for planting, and oversees the regular watering and tending of the garden until the plant emerges. Rarely does project supervision revolve around the supervisor simply providing a set of rules which the student unbendingly follows. The nature of research does not lend itself to that. Problems fall into one of two categories: the open and the closed (Poulton, 1957). The closed problem is a self-limiting system, with little or no room for imagination or lateral thinking required to solve it. Algebraic equations are closed problems. Cooking a dish from three given ingredients is a closed problem. There are a limited number of things one can do with three ingredients and a set of rules to follow about how to cook things, and in what combinations and so on. Open problems are, as they sound, entirely open, and there are potentially infinite combinations and permutations of ideas and givens that can occur on the way to the goal. There are, typically, many solutions possible, rather than one. Research projects fall into this category, because there are infinite ways to research a given topic. It is possible to provide heuristics, but not algorithms, to meet the challenge of guiding a student from idea to written-up project.

Coaching can be referred to as a process of incremental encouragement. In good supervision, this is exactly what occurs. Anatole France is reputed to have said that nine tenths of education is encouragement. When the student approaches with an idea, it is our aim to foster that, or to quash it where it is a poor idea likely to lead to a disastrous outcome. Often, we cajole and praise, but need to push the student lightly in another direction, so that they leave without feeling dejected but with some new thoughts on the subject and with guidance for their independent work. Each time they visit us, or communicate via e-mail or telephone, we hope to see progress in their goal-seeking behaviour, and we direct and redirect appropriately. Like problems (and missiles), movements come in two forms: ballistic or guided. Good project supervision is guided. Many lecturers will have encountered the student who effectively, through non-attendance or extreme independence, chooses a ballistic process for their project. After an initial meeting, they become incommunicado, and eventually return, often with one of two outcomes: a work of genius, or a catastrophe. Sometimes, students refuse to take on board advice and pursue a single course of action regardless of all contingencies. However, the vast majority of projects are guided in nature. The student seeks advice, acts on it, returns, seeks more advice, each time mapping out for the supervisor the status quo and adapting and moderating as time goes on. That, after all, is the purpose of a series of meetings over the course of the supervision period.

Coaching, or guiding, has to be incremental. It is no different from most learning in that a period of consolidation and reflection is required before the next 'instalment'. Judging when to push a student further and when to leave them to their own devices is a subtle and ill-defined dance between two time-management systems: that being employed by the supervisor and that by the student. Often, when clashes occur, they do so because of incompatible time management.

Good coaches often find themselves working with clients on time management issues, but our problem as lecturers is that we are usually no more qualified in such things than the students are, although one would hope that the greater experience and knowledge that a supervisor naturally has inclines them more towards superiority in planning, judging how long tasks will take, and in meeting deadlines and setting and adjusting realistic milestones. Unfortunately, as human beings, we all must admit that occasionally we fail to manage our time effectively and some of us more than others. For some, it is a trait, a characteristic of their working life. Such things are part of life's splendid diversity, naturally, but it does make for the potential for a vastly different experience from student to student, supervisor to supervisor. If one were to conduct a study of experiences of project students, one might hazard a guess that differences between departments are swamped by differences within, due to the range of personalities and experiences that staff might have. This is not to be overly critical, since the 'system' seems to work for its purpose, but there is a difference between something that works and something that works *better*. We should aim higher, perhaps. The only way that can be achieved is by giving lecturers more time and resources to reflect, identify weaknesses and strengths in their profile, and to adapt and develop. After all, that is what continuing professional development is all about.

One key fact of coaching is that it is 'supportive'. The purpose is to move people on. In many respects the undergraduate research project is about learning to work on a longer-term task, working with others and developing expertise, and about making mistakes and learning from them. All of these things are central to the types of task that graduate professionals need to undertake. It is an apprenticeship in doing real-world tasks. Furthermore, for those who want a career in research it is an essential starting point, and should not be underestimated in its importance in setting the agenda for an entire career. A bad research experience can put someone off for ever, just as a good one can inspire. The supportive, coaching model of research supervision is about inspiration as much as it is about methods and materials and analysis. Love *et al.* (2007) discuss the concept of research self-efficacy (RSE) as an important determinant in careers of would-be researchers. They admit that many students detest research, but others relish it. The difference between some of them is to be found in their research self-efficacy, and the best thing a supervisor can do for a student, arguably, is promote and encourage RSE. They found that early experiences of research predicted variance in RSE but, interestingly, this included both team and individual experiences. When separated, only team experiences of research predicted RSE. Individual experiences did not contribute significantly to variance prediction. This leads us to wonder what exactly undergraduate project supervision would count as. It certainly is *independent*, and 'independent' would imply 'individual' (although some projects are completed on a group, cooperative basis in some departments, with distinct write-ups). However, the supervisor and student surely act as a team? Using this logic, by creating an environment where the student is encouraged to see the dyad as a team, one could, possibly, promote future research interest in a way that is life-changing. Love *et al.* (2007) also conducted a qualitative analysis to understand research motivations, and they discovered that the strongest theme in explaining students being put off research was an unsupportive advisor or supervisor. Almost all other themes were considerably weaker in their relative contribution to discourse. The conclusions are obvious: we, as supervisors, have a great deal of influence on the experience of the student and indeed their future engagement with research. We return to the concept of inspiration: we work best when we are inspiring, but unfortunately no part of our own training teaches us how to inspire.

Hamman *et al.* (2000) looked at teachers in relation to their ability to 'coach' learning, that is, to support learning specifically, over and above imparting knowledge. All teaching activity, ideally, involves both the handover of information, and the encouragement and support needed, along with some reflection on student learning, so that the student in turn reflects on their own learning style, ability to engage with the material and so on. Hamman *et al.* found that there was a direct relationship between students' spontaneous learning activities that were structured, thought out and relevant and the amount of coaching of learning that teachers had engaged in. In other words, when we make students aware of their learning, they think about it, and learn better. The research supervision meeting is the best place for this to happen. There is less time needed for traditional 'instruction'. We are not there to teach a student the details of a particular theory, but to hammer out a solution to a practical problem, most of the time. It is also one-to-one instruction, which means that it is effectively bespoke. At no other time in the typical, modern degree does that really occur. We are, therefore, ideally placed in the arena of research project supervision to spend time on the concept of learning to learn. When the student tells us that they have not completed their literature search because they are not very good at using the electronic databases, that instant is precisely when we can address the issue and probe the reasons why the student has encountered this barrier. What does it mean to be 'poor' at something? What are the student's motivations? What does the student need from us to progress? These are the questions a coach asks of themselves and their client; the gap between coach and teacher becomes invisible at these moments.

## Student Characteristics

Students themselves reflect the diversity of humankind, as one would expect. What one could find unusual is the lack of training we typically receive in dealing with the range of working styles and personalities that we encounter. The average lecturer supervises a handful of undergraduate projects in the course of a year, potentially hundreds in a career. Within that portfolio the range of characters is vast. It is easy to work from the premise that being a human being makes one well equipped to engage with and support other human beings, and to an extent this is true, but supervision is not normal, everyday human interaction. Nor is it, as we have firmly made clear in our discussion of coaching, an entirely formal, predictable and rule-bound set of exchanges. Of course, this view that people deal well with people, coupled with the fact that as psychologists we could argue that we have better understanding of human behaviour than most, has perhaps kept us away from pursuing continuing professional development in 'people skills'. Time has come, perhaps, for that view to change. There was a time, perhaps, when students were rather more homogenous. The vast majority came from a particular type of family, and were of a particular mindset. Things in common (between students and students and between students and lecturers) far outweighed the differences. However, the widening participation agenda is changing all of that (and, indeed, has changed it markedly already). A greater range of people pursue university study than ever before in history, and one could argue that universities were ill prepared for that. Like so many initiatives, the change comes before the preparation for it. This sounds like a contradiction in terms, but will resonate with a great many readers. Resources tend to follow the need for them; rarely are they put in place in advance. However, regardless of the reasons for expansion in universities and changes to the make-up of the 'customer', there is a good argument for supporting training of lecturers that is focused on dealing with people, and finding the best ways to provide for those customers. A one-size-fits-all approach to supervision is not necessarily the best. It is crucial that we treat our students equally, and are fair, but that does not mean that we should literally follow a set pattern of supervision, never straying from the path or rulebook. Some people are more lively than others in their demeanour, some more intelligent than others, some fear challenges whilst others embrace them, some detest all research, others have their careers as lecturers mapped out from an early age, and to suggest that equity would be to treat them all in the same fashion, offering the same type of support and supervision across the board, would be foolish. The problem arises in that we are simply not trained to deal with this array of personalities, and we are largely left to our own devices to negotiate a route through supervision. It is testament to the skill of the vast majority of lecturers that this process works at all, since it is essentially little more than Lindblom's (1959) 'muddling through'. Lindblom's view resonates somewhat with our discussion of coaching, in that he is also associated with describing a form of 'incrementalism'. Big decisions, he argues, occur through small steps, hopefully in the right direction, often through trial and error. Working with a student on a big project when we might have never met them previously, or know them only fleetingly, is quite an undertaking, and the room for error is vast. Whilst Lindblom was initially writing about matters of public administration, it is the nature of complex problems, whether they be research projects or town planning schemes, which creates the climate for muddling to occur. Of course, we should not accept muddling through as our modus operandi. In fact, a great deal of supervision probably occurs in accordance with plans and structures put in place early on in the initial meetings with the students, and again this is testament to supervisors' skills. However, it is *not* due to mandatory training in supervision and dealing with people. How many supervisors experience difficulties over the years with students who won't communicate, or particularly demanding individuals, or those who have little or no ambition, or those who believe they are more capable than evidence attests, or those who are overly informal, or indeed any number of other possibilities? Generally, we either already know what to do in these cases, or we learn from consultation with more experienced colleagues, or, possibly, we never learn. Over and over, we muddle through, however successfully.

Diversity in the student population probably means diversity in learning styles. West *et al.* (2007) state that 'In order to provide maximally effective research training, educators need to understand how person factors affect a student's scientific development' (p.175). At the time of their study, there had been no published data on learning styles and their relationship with research interest, and research self-efficacy. What they discovered is that greater RSE was found in those people who gain knowledge through doing and working in teams (rather than alone), and RSE was positively related with a tendency towards abstract rather than practical, fact-based thinking. The variance predictions of these styles on RSE were small, but nevertheless significant. Their recommendations were that we should actively assess students' learning styles, and that we should use varied methods to engage them with research. We would argue that good supervisors do exactly this without thinking about it. Early on, they ascertain how a student learns, from reflecting on discussions and asking pertinent questions, and they use a range of approaches to support the student. It is time, perhaps, that we recognise this formally, and we disseminate this good practice as a matter of course.

In thinking about modern universities, we soon meet an astonishing irony. There have been two distinct strands in the recent history of higher education in the United Kingdom in particular. One is the widening participation initiative, and the other the increase in student numbers. The two are, of course, interlinked, since one of the main reasons for an increase in student numbers, it can be argued, is because universities have 'widened the net'. If we accept the premise that greater diversity in students means that we must develop new skills in supervision, we run up against a curious fact. Bluntly, we rarely have time for this, because student numbers have increased. We are too busy supervising the larger numbers of students to take training to help us supervise the larger numbers of students. Something is amiss here. A further irony then emerges. Working out how to do more and increase our skill base, in less and less time, is an issue of time management and efficiency, something which we have identified in this chapter we often lack. There is probably a limit to how much muddling through any system can tolerate, and it can be posited that that limit has been reached. Higher education has many challenges ahead, and this is one of them. Project supervision is particularly interesting in this respect because it is unavoidably labour intensive. We can build larger lecture theatres to accommodate more students. We can convert materials to engage more with distance learning, create 'podcasts' and rely more on students' independent directed learning, but when it comes to research supervision there is no conceivable substitute for one-to-one guidance and support, in real time. Again and again, we see just how special the undergraduate research project is.

## Challenges Particular to the Supervision of Qualitative Research Projects

In addition to these considerations generic to good practice in the supervision of undergraduate projects, there are also a number of challenges that are perhaps particular to the effective supervision of *qualitative* research projects. The first of these is located in students' very selection of a qualitative research method, and of a supervisor with expertise in qualitative research methods, for their final year project. Despite significant progress in the introduction of qualitative methods across psychology degree programmes, and the inclusion of growing numbers of academic staff with qualitative expertise, there remains a pernicious misconception, amongst both a minority of academic staff and some members of the undergraduate student body, that qualitative methods in some way represent a 'softer' or 'easier' option for a student's final-year project than do quantitative research methods (Hansen & Rapley, 2008). There is, thus, often a small, but noteworthy, proportion of students who appear to select a qualitative research project on this erroneous and problematic basis. Such students are usually identifiable during the opening stages of any pre-supervisory interaction, and indeed, it is always worthwhile to ask, as an initial question for a first meeting, 'Why do you want to use (this particular) qualitative method?'; 'What makes (this particular) qualitative research method the most appropriate method for studying X?' Students who are unable to answer such questions should be gently encouraged to reflect upon the basis for their methodological choices.

Besides the more general long-term project of addressing this misconception as it arises in student–academic and academic–academic interaction, and of increasing the visibility and diversity of qualitative methods in the curriculum, there are a number of more concrete strategies for dealing with this issue. Indeed, these strategies are readily generalisable for use with any final-year student indicating an interest in pursuing a qualitative research project. The first of these we have already raised – that is, in any pre-supervisory meeting, it may be prudent to pose some 'sticky questions', and to lead a guided discussion regarding the student's rationale for their choice of qualitative methodology. It may also be helpful to encourage prospective students to read some best-practice examples of qualitative research theses written by previous students, to give a concrete sense of the rigour and quality of work they might aim to achieve.

Further, it may be advisable to talk frankly about the considerable work involved in qualitative data collection, transcription and analysis. Many students are surprised at the sheer number of hours involved in transcribing even one hour of recorded data in sufficient detail to enable some forms of finer-grained qualitative analysis (e.g. conversation analysis and discursive psychological analysis). Many forms of qualitative data analysis involve an iterative process of reflection and analysis, and of refining and reframing one's earlier analysis, and so on, which may continue throughout the course of supervision until close to the deadline for submitting a project draft. Needless to say, any such 'warning' about the demanding time investment necessary to undertake a successful qualitative research project should, as per Gough *et al.*'s (2003) recommendations, be offset with some mention of the commensurate rewards inherent in undertaking such a project: the satisfaction that resides in successfully collecting, transcribing and analysing one's own unique dataset, and in mastering a challenging and demanding set of relatively novel methodological skills.

As with the supervision of quantitative undergraduate research projects, it goes without saying that the faculty charged with supervising any qualitative research project should ideally be specialists in the methodological area attempted by the student. However, perhaps due to the widespread assumption of homogeneity between qualitative approaches, and the considerable divergence in practice between certain qualitative methods – and as, in part, a product of the normatively lower numbers of members of staff with expertise in qualitative, rather than quantitative, methods – this ideal is not always satisfied, in practice. Indeed, student 'demand' for qualitative project supervision often exceeds the 'supply' of academics who are equipped and confident to supervise (and assess) such projects – which of course has repercussions in terms of the availability of fully trained staff for supervision, and indeed on the personal research time of such staff members – as the supervision of qualitative research projects is a time-consuming matter. Gough *et al.* (2003) suggest that one solution, for divisions seeking to widen the availability of qualitative supervision in response to student demand, would be to arrange for more experienced qualitative researchers to provide consultation and advice to staff newer to the supervision of qualitative project students. Other strategies for dealing with this issue include the practice of various forms of group supervision, where two or more academics will advise a small group of students on methodological issues. This is of clear benefit to both less experienced members of staff and to students as this enables the transfer of methodological expertise and fosters an inclusive community of scholarship. Of course, this need not be restricted to qualitative research!

Many forms of qualitative data analysis benefit significantly from peer review and support during the course of a research project – perhaps more so than quantitative forms of analysis, for which students have received exhaustive training as part of their undergraduate studies, and where the results of one's analysis may be more 'black and white' – requiring only considered feedback from one's supervisor to ensure 'correct' conclusions are drawn. Undoubtedly, the undergraduate research project can be a somewhat isolating experience for students, one that often involves one-to-one contact with a supervisor only, and little contact with other undergraduates or even postgraduates or staff members employing similar methods or engaged in studying a similar topic area. The group supervision of qualitative research projects, and the associated practice of holding group data analysis sessions, can help to provide qualitative undergraduate project students with a level of peer and faculty support, and to feel part of a community of scholars engaged in qualitative research. Such groups can enable students to validate their own ongoing analysis, and may provide vital feedback on technical aspects of their transcripts – for instance, in identifying 'errors' in transcription, etc. Such practices also assist less experienced faculty members in mastering the effective supervision of qualitative research projects. The incremental process of 'coaching' and guidance so crucial to dyadic project supervision (as discussed earlier) can be effectively supplemented, for qualitative student research projects, by such small groups since qualitative methods, unlike quantitative methods, are arguably a set of 'craft skills' (Potter & Wetherell, 1987) that cannot be taught in a codified manner, nor mastered without such 'social' forms of support and validation.

## Assessment

Assessing undergraduate psychology research projects is a minefield of its own, and most departments have discussed, debated and struggled with this issue for decades, possibly visiting and revisiting the same thorny arguments. Put simply, the nature of research work is such that there is no level playing field upon which we can judge the efforts of our students. We are particularly burdened by the fact that we have two approaches to research which are of equal importance but which have very different underpinnings, different views on research, and often varying views on what constitutes value, good research, rigour and indeed the right way to do things. Of course, these two strands are the quantitative and the qualitative.

Quantitative research is a vast field in itself, but it is important to note that there is also nothing homogeneous about qualitative methods of enquiry. Indeed, even within the field of qualitative research, there can be significant differences between methodological approaches – for example, between interpretative phenomenological analysis and discursive psychological analysis. It is an issue of considerable frustration to many qualitative researchers that such – to us – clear and fundamental epistemological differences are often elided by quantitative researchers. Indeed, as Gough *et al.* (2003) note, it remains common, in the predominantly quantitative research culture of many contemporary psychology departments, to assume homogeneity between distinct qualitative approaches in terms of standards of 'value, good research, and the "right" way to do things'. In practice, however, different qualitative methods have quite distinct standards for data collection, presentation and analysis. For instance, some qualitative methods (e.g. interpretative phenomenological analysis) require the collection of a considerable volume of data for transcription and analysis (Gough *et al.* (2003) suggest at least five hours of transcribed material); whereas other, more fine-grained methods (e.g. conversation analysis) require perhaps only an hour of transcribed audio or video recording. Some methods of qualitative analysis are designed primarily for use with interview data, whilst other methods prefer to draw upon naturally occurring, or secondary, data. Further, some qualitative methods require only a simple orthographic transcript, whereas other methods demand a more detailed transcription method, with attention to aspects of prosody, gesture and dysfluency in speech production.

Furthermore, various qualitative methods also differ in terms of the normative standards for the presentation of qualitative data extracts within the body of an undergraduate thesis. Some methods require only the provision of very brief extracts from the data corpus, to illustrate key themes or sub-themes (e.g. thematic analysis or interpretative phenomenological analysis); whereas other methods (e.g. discursive psychological analysis and conversation analysis) rely upon the presentation of extended data extracts for detailed analysis. This can, in turn, have a considerable impact on such factors as the relative ease or difficulty with which a student will be able to achieve the suggested word length for their project. Of course, this is a difficulty experienced by students undertaking both quantitative *and* qualitative projects. However, arguably methods that demand the inclusion of lengthy data extracts make it proportionately more challenging for students to present their analysis in a concise yet systematic fashion, given that the standard regulations for undergraduate projects often specify that all extracts be included in the final word count. This presents concomitant difficulties for the assessors who have to try to mark projects equally and fairly across methods and topics.

Putting aside differences arising from the qualitative/quantitative debate, there are still substantial differences between potential and actual research projects which can prove to be extremely difficult for assessors to align. Any two projects can be judged against each other with a high degree of concordance between markers when all things are equal. Imagine two students having conducted two identical projects, but one student had obtained the necessary number of participants for a given power and effect size, whereas the other had obtained half that number. Clearly, the former deserves a higher grade. But, all other things being equal, it would obviously be inappropriate for the first to gain double the mark of the second, albeit that they have found twice the participants. So, what should the mark discrepancy be? Some might argue that the answer depends on the overall effect on the quality of the project, but would rarely wish to venture a quantification of that effect. This makes it especially difficult explaining project marks to students. All too often, our judgements are impressionistic, no matter what efforts we take to avoid that. We have safety measures in place, in that we tend to double-mark projects, and most departments are proud of the high degree of consistency they find between markers. This is laudable and reassuring, and the comments of our external examiners prop up the system. However, this still does not allow us to give clear feedback to students on their performance. We are trapped in this nebulous field and saved often only by the fact that undergraduate projects are, by their nature, final-year projects. By the time students receive feedback or a mark, their courses are finished. Generally, they rarely expect detailed feedback or even more rarely seek it.

It is clear that we do need to justify our actions and impressions, not only to students but to ourselves. Imagine the above-mentioned issue of participant numbers, and apply it to a qualitative project. Now we have a different pack of cards on the table. Does a student who interviewed ten people deserve a higher mark than one who interviewed five, again *all other things being equal*? Numbers concern qualitative researchers much less than they do the experimentalists (except perhaps for line numbers in transcripts), but nevertheless one should surely give students credit for hard work, and harder work still, and harder, and so on. Of course, this is a self-limiting concept. Eventually, the added value of doing more work changes according to the law of diminishing returns. There comes a point when a hardworking, keen student simply becomes an obsessive one who does not know when to stop. Overwork, arguably, should be penalised because it represents poor scholarship, shoddy planning and a waste of resources, which is actually unethical. Again, most of the time our answers to these conundra are impressionistic ones.

A further, less often discussed and more delicate issue may arise when a student is pursuing an unrealistically large sample size, or too extensive corpus of qualitative data, at the behest of a supervisor who is hoping to jointly publish work on the basis of the study. In such cases, it is, obviously, not to the student's benefit to continue with data collection when their timescale for project completion does not allow a long period of data collection, and when this eats into time set aside for data analysis and writing up. We need to balance our aspirations for our brightest students with our diligent attention to the strictures imposed by the relatively tight time frame for the final-year research project. Much as they may represent future productive members of our research teams, our project students are not unpaid research assistants.

Let us consider one more argument. Who has not argued over the relative importance of the various sections of a research report? Some hold that replicability, in the case of quantitative work, is the crucial factor in determining success of a report. After all, a write-up of research which lacks information that allows the reader to understand what happened, or what the results imply, and which prevents construction of a similar study by a naive reader, is undoubtedly problematic. But exactly how problematic should we view this as being? Does a student deserve to fail on account of a poor methods section? What about a results section? Should, indeed, any section alone dictate the outcome in such a situation? It is possible to argue that a report missing an Introduction could still be understood, and the appropriate literature review could be conducted by someone based upon what they read elsewhere in the report. Therefore, on this basis, the Introduction is surely worth less than other parts? This is where we have the beauty of Gestalt to fall back on. What we tend to mark is the entire project, not the parts of it in isolation. This allows us to conveniently evade the issue of relative salience of sections, and further establishes the 'right' to vagueness when we assess 'big' pieces of work like this one.

This is yet another reason why the project is special, and worth considerable discussion, perhaps more than any other piece of work in the catalogue of assessments. It presents assessment challenges which are stronger, less deniable, and of greater import than anything else we do. The purpose of this chapter is not to present answers. If anything, entire symposia and volumes of text on this matter are required, and are to be welcomed. Our aim is to make concrete and reify the arguments and struggles we all have, perennially, in our work. Pointing something up is the first step in addressing it.

Dennis (2007) has drawn our attention to another problem in the assessment of student projects, that of halo effects. By necessity, there is a supervisor who usually is one of the markers of a student's project. Contrary to expectation, Dennis's study showed that this supervisor-marker is not prone to significant halo effects, that is, they are not likely to overestimate the value of project reports submitted by their own students. However, halo effects are to be found within markers in relation to what we often term 'grade inflation'. Where projects are marked section by section, or multiple marks given to work for different aspects of it, there emerge trends in giving higher marks to poorer sections where other sections have been judged very good, and vice versa. Interestingly, this seems to provide evidence that those departments using overall marking schemes are less prone to problems than those who have opted for awarding marks for individual report sections and then creating some sort of composite mark at the end. Whilst we can be encouraged that there is little evidence that knowing a student changes our judgement of their work, we should pay attention to the nature of the marking schemes that we use, since both first and second markers are potentially both subject to carry-over effects. From the point of view of a student, one could argue that it makes a good sense to create a good first impression, since a good title and introduction will set the tone for the markers to unconsciously view the rest of the work as equally or more good.

One reason alone justifies the amount of care and caution we should take in marking projects. Typically, it is impossible to mark anonymously. We know which student did which project, and so we begin with the potential for bias. Even second markers can sometimes be slightly familiar with a project student's work, either through participant recruitment e-mails sent around the department, advice sought by the student or supervisor that brings in other members of a department, and so on. Without the fail-safe of complete anonymity, we owe it to ourselves and the student to examine, face up to and work to eradicate, possible sources of inequity, bias, or halo.

## The Joy of Projects

So many students find research methods and statistics unexciting or difficult, and yet the undergraduate research project is something that the majority find the greatest pleasure in the entire degree. We should reflect on that apparent contradiction. What is noteworthy is not that the student should find an independent piece of research to be fascinating and worthwhile, but that this feeling does not usually attach itself to their previous experiences with research and analysis. What this tells us is that either we are doing something wrong in teaching research methods, or that the project is something over and above that. The answer is relatively obvious. The research project is independent and, unlike most tasks we ask students to engage in for research methods or statistics, not driven by assessment. Arguably, it is not even driven by learning outcomes in the same way that other 'modules' are. Learning outcomes for projects are often necessarily vague and are focused on students demonstrating independence and the ability to carry out work to address a problem and to apply relevant and appropriate methods and analysis. There is rarely anything more specific than that. One can argue that this is where the joy is to be found. Again, the word *independence* strikes us. The undergraduate research project allows the student to express themselves, relatively free from constraints compared with other, taught, components of a degree, and to move around the problem space, selecting what to focus on, what to ignore, and making choices. That, it seems, is what people like to do. It is that which makes the psychology research project enjoyable, but also which, anecdotally, leads us to consider it a valid predictor of a whole range of transferable skills for future success in academia and the employment marketplace. Whether this anecdotal picture holds true is a research project in itself.

If we analyse students' distaste for research, it often is a misdirected dislike of statistics which is directed at research because research and statistics go hand in hand so often. This is possibly why there has been such a rise in the number of qualitative projects in departments' undergraduate research throughput. Students do not necessarily hate research; they simply struggle with or detest statistics. This leads us to two conclusions. On the one hand, this suggests that perhaps there are better ways to teach statistics than those we currently use, although just about every permutation and approach has been tried over the years, and only with modest success. Few departments can claim to have sorted this out once and for all. Secondly, it would be a sorry state of affairs if qualitative projects are becoming popular because they are a way of avoiding statistics, rather than a different and useful way to approach research per se. It is too early to tell if this is indeed happening but no one would be satisfied with this, least of all qualitative researchers who naturally want their project students to be fully engaged and to have actively chosen qualitative work because it suits their research *ethos, not* because it matches their research skills. The very nature of the project as an independent piece of research work means that the best results are achieved when the student makes reasoned decisions. Which is worse, the student who says that their supervisor made them do 'something that would fit an ANOVA', or the student who conducted a qualitative project because they perceive themselves as 'no good with numbers'? In neither case is there proper choice and in neither case is a rounded, successful project likely to be the outcome. As with all research, the crucial element is *ownership*. When something is yours, you are likely to value it most and enjoy it, but also most likely to understand it best.

We should end, as we began, with a Chinese proverb, which sums up what the project is about: 'Tell me and I'll forget; show me and I may remember; involve me and I'll understand.'

## Tips for Practice

- Consider setting up small 'support' groups for students, and indeed for graduate students and staff. These could be targeted at quantitative or qualitative research.

- Mentoring of staff new to supervision is a key to the dissemination of good practice. This should include occasional peer observation of supervisory meetings.
- Keep a careful watch on the potential for grade inflations, either because of section-by-section marking schemes, or more general halo effects. Projects require much more energy devoted to reliability and consistency between markers, and moderation since they are the most open to variability due to large team marking.
- Make a case for activities around project supervision to be considered in departmental staff development budgets as an essential item rather than a luxury.
- Keep logs of supervisory activity, signed by staff and students, in order to have an accurate paper trail should things go awry. Keep e-mails concerning supervision, missed appointments, advice given, drafts with tracked changes and the like.
- Ensure at the outset that students are realistic about their aims, their skills and their needs. This includes assessing motivations for conducting particular projects employing specific methods. If someone is dead-set on grounded theory, is it for the 'right' reasons?

## Key Messages

- The research project is a fundamental part of psychology 'graduateness'.
- The nature of supervision places it in the category of coaching activity.
- Psychology departments would benefit from regular debates and moderation meetings concerning the undergraduate psychology project.
- Many staff members would appreciate and benefit from continuing professional development courses and training in relation to research supervision and assessment.
- The student choice between qualitative and quantitative work should be driven by ethos rather than perceived expediency.

## Research Questions

1. What drives student choice of topic and method?
2. What are the real and perceived barriers to communication within supervision?
3. What do lecturers feel are the greatest challenges in assessing undergraduate research?
4. Can you teach others how to supervise?
5. Is a good supervisor a good researcher and vice versa?

# References

Cope, M. (2004). *The seven Cs of coaching.* Harlow: Pearson Prentice Hall.

Dennis, I. (2007). Halo effects in grading student projects. *Journal of Applied Psychology, 92,* 1169–1176.

Forshaw, M. (2004). *Your undergraduate psychology project: A BPS guide.* Oxford: BPS Blackwell.

Gough, B., Lawton, R., Madill, A. & Stratton, P. (2003). *Guidelines for the supervision of undergraduate qualitative research in psychology.* LTSN Psychology Report and Evaluation Series No. 3 May 2003.

Hamman, D., Berthelot, J., Saia, J. & Crowley, E. (2000). Teachers' coaching of learning and its relation to students' strategic learning. *Journal of Educational Psychology, 92,* 342–348.

Hansen, S. & Rapley, M. (2008). Editorial: Special issue of qualitative research in psychology on 'teaching qualitative methods'. *Qualitative Research in Psychology, 5*(3), 171–172.

Lindblom, C. (1959). The science of muddling through. *Public Administration Review, 19*(1), 79–88.

Love, K.M., Bahner, A.D., Jones, L.N. & Nilsson, J.E. (2007). An investigation of early research experience and research self-efficacy. *Professional Psychology: Research and Practice, 38,* 314–320.

Potter, J. & Wetherell, M. (1987). *Discourse and social psychology: Beyond attitudes and behaviour.* London: Sage.

Poulton, E.C. (1957). On prediction in skilled movements. *Psychological Bulletin, 54,* 467–478.

West, C.R., Kahn, J.H. & Nauta, M.M. (2007). Learning styles as predictors of self-efficacy and interest in research: Implications for graduate research training. *Training and Education in Professional Psychology, 1,* 174–183.

# 8

# How Do You *Really* Know?

## Kathy Harrington

ID BEEN GETTING QUITE DEPRESSED WITH MY SELF ASSESSMENT ESSAY GRADES ....
SO IVE RE GRADED THEM UPWARDS AND FEEL MUCH BETTER

This chapter covers the following areas:

- recent developments in research and the practice of assessment in higher education and their relevance to teaching psychology;
- raising awareness of the potential for assessment to be a powerful driver of student learning;
- principles and methods that enable assessment to facilitate students' disciplinary understanding and writing development in psychology;

- contextual factors affecting assessment in higher education (e.g. increasing class sizes, constraints on staff time, concerns about plagiarism) and ways of responding effectively;
- encouraging reflection on opportunities for local development of relevant, creative and effective assessment practice that can foster a more rewarding and beneficial engagement with the assessment process amongst students and staff.

## Introduction

The importance of assessment in determining students' experiences of higher education is supported by a substantial and growing body of research, and it is also well documented in the scholarly literature and practical guides written for teachers in higher education. Gibbs & Simpson (2004–5), for example, draw on research by Snyder (1971) and Miller & Parlett (1974) to argue that what influences learning most is not the teaching students receive, but the assessment: what, how and how much students learn is determined by their perceptions of what the assessment system demands of them. Ramsden (2003) cites a study by Laurillard (1984) and some of his own research conducted at Lancaster in the 1970s to show how the method and amount of assessment has an especially powerful influence on the quality of students' learning, and thus how unsuitable methods and excessive amounts of assessment can have harmful effects on students' attitudes to studying and their approaches to learning. These findings are corroborated by a number of other studies (e.g. Biggs, 2003; Brown *et al.*, 1997; Brown & Knight, 1994), leaving little doubt about the centrality of assessment in shaping students' learning experiences.

Yet, it is also well documented that current assessment practice in higher education tends to lag quite a way behind the insights achieved through research, and to some extent behind lecturers' own awareness of the relationship between assessment and student learning gained through reflection on their individual experiences of teaching. In their review of assessment research in higher education, Elton & Johnston (2002) record the 'persistence of a largely unreflective traditionalism in spite of the existence of proven innovations and much relevant research over the past 35 years' (p.6). Assessment seems to stand somewhat apart from other aspects of learning and teaching in this respect. Increasing awareness amongst educational practitioners of learning as a constructivist process of knowledge creation rather than knowledge reproduction has led in recent years to the exploration and adoption of many new teaching methods (e.g. problem- and enquiry-based learning) (Maclellan, 2001), but has often failed to lead to a similar shift in the conceptions (Samuelowicz & Bain, 2002) and practice (Nicol & Macfarlane-Dick, 2006) of assessment. Another study found that contextual factors (e.g. institutional use of examinations in response to concerns about plagiarism) constrained lecturers' ability to choose methods that aligned with their beliefs about the pedagogical value of assessment (Harrington *et al.*, 2007).

There is also evidence of persistent student dissatisfaction with their experiences of assessment in higher education. Results of the National Student Survey, commissioned by HEFCE annually since 2005, have consistently shown assessment and feedback to be the most poorly rated area of students' experiences regardless of institution type, with over one third of survey participants in 2008 expressing dissatisfaction (36 per cent), compared with less than one fifth of participants expressing dissatisfaction with the quality of teaching on their courses (17 per cent) (National Union of Students, 2008). In a survey of psychology departments in the UK and focus groups with students to investigate the organisation and perception of coursework assessment, Crook *et al.* (2006) also found evidence of student unease with assessment processes. This contrasted with their finding of staff contentment with the same processes. They suggest that the mismatch may result from an increasing proceduralisation of assessment and attention to managing the process for reasons of transparency and accountability, giving an outward appearance of quality and fairness whilst encouraging students to take a procedural approach to what should be a creative practice of studying, and leading to student dissatisfaction when they find that tutor instructions about assessment do not extend as far as the desired advice to 'look at this and this and this, go and find this and that' (quoted words from a focus group student, p.111).

Others have commented on the way a changing higher education context has created a tension between different purposes of assessment. Elton & Johnston (2002) describe the basic assessment dilemma in UK higher education as a conflict between two aspects that are not easily reconciled. The first is an increasing importance of educational qualifications in determining subsequent employment opportunities and, coupled with increasing student numbers, the pressure for higher education institutions to develop assessment systems that are efficient and economical to run and that provide consistent results useable by employers. The second aspect focuses on assessment as a developmental process that is informed by current thinking on the nature of learning and is responsive to increasing student diversity through adoption of more varied approaches. These two understandings of assessment are not readily consistent with one another, and it often happens that the first aspect stifles development of the second. Gibbs (2006) has also looked in detail at recent changes to assessment in higher education and identifies several contextual factors, including declining resources, increasing student numbers, reduction in class contact time, reduced study time arising from students' working lives and financial pressures, declining student retention, more frequent summative assessment as a result of modularisation, and the fact that gaining approval for changes to assessment is often difficult and more time consuming than gaining approval for changes to other aspects of a course. The Quality Assurance Agency Scotland (2007a,b) similarly acknowledges many of these factors as affecting the development of assessment practice, and adds that staff cautiousness about innovation is often associated with fears about declining standards.

Within this environment, staff can often feel burdened by assessment, and it can be difficult for individual lecturers to effect meaningful change in their practice even when they have the desire to and recognise sound pedagogical reasons for doing so. However, the current context can also provide a helpful stimulus to reflection. Opportunities for developing relevant and effective assessment practice remain, and there are many inspiring examples, supported by a rich and growing body of theory and evidence, on which the interested lecturer can draw. This chapter will present some of these examples and discuss them in the context of underlying principles that can enable assessment to facilitate students' learning. It also aims to show how reflecting on one's practice and engaging in a search for local possibilities to develop and refine relevant, creative and effective assessment practice can lead to a more rewarding and beneficial engagement with assessment for both students and lecturers.

## Understandings of Assessment

Ramsden (2003) argues that assessment comprises three interlinked functions; it is (a) a means of helping students learn; (b) a way of reporting on student progress; and (c) a way of making decisions about teaching (p.205). The first two of these functions map onto the tension outlined by Elton and Johnston above, and they also accord with the concepts of using assessment for 'formative' and 'summative' purposes widely referred to in literature on student assessment. Assessment for a formative purpose refers to assessment that is used to support students' learning processes (providing feedback on an essay draft, or a self-assessment exercise, are typical examples), whereas assessment for a summative purpose refers to using assessment to measure an amount of learning that has already taken place (such as an end-of-module examination). The distinction between these two purposes is often characterised as assessment *for* learning versus assessment *of* learning; however, as many, including Ramsden, point out, formative and summative aspects of assessment rarely exist separately in practice. Often they occur in relation to the same assignment, as for example when an assessed piece of coursework or a final module examination leads to study activity and learning through the processes of reading, note-making and drafting. Use of the concepts is nevertheless beneficial in that they can promote healthy reflection on the purposes of assessment in specific teaching situations, and on how different assessment practices can facilitate meeting different pedagogical goals, and can thus help assessment fulfil the third function identified by Ramsden above, that of aiding tutors in reviewing and developing their own teaching practice. Reflecting on assessment opens up possibilities for seeing freshly what would otherwise remain habitual, and can enable an ongoing process of thoughtful change and development that is responsive to the individual, practical contexts in which we work.

## A few words about validity and reliability

Reliability in assessment refers to measures that are without marker bias, accurate and able to produce consistent results when repeated, and validity refers to the assessment of what is deemed valuable or important to assess. Both are important aspects of a well-functioning assessment system. However, if an assessment is not measuring or evaluating something that it is worthwhile to evaluate, there is little point in its being a consistent measure of achievement. Hence, many have argued for the primacy of validity when thinking about designing assessments supportive of student learning (Gibbs & Simpson, 2004–5; Ramsden, 2003). This is not to downplay the importance of reliable assessment for maintaining appropriate and recognisable standards of achievement in higher education but, as Gibbs (2006) has argued, 'standards will be raised by improving student learning rather than by better measurement of limited learning' (pp.3–4). In addition, a number of studies have shown a high degree of unreliability in current assessment practices (Laming, 1990; Newstead & Dennis, 1994), and questions have been raised about the possibility of achieving perfect reliability, and indeed about the value of striving to do so. Dracup (1997), for example, has argued that the practice of double-marking prevalent across psychology degree programmes as a strategy to increase the fairness of marking is actually of questionable worth, and Newstead (2002) has suggested that double-marking could be abandoned without adverse effects on students' grades.

Similarly, Bloxham (2009) has argued that in attempting to create robust moderation procedures, staff workload around marking has increased dramatically, assessment choices have been restricted and the time taken to provide feedback to students has increased, with no real improvement in the accuracy of marking. She has also suggested that the potential for improving reliability is likely to lie in attempts to reach shared understandings through dialogue between students and staff not only about assessment standards but also about the inherently subjective nature of the process of making judgements about students' work. In this suggestion, striving for reliability and validity have the potential to overlap, as such dialogue is also likely to consider the degree to which stated criteria match the judgements that are actually applied to student work and how far these criteria are helpful and appropriate (i.e. valid) measures of student learning.

This chapter focuses on the validity of assessment, that is, on developing assessment methods that are able to measure what it is most important to measure as determined by the educational goals lecturers have for their students.

## Assessment for Learning

Murphy (2006) defines 'assessment for learning' as having two main elements. The first is an alignment of assessment goals with learning goals, so that assessment is used to drive learning in a meaningful way towards intended learning priorities. The second element is the use of assessment to give students feedback on their learning as they are progressing, so that assessment is used to support their learning development. The emphasis here is on the formative purpose of assessment, and research has shown substantial benefits for student learning and motivation of conceptualising assessment in this way (Black & William, 1998).

Liz McDowell and Kay Sambell have worked extensively with students and staff at the University of Northumbria to develop and evaluate assessment for learning approaches in a variety of academic subjects, and they identify six characteristics of assessment that are used to facilitate students' learning. Four of these refer to students receiving some form of information about their learning as they progress, whether the source of this feedback is the tutor, peers or themselves, or comes in written or verbal form. Drawing on

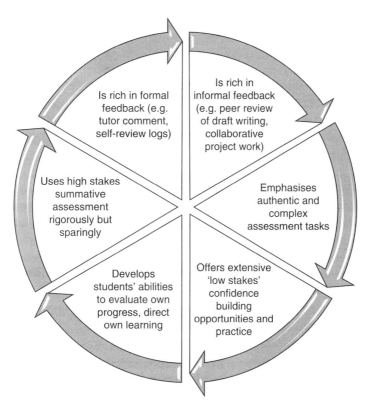

**Figure 8.1** Six characteristics of assessment for learning
*Source*: Assessment for Learning Centre for Excellence in Teaching and Learning, Northumbria University

a thorough review of theoretical and empirical research on assessment as well as on practical experience, Gibbs & Simpson (2004–5) identify 10 conditions under which assessment can support student learning, later refined to 11 conditions in Gibbs (2006), and the majority of these conditions also relate to feedback (see Table 8.1). The authors suggest that these conditions can be used by lecturers to evaluate the effectiveness of their own assessment practice, and they have also developed an Assessment Experience Questionnaire to assist with this process of diagnosis, which is freely available and has been used widely in the UK as well as in South Africa and Hong Kong (www.open.ac.uk/fast). Table 8.1 provides a summary based on information from both iterations of the conditions and includes some practical examples of meeting the conditions as identified by the authors.

**Table 8.1**  Conditions under which assessment supports student learning, with some practical examples (from Gibbs & Simpson, 2004–5 and Gibbs, 2006)

**Quantity and distribution of student effort**

| | | |
|---|---|---|
| 1 | Assessed tasks capture sufficient study time and effort | • Unseen examinations that unpredictably sample course content |
| | | • Self- and peer-assessment |
| 2 | Tasks distribute student effort evenly across topics and weeks | • Sampling assignments for marking (e.g. from a portfolio) |
| | | • Frequent short assignments or tests (e.g. computer-based assessment, problem sheets) |

**Quality and level of student effort**

| | | |
|---|---|---|
| 3 | Tasks engage students in productive learning activity | • Complex, open-ended assignments requiring demonstration of understanding (e.g. extended essay) are more likely to induce a deep approach to study |
| | | • Collaborative or group work can engage students in discussion and confront them with alternative viewpoints |
| 4 | Assessment communicates clear and high expectations to students | • Clear specification of goals, criteria and standards, along with modelling and discussion of exemplars |
| | | • Making assessment products public (e.g. posters, use of peer assessment) may induce more pride and care in work |

**Quantity and timing of feedback**

| | | |
|---|---|---|
| 5 | Sufficient feedback is provided, often enough and in enough detail | • Computer-generated feedback and marking can provide frequent, regular information on progress |
| 6 | Feedback is provided quickly enough to be useful to students | • Practice tests with computer-based feedback offered sufficiently in advance of summative assessment has enabled weaker students to outperform initially stronger students in the final examination (Sly, 1999) |

**Quality of feedback**

| | | |
|---|---|---|
| 7 | Feedback focuses on learning rather than on marks or on students themselves | • Feedback on the content of work with suggested actions students can take |
| | | • Critical feedback on personal characteristics can negatively effect self-efficacy, which in turn is related to academic achievement (Thomas *et al.*, 1987) |
| | | • Grades without feedback can be especially harmful |

**Table 8.1**    (*Cont'd*)

| 8 | Feedback is linked to the purpose of the assignment and to criteria | • Feedback is structured around goals of the assignment and relates to criteria and standards |
|---|---|---|
| 9 | Feedback is understandable to students, given their sophistication | • Provision of feedback which is sensitive to students' possible (mis)conceptions of the task and unsophisticated conceptions of learning, knowledge and disciplinary discourse |

**Student response to feedback**

| 10 | Feedback is received by students and attended to | • Provision of marks only after self-assessment and tutor feedback have been completed |
|---|---|---|
| 11 | Feedback is acted upon by students to improve their work or their learning | • Provision of feedback on drafts before the final submission<br>• Multi-stage assignments where each stage builds towards a larger final assignment, with feedback at each stage<br>• Ultimately this may rest more with the student than the teacher, but it can help to avoid feedback that is: too late, backward-looking, unspecific, not generalisable to other assignments, discouraging, without follow-up to check whether students have taken any action |

The emphasis on feedback as a key aspect of learning environments that use assessment to support students' learning is not surprising, given that research has shown feedback to be the most significant aspect of the assessment process in improving student attainment (Black & William, 1998; Hattie, 1987). Initially, the word 'feedback' may evoke thoughts of the traditional, time-honoured process of a tutor providing written comments on student work before or after it is submitted for a grade. However, as the examples in the table above show, 'feedback' is helpfully understood more broadly as any kind of information on the progress of one's learning, whether that comes from a tutor, peers or one's own reflections, and which has a formative influence on subsequent learning. This would include, for example, formal tutor comments on draft coursework and structured exchange amongst students and staff on an online discussion board, as well as informal discussion amongst peers about each other's work-in-progress and reviewing one's own learning journal or reflective log to self-assess progress over time. In this, feedback and formative assessment are largely synonymous in concept, and they are used as such in this chapter. It is worth noting the caution sounded by Yorke (2003) that we should not assume formative assessment is automatically helpful; if not designed and implemented appropriately, it can also hinder students' development, and he calls for more discussion and elucidation of the theoretical underpinnings of effective formative assessment.

Nicol & McFarlane-Dick (2006) argue that the importance of formative assessment and feedback lies in its ability to promote student autonomy and enable the development of self-regulated learning. They see feedback as having an empowering influence on students, enabling them to take control of their own learning in ways which will benefit them in their studies as well as outside formal education and throughout their lives. Their thinking about the power of feedback follows from a constructivist theory of learning, in which feedback is not about a one-way transmission of messages that are then acted upon by students. Instead, students inhabit a central, actively creative role in the feedback process, 'monitoring and regulating their own performance, both in relation to desired goals and in terms of the strategies used to reach these goals' (p.210). Conceptualising feedback in this way means being able to see that 'students interact with subject content, transforming and discussing it with others, in order to internalise meaning and make connections with what is already known' (p.200). They also suggest that with growing pressure on staff time (workload increases, larger classes), looking at ways of enhancing student learning that do not simply imply more time spent by tutors on generating feedback (which in any case may not be understood or applied) has pragmatic as well as pedagogical benefits. Table 8.2 provides a summary of their findings from a survey of empirical and conceptual research on feedback, which resulted in the formulation of seven principles of good feedback practice substantiated by numerous examples from the literature.

### *Establishing shared understandings of criteria and standards*

There is good reason not to work with the 'transmission' model of feedback. Hounsell (1987) showed that many students do not understand or do not attempt to read tutor feedback, and similarly Higgins *et al.* (2001) found that when students do read tutor feedback, they often do not understand

**Table 8.2**  Seven principles of good feedback practice with some practical examples (from Nicol & MacFarlane-Dick, 2006)

| No. | Principle | Practical examples |
|---|---|---|
| 1 | Helps clarify what good performance is (goals, criteria, expected standards) | • Provision of explicit written descriptions of criteria and standards accompanied by exemplars of performance<br>• Class discussion of criteria and standards<br>• Simulated marking exercises in which students comment on and mark sample written work in relation to criteria<br>• Lecturer-facilitated workshop where students negotiate own assessment criteria |
| 2 | Facilitates the development of self-assessment (reflection) in learning | • Provision of opportunities for peer review and feedback<br>• Having students request the kind of feedback they would like when submitting work<br>• Identification of strengths and weaknesses in own work before submission to the lecturer |
| 3 | Delivers high-quality information to students about their learning | • Provision of feedback whilst students still have time to make changes to their work<br>• Provision of corrective advice, rather than just comments on strengths and weaknesses<br>• Limiting the amount of feedback to encourage students to act on it<br>• Provision of online tests that can be accessed anytime and as often as students wish |
| 4 | Encourages teacher and peer dialogue around learning | • In large classes, use of small group discussions of written feedback students have received on individual assignments<br>• Use of in-class questions and electronic voting systems<br>• Asking students to identify examples of good feedback received and explain how they helped<br>• Group projects where students discuss criteria and standards at the outset |

(*Cont'd*)

**Table 8.2**    *(Cont'd)*

| No. | Principle | Practical examples |
|-----|-----------|--------------------|
| 5 | Encourages positive motivational beliefs and self-esteem | • Provision of marks only after students have responded to feedback comments<br>• Allocation of time for rewriting selected pieces of work<br>• Automated testing with feedback |
| 6 | Provides opportunities to close the gap between current and desired performance | • Provision of feedback on work-in-progress<br>• Use of two-stage assignments where feedback on the first stage is used to improve in stage two<br>• Provision of 'action points' alongside usual feedback<br>• Involving students in identifying their own action points in class after receiving feedback on their work |
| 7 | Provides information to teachers that can be used to help shape teaching | • Use of one-minute papers<br>• Having students request the kind of feedback they would like when submitting work<br>• Having students identify where they are having difficulties when they submit work |

terms used in the comments in the same way that their lecturers do. A similar problem has been identified with the terms used in assessment criteria. For example, Harrington, Elander, Norton *et al.* (2006) found that students interpreted 'developing an argument' as expressing one's personal views on a topic, while tutors understood the criterion to refer to the development of a point of view in relation to evidence found in published literature. Lea & Street (1998) argue that differing understandings of words such as 'argument' are rooted in the epistemological gap that exists between students and tutors, and Read *et al.* (2001) point out that this gap can be quite wide and potentially daunting for students struggling to adopt the specialist discourse of their expert tutor readers. It cannot be assumed that students understand or know what to do with tutor comments or assessment guidelines, including explicit criteria, when they are provided, and there is a need to create opportunities for students to construct their own understandings within the context of their discipline and in dialogue with tutors. The key to successful formative assessment is the quality of engagement with feedback (again, broadly understood to include that from peers and oneself as well as from tutors), and the challenge is to create a learning environment that encourages students' active engagement.

Prompted by the relatively recent quality assurance emphasis on the constructive alignment (Biggs, 1996) of learning outcomes and assessment (Bloxham & Boyd, 2007), the development of assessment criteria applicable to individual assignments, as well as modules, courses, departments and even institutions as a whole, is widespread practice in UK higher education. This emphasis on assessment as the valid, reliable and transparent measurement of outcomes is not without criticism (see Bloxham & Boyd, 2007, pp.28–29 for an excellent overview of the debate). However, the provision of clear guidelines and information about what tutors are looking for in assessed work is widely regarded as a necessary, though not sufficient, aspect of the process of enabling students to understand what is required of them and what markers will take into account when making judgements about the quality of their work (Norton, 1990; O'Donovan *et al.*, 2000). Sadler (1989) has identified three conditions necessary for effective feedback which acknowledge the importance of clear guidelines but also the need to provide opportunities to understand and act on the guidelines in relation to one's own work. What is required is: (a) knowledge of the standards that will be applied in assessment; (b) comparing those standards with one's own work; and (c) taking action to close the gap between standards and the achievement of them. These conditions can be met through a variety of activities, many of which are listed in the tables above.

Research has established that facilitating students' active engagement with the assessment criteria applied to their work can enable standards of achievement to be internalised and learning and performance to be demonstrably enhanced. Rust *et al.* (2003) delivered an embedded programme of workshops in a first-year introductory business module with over 600 students in which tutor-led discussion of assessment criteria combined with small-group marking exercises using the criteria and sample assignments resulted in significant improvements in module performance amongst those who attended the workshops compared with those who did not. In addition, the improvement in performance was sustained at a significant level when investigated one year later. Similar interventions conducted in psychology have also led to improved module performance, as well as the adoption of a deeper approach to learning, improved confidence and a greater sense of belonging at university (Harrington, Elander, Lusher *et al.*, 2006; Lusher, 2007; Norton *et al.*, 2005).

Norton (2004) has shown how conceptualising assessment criteria as 'learning criteria' in an undergraduate counselling psychology module helped steer students away from adopting a mechanistic, instrumental approach to using the criteria and instead supported a focus on the process of learning and developing students' understanding and functioning knowledge.

# Methods of Assessment

Traditionally, coursework and examination essays have been the primary means of assessing psychology students in UK higher education. More recently other forms of assessment have begun to emerge, including multiple-choice questions, posters, reflective logs, presentations and group projects, used for both formative and summative purposes, and integrating peer and self-assessment elements alongside, and sometimes instead of, tutor-produced marks and feedback. Whether traditional or newer forms of assessment are used, the criteria for choosing a particular method should be the same if the goal is to use assessment to improve students' learning. As already discussed, a number of contextual and institutional factors will impinge on your choice of assessment method; however, it is still important to consider, within the reality of the specific context where you are working, the degree to which the assessment you use is both fit for purpose (i.e. it assesses what you think is important to be assessed) and provides an opportunity for students to develop their learning.

There is some evidence that the choice of assessment method can have an influence on the quality of student learning by encouraging behaviour that is more or less helpful for reaching the educational goals you have for your students. Below is a brief overview of some of the research findings in this area with respect to traditional assessment methods of coursework essays and examinations, followed by consideration of potential advantages of innovating in assessment and some examples of how newer assessment methods have been implemented in practice.

### *Coursework essays and examinations*

Taking a deep approach to learning has been described as an intention to understand (rather than memorise), integrating new knowledge and concepts with what is already known and making connections between subject content and everyday life (Entwistle, 1988; Marton & Saljö, 1976; Ramsden, 1992).

In addition, students who adopt a deep approach are intrinsically interested in their studies, which leads to a higher quality of learning outcomes than when a surface approach is adopted (Bloxham & Boyd, 2007). Assessment has been identified as one of the most important features of course design that can encourage students to take a deep approach (Bloxham & Boyd, 2007).

Some research has shown that the traditional coursework essay remains one of the more relevant, and valid, methods of assessment because of its ability to enhance and deepen students' learning experiences, and because it also enables the outcomes of this learning to be most easily and accurately assessed (Gibbs & Simpson, 2004–5). One study found that students were more likely to adopt a deep approach for essay assignments than for multiple-choice examinations (Scouller, 1998), and similarly Tynjälä (1998) found that, when compared with traditional instruction concluding with an examination, constructivist learning tasks produced higher-level learning outcomes. Examinations have also been identified as poor predictors of students' subsequent performance, including in the workplace (Baird, 1985, cited in Gibbs & Simpson, 2004–5). In comparison, coursework marks are a better predictor of long-term learning of course content, and Gibbs (2006) cites a study that showed that students' recall of content on a cognitive psychology module 12 years after finishing the module was not correlated with examination marks but was positively correlated with coursework marks.

## Why innovate in assessment?

McDowell & Sambell (1999) argue that thoughtful and relevant development of assessment practice, instead of an automatic reliance on more traditional forms, brings many benefits for student learning. They suggest that students appreciate assessment tasks which help them develop knowledge, skills and abilities they can take with them to other contexts such as employment. They also suggest that innovation which allows students an element of choice in determining an assessment topic or method of approaching a task can give them a greater sense of ownership and personal involvement in the work, and that collaboration with fellow students can be linked to motivation and an improved quality of learning. They argue that overall there is high potential for innovative assessment to encourage students to take genuine interest in their studies, work hard and produce good outcomes with lasting benefits. Others have similarly argued for the value of diversifying assessment practice in the interest of improved student learning (Brown & Glasner, 1999).

*Authentic assessment*

MacAndrew & Edwards (2002) suggest that the rationale for diversification of assessment methods is that traditional practices can lack relevance and effectiveness compared to newer, alternative forms of assessment, and they make a plea for the use of more authentic forms which resemble the kinds of tasks students will be asked to undertake in future employment situations. Authentic assessment can be used for formative or summative purposes, and can take a wide variety of specific forms, limited only by the ingenuity, and time, of the designer. Mcgann *et al.* (2008) have shown that the creation of information leaflets can be used as an innovative form of summative assessment, enabling students to attain learning outcomes, enhance writing and thinking skills and deepen their understanding of the topic area. Problem- and enquiry-based learning activities have also been used to enhance the authenticity and relevance of assessment. Helman & Horswill (2002) showed that, when combined with peer mentoring and feedback, problem-based learning activities led to improved student achievement in psychology statistics classes.

Authentic assessment is of particular relevance in applied psychology postgraduate programmes where the recent development of National Occupational Standards by the British Psychological Society emphasises a competence-based approach to the assessment of required standards, and the implementation of competence-based training and portfolio assessment is an emerging area within health psychology programmes (Elander *et al.*, 2007). In training clinical psychologists, where assessment of 'fitness to practice' in clinical settings including the National Health Service is relevant, problem-based tasks have been used to promote self-directed learning and help bridge the gap between conceptual, university-based study and experiential learning through placements (Stedmon *et al.*, 2006). Simulated patient role-plays have also been used successfully in the teaching and assessment of clinical psychologists, leading to improved self-reflection skills and the transfer of clinical skills into placement settings (Melluish *et al.*, 2007).

*Peer and self-assessment*

The aim of involving students in the assessment of each other's and their own work is to provide opportunities for students to learn how to take on the role of self-assessor, that is, 'someone who is able to provide their own feedback because they understand the standard they are aiming for and can judge and change their own performance (that is, self-regulate) in relation to the standard' (Bloxham & Boyd, 2007, pp.21–22). This is a valuable educational goal in itself. As Gibbs (2006) argues, the value of peer- and self-assessment is the internalisation in students of academic standards and their subsequent ability to self-regulate, not the grading that takes place or the reliability of the grading. Through well-designed peer- and self-assessment activities, students can be helped to close the gap identified by Sadler (1989) between their knowledge of standards and their ability to meet these standards in their own work.

Both peer and self-assessment can be performed for summative or formative purposes, using various combinations of student- and tutor-generated marks and feedback. Falchikov (2005) provides a thorough analysis of the features, benefits and challenges of involving students in peer- and self-assessment practices, and there are a growing number of examples of successful practice to be found in the pedagogical literature on student assessment (e.g. Brown & Glasner, 1999, Part 4). In her meta-analysis of self-assessment studies, Falchikov found that good levels of agreement between students and tutors on the quality of student work occurred when students were well prepared for the self-assessment task, students and tutors engaged in discussion and agreement of criteria, and students had some experience of a subject area and so had already internalised some standards of the discipline. One study with second-year psychology students, designed to investigate whether students who take a deep approach to their learning and assignment writing are rewarded by their tutors for doing so, found that students' grades for their own essays correlated positively with the grades their tutors gave, and that thus students were indeed rewarded for taking a deep approach (Longhurst & Norton, 1997).

Falchikov's (2005) meta-analysis of peer assessment studies found that agreement between students and tutors was highest when assessment was based on a global consideration of well-understood criteria, rather than on marking in relation to several individual criteria, and when students were familiar with and had a sense of ownership of the criteria; and she offers several recommendations for good practice in peer assessment, including not using very large numbers of peer assessors per group.

## *Using technology to facilitate learning, feedback and assessment*

The use of technology to support learning in higher education has increased rapidly in recent years, owing in part to the development and expansion of Web 2.0 capabilities, and there have been many innovative ways in which such technology has been used to facilitate student assessment. The use of computer assisted technology (CAA) to deliver short quizzes or multiple-choice questions with feedback easily and frequently is perhaps one of the most widespread uses of technology in assessment (Brown *et al.*, 1999). Such tests are relatively simple to design and administer and can be delivered through institutional virtual learning environments. Regular testing with feedback has been shown to aid recall of information more successfully than rereading study material (e.g. Karpicke & Roediger, 2008), and online testing provides a ready source of information to the tutor on students' progress throughout a course (Hardman, 2009).

As part of the Re-engineering Assessment Practices (REAP) project at the University of Strathclyde, a large first-year basic psychology course was redesigned in line with the conditions in Table 8.1 and the principles in Table 8.2 above, making use of an online discussion board and structured tasks to replace half of the standard lectures (including online discussion, directed reading, collaborative writing and provision of exemplars with tutor commentary) (Nicol, 2009). The overall aim of the redesigned course was to improve the students' learning experiences while creating efficiency gains with regard to staff workload. More specifically, the new course was intended to encourage students' even engagement over the duration of the course, promote deeper reading of psychology texts, and provide feedback and writing practice in preparation for the final examination. Student evaluation of the redesigned course showed that they read more and learned more about psychology due to the online projects, and that they felt reading others' contributions online supported the development of their own understanding of psychology. Examination performance also improved significantly compared to previous years, and the failure rate declined. The success of this new design has led to rethinking the format of teaching across the whole psychology degree programme.

Wikis, or editable websites, have also been used to support assessment for learning. Collaborative learning through the process of co-writing has been shown to provide substantial benefits to students, including the promotion of critical thinking, reflection and knowledge building, and wikis have been used successfully to facilitate as well as evaluate such learning (Trentin, 2009). The benefits of using a wiki include being able to distribute the final editing of a document amongst all members of a group, ease of motivating individuals to collaborate in each stage of text production, and a record of all interaction on the wiki allowing assessment of individual contributions, interactions amongst participants and the final work overall.

Richard Buckland has been using wikis with large classes of up to 500 students for over eight years in the Faculty of Computer Science and Engineering at the University of New South Wales. He uses them to facilitate collaborative writing assignments and enable the assessment of groupwork. In addition, appropriate permissions settings allow students to create reflective diaries that only the tutor can see, which promotes students' engagement with their learning and also provides the tutor with continuous feedback on students' progress that can be used to inform teaching throughout the semester. For example, students' misconceptions and difficulties can be spotted as they develop, allowing the tutor to respond in a timely way to individual students or to the class as a whole, rather than discovering problems only once an assignment has been submitted and there is no longer an opportunity for students to respond to the feedback within the current module. Students are also encouraged to keep notes and compose written assignments directly on the wiki, whether individual or collaborative, which can eliminate the need for a paper-based submission process and the problem of lost work. Once assignments have been marked, use of the wiki enables efficient release of feedback to students, including anonymised assignments with tutor marks and comments (Buckland, 2009).

## Writing, Thinking and Assessment

Psychology is a writing-intensive subject and students are asked to write in a wide range of genres throughout their degree studies (e.g. coursework essays, practical reports, reflective logs, problem-based case studies, posters, third-year dissertations and projects), and the vast majority of assessed work involves a substantial amount of writing. Through writing, and opportunities to practise writing, students learn to adopt the conventions of the discipline and participate as members of the psychology academic community, that is, to think and communicate like a psychologist. It is helpful, therefore, to conceptualise the act of writing as an aid to thought, and as an integral part of the process of thinking itself, rather than seeing it simply as the translation of already-formed thought into appropriate words. This view of writing aligns with the constructivist view of learning discussed above, and it opens up possibilities for using writing to support students' cognitive development and facilitate their active role in coming to understand and meet the disciplinary requirements and standards applied to their assessed work.

When confronted with regular occurrences of poor grammar, spelling, sentence construction and punctuation in students' written work, it may be tempting to see helping students learn to write well as a matter of remediating deficiencies in specific writing skills, and to see providing this kind of support as beyond the remit and expertise of the psychology lecturer. With increasing student numbers, this is an understandable response (Newman, 2007), but there is evidence to suggest that separating the teaching of writing from learning subject content may not be the most effective way of enabling students to express themselves effectively in academic work, and there are valid pedagogical reasons for integrating writing, and learning to write, within disciplinary teaching (Lillis, 2006; Wingate, 2006). Castelló (2009) conducted an intervention study using peer revision exercises and exemplar texts with psychology students writing their final-year dissertation, and found that by the end of the intervention students had learned how to revise each other's and their own writing, text quality was better for the intervention groups than for the control group, and better texts were correlated with higher rates of revision and student satisfaction with the course.

As mentioned already, the provision of model answers accompanied by tutor feedback and discussion of assessment criteria can aid development of students' understanding of what is expected in their written assignments. However, it can also be helpful to focus attention on the writing process behind the finished product. A third-year undergraduate psychology student at London Metropolitan University led the Evolving Essay Project, in which she used wiki and blog technology to write an essay online over the course of six weeks, exposing each step in the process by publishing her reflections and successive drafts online. Several students and tutors across the UK and internationally contributed to the project by posting comments on the wiki and blog, which were responded to as part of the essay writing process. The finished essay was then marked by a psychology lecturer, using assessment criteria that had been provided to the student at the outset of the project, and his mark and feedback were made available on the wiki, leading to further discussion of criteria, standards and the process of meeting them in written work. The wiki and blog are now a repository of reflections on various aspects of the writing process (e.g. finding sources, drafting, staying on topic, using research evidence in one's own writing), some of which have been integrated into classroom teaching, and are freely accessible at http://evolvingessay.pbworks.com/ and http://anessayevolves.blogspot.com/ (Harrington *et al.*, forthcoming).

The Assessment Plus project conducted interviews and focus groups with psychology lecturers and students to investigate understandings of assessment criteria applied to written work, and has produced an evidence-based guide to writing academic essays in higher education which looks at common misconceptions amongst students and provides accessible guidance that draws on the views of students and tutors to help demystify the process of writing for assessment. A full-text version of the guide is freely available from www.writenow.ac.uk/.

## Helping students avoid plagiarism

There is evidence that choice of assessment method is determined by more than considerations of pedagogical merit, and concerns about plagiarism have been cited by lecturers as reasons for preferring timed examinations to written coursework (Harrington *et al.*, 2007). It is hard to determine the extent of plagiarism in higher education, and in psychology specifically, but there are indications that it is a growing phenomenon. One study with psychology students found that 57 per cent of students surveyed admitted to paraphrasing without referencing the source of the information, and 53 per cent admitted to copying information directly without citing the source (Franklyn-Stokes & Newstead, 1995). However, much plagiarism is inadvertent and due to a lack of understanding amongst students about what it is. It is possible to design assessment in such a way as to deter plagiarism and to deliver simple learning activities that are effective in promoting student understanding of, and their ability to avoid, plagiarism.

An intervention study with students learning to write an APA-style research report showed that admonishment is the least effective method of helping students detect and avoid plagiarism (Landau *et al.*, 2002). Participants in all conditions (receiving feedback, plagiarism examples, or a combination of both) other than the control group were better able to identify plagiarism, and the authors conclude that it is neither difficult nor time-consuming to effect a change in students' ability to detect and avoid plagiarism. Another method of helping students avoid plagiarism is the delivery of workshops that aim to develop students' understanding of authorship and improve their sense of authorial identity in their own work (Pittam *et al.*, 2009). These workshops and an accompanying questionnaire designed to measure students' beliefs and attitudes to writing, authorship and plagiarism have been used in interventions to reduce the incidence of unintentional plagiarism and are freely available for lecturers to use in their own teaching (www.writenow.ac.uk/

authorship). Ryan (2001) has tackled the problem of plagiarism in course-work essays by designing a form of assessment that requires students to produce concise written work during class time using notes based on prior reading, which has resulted in better outcomes in terms of student understanding and writing as well as reduced marking time.

## Specific Issues in Assessment with Large Groups

Large groups pose particular problems for the design of assessment supportive of student learning, namely the constraint on time tutors have for providing individual feedback, creating a need for efficient use of formative assessment that increases learning while reducing staff time spent on feedback and marking. Many of the examples of formative and innovative assessment provided earlier in the chapter have been used or would be applicable with large groups, such as the marking exercise used with a large business studies cohort (Rust *et al.*, 2003) and the redesigned introductory psychology course making use of online discussion and activities (Nicol, 2009). In addition, as noted above, wikis can be used to facilitate collaborative learning effectively in large classes, providing an accessible forum for peer feedback and learning as well as the efficient provision of tutor-generated feedback for the group as a whole or for individual students in need of specific attention. Peer assessment has also been used successfully in large classes. Forbes & Spence (1991) used peer assessment of model examination answers in a large engineering class, resulting in improved final grades. Chapters 2 and 3 of this volume also address the issue of dealing with large groups, and they include additional examples of using peer assessment as well as discussion of how electronic voting systems have been used to encourage formative assessment during class time.

## Conclusion

The aim of this chapter has been to raise awareness of the great potential for using assessment to support students' learning development, and to discuss the underlying principles and some specific methods that can enable assessment to be used in this way. However, perhaps one of the most motivating reasons for reflecting on one's assessment practice is the benefit this can bring not just to students but also to our own sense of being able to engage creatively with a central aspect of our work as educators. I hope this chapter has illustrated some of the ways that reflecting on assessment can lead to innovative development of relevant and effective assessment practice which improves the quality of student learning whilst rewarding staff with a greater level of engagement with and enjoyment of the experience of teaching and assessing in higher education.

## Key Messages

- Assessment is an important determinant of students' experience of higher education but practice remains largely unreflected and traditional;
- Assessment can, and should, be used to drive learning;
- The main value of effectively designed assessment for learning lies in its ability to enable students to internalise standards and empower them to take control of their own learning; Choice of assessment method influences student learning and requires careful consideration to ensure positive outcomes;
- Reflecting on local assessment practice in the context of current educational theory and research can open up possibilities for more creative and rewarding engagement with assessment for tutors and students.

## Research Questions

1. What impact does assessment have on the quality of your students' learning?
2. How can good feedback be provided to all your students, given the size of cohort?
3. How can a shared understanding between students and tutors on the purpose and value of assessment practices be facilitated?
4. What is the role of the new technologies in supporting assessment for learning?
5. How can you design out plagiarism within an assessment strategy?

## References

Biggs, J.B. (1996). Enhancing teaching through constructive alignment. *Higher Education*, *32*(3), 347–364.

Biggs, J.B. (2003). *Teaching for quality learning at university* (2nd edn). Buckingham: Open University Press.

Black, P. & William, D. (1998). Assessment and classroom learning. *Assessment in Education*, *5*(1), 7–74.

Bloxham, S. (2009). Marking and moderation in the UK: False assumptions and wasted resources. *Assessment & Evaluation in Higher Education, 34*(2), 209–220.

Bloxham, S. & Boyd, P. (2007). *Developing effective assessment in higher education: A practical guide.* Maidenhead, England: Open University Press.

Brown, G., Bull, J. & Pendlebury, M. (1997). *Assessing student learning in higher education.* London: Routledge.

Brown, S. & Glasner, A. (1999). *Assessment matters in higher education: Choosing and using diverse approaches.* Guildford: Society for Research in Higher Education and Open University Press.

Brown, S. & Knight, P. (1994). *Assessing learners in higher education.* London: Kogan Page.

Brown, S., Race, P. & Joanna, B. (Eds.) (1999). *Computer-assisted assessment in higher education.* Herndon, Virginia: Stylus Publishers.

Bryan, C. & Clegg, K. (Eds.) (2006). *Innovative assessment in higher education.* London: Routledge.

Buckland, R. (2009). Wikis in university teaching and learning. Workshop delivered as part of the Foundations of University Learning and Teaching programme, University of New South Wales. www.youtube.com/watch?v=m1-8OOrBi0o. Accessed on 30 June 2009.

Castelló, M. (2009, July). *Tutoring the end-of-studies dissertation: Helping psychology students find their personal voice when writing academic texts.* Paper presented at the European Congress of Psychology, Oslo.

Crook, C., Gross, H. & Dymott, R. (2006). Assessment relationships in higher education: The tension of process and practice. *British Educational Research Journal, 32*(1), 95–114.

Dracup, C. (1997). The reliability of marking on a psychology degree. *British Journal of Psychology, 88,* 691–708.

Elander, J., Towell, T. & Fox, P. (2007). Competence-based training and assessment by portfolio: The health psychology model. *Psychology Learning and Teaching, 6*(2), 73–79.

Elton, L. & Johnston, B. (2002). *Assessment in universities: A critical review of research.* York: Higher Education Academy. www.heacademy.ac.uk/resources/detail/id13_assessment_in_universities. Accessed on 6 May 2009.

Entwistle, N. (1988). *Styles of learning and teaching.* London: David Fulton.

Falchikov, N. (2005). *Improving assessment through student involvement: Practical solutions for aiding learning in higher education.* London: RoutledgeFalmer.

Forbes, D.A. & Spence, J. (1991). An experiment in assessment for a large class. In R. Smith (Ed.) *Innovations in engineering education.* London: Ellis Horwood.

Franklyn-Stokes, A. & Newstead, S.E. (1995). Undergraduate cheating: Who does what and why?, *Studies in Higher Education, 20*(2), 159–172.

Gibbs, G. (2006). Why assessment is changing. In C. Bryan & K. Clegg (Eds.) *Innovative Assessment in Higher Education.* London: Routledge.

Gibbs, G. & Simpson, C. (2004–5). Conditions under which assessment supports students' learning. *Learning and Teaching in Higher Education, 1*, 3–31.

Hardman, D. (2009). Practice makes perfect: Testing the testing effect in a naturalistic setting. Presentation to the 2009 Teaching and Learning Conference, London Metropolitan University, 7 July. http://tinyurl.com/nvtok2. Accessed on 3 November 2009.

Harrington, K., Bakhshi, S., Shannon, L., Norton, L., Norton, B., Elander, J. & Reddy, P. (2007). University lecturers' beliefs about how examinations help students learn. Presentation at the EARLI conference, Budapest, August 2007. Poster available at: www.writenow.ac.uk/research. Accessed 20 May 2009.

Harrington, K., Elander, J., Lusher, J., Aiyegbayo, O., Pitt, E., Norton, L., Robinson, H., & Reddy, P. (2006). Using core assessment criteria to improve essay writing. In C. Bryan & K. Clegg (Eds.) *Innovative Assessment in Higher Education*. London: Routledge.

Harrington, K., Elander, J., Norton, L., Reddy, P., Aiyegbayo, O. & Pitt, E. (2006). A qualitative analysis of staff–student differences in understandings of assessment criteria. In C. Rust (Ed.) *Improving student learning through assessment*. Oxford: Oxford Centre for Staff and Learning Development.

Harrington, K., O'Neill, P. & Reynolds, L. (forthcoming). Using wikis and blogs to support writing development: The online evolving essay project. In S. Little (Ed.) *Developing staff–student partnerships in higher education*. London: Continuum.

Hattie, J.A. (1987). Identifying the salient facets of a model of student learning: A synthesis of meta-analyses. *International Journal of Educational Research, 11*, 187–212.

Helman, S. & Horswill, M.S. (2002). Does the introduction of non-traditional teaching techniques improve psychology undergraduates' performance in statistics? *Psychology Learning and Teaching, 2*(1), 12–16.

Higgins, R., Hartley, P. & Skelton, A. (2001). Getting the message across. *Teaching in Higher Education, 6* (2), 269–274.

Hounsell, D. (1987). Essay writing and the quality of feedback. In J.T.E. Richardson, M.W. Ezsenck & D. Warren-Piper (Eds.) *Student learning: Research in education and cognitive psychology*. Milton Keynes: Society for Research in Higher Education and Open University Press.

Karpicke, J.D. & Roediger, H.L. (2008). The critical importance of retrieval for learning. *Science, 319*, 966–968.

Laming, D. (1990). The reliability of a certain university examination compared with the precision of absolute judgements. *Quarterly Journal of Experimental Psychology, 42*(A), 239–254.

Landau, J.D., Druen, P.B. & Arcuri, J.A. (2002). Methods for helping students avoid plagiarism. *Teaching of Psychology, 29*(2), 112–115.

Laurillard, D.M. (1984). Learning from problem-solving. In F. Marton *et al.* (Eds.) *The experience of learning*. Edinburgh: Scottish Academic Press.

Lea, M. & Street, B. (1998). Student writing in higher education: An academic literacies approach. *Studies in Higher Education, 23*(2), 157–172.

Lillis, T.M. (2006). Moving towards an 'academic literacies' pedagogy: Dialogues of participation. In L. Ganobcsik-Williams (Ed.) *Teaching academic writing in UK higher education* (pp.30–45). Houndmills: Palgrave Macmillan.

Longhurst, N. & Norton, L.S. (1997). Self-assessment in coursework essays. *Studies in Educational Evaluation, 23*(4), 319–330.

Lusher, J. (2007). How study groups can help examination performance. *Health Psychology Update, 16*(1 & 2).

MacAndrew, S.B.G. & Edwards, K. (2002). Essays are not the only way: A case report on the benefits of authentic assessment. *Psychology Learning and Teaching, 2*(2), 134–139.

Maclellan, E. (2001). Assessment for learning: The differing perceptions of tutors and students. *Assessment and Evaluation in Higher Education, 26*(4), 307–318.

Marton, F. & Saljö, R. (1976). On qualitative differences in learning, I: Outcome and process. *British Journal of Educational Psychology, 46*, 4–11.

McDowell, L. & Sambell, K. (1999). The experience of innovative assessment: Student perspectives. In S. Brown & A. Glasner (Eds.) *Assessment matters in higher education: Choosing and using diverse approaches* (pp.71–82). Guildford: Society for Research in Higher Education and Open University Press.

Mcgann, D., King, S. & Sillence, E. (2008). Information leaflets: An evaluation of an innovative form of assessment. *Psychology Learning and Teaching, 7*(1), 19–22.

Melluish, S., Crossley, J. & Tweed, A. (2007). An evaluation of the use of simulated patient role-plays in the teaching and assessment of clinical consultation skills in clinical psychologists' training. *Psychology Learning and Teaching, 6*(2), 104–113.

Miller, C.M.I. & Parlett, M. (1974). *Up to the mark: A study of the examination game.* Guildford: Society for Research into Higher Education.

Murphy, R. (2006). Evaluating new priorities for assessment in higher education. In C. Bryan & K. Clegg (Eds.) *Innovative assessment in higher education.* London: Routledge.

National Union of Students (NUS) (2008). National Student Survey Results 2008. Education information, EI/08/35. http://resource.nusonline.co.uk/media/resource/EI%20NSS%20Results.pdf. Accessed on 4 May 2009.

Newman, M. (2007, 7 May). 'Appalling' writing skills drive tutors to seek help. *Times Higher Education.*

Newstead, S. (2002). Examining the examiners: Why are we so bad at assessing students? *Psychology Learning and Teaching, 2*(2), 70–75.

Newstead, S.E. & Dennis, I. (1994). Examiners examined: The reliability of exam marking in psychology. *The Psychologist: Bulletin of the British Psychological Society, 88*, 229–241.

Nicol, D. (2009). Assessment for learner self-regulation: Enhancing achievement in the first year using learning technologies. *Assessment and Evaluation in Higher Education*, *34*(3), 335–352.

Nicol, D. & Macfarlane-Dick, D. (2006). Formative assessment and self-regulated learning: A model and seven principles of good feedback practice. *Studies in Higher Education*, *31*(2), 199–218.

Norton, L.S. (1990). Essay writing: What really counts? *Higher Education*, *20*(4), 411–442.

Norton, L. (2004). Using assessment criteria as learning criteria: A case study in psychology. *Assessment and Evaluation in Higher Education*, *29*(6), 687–702.

Norton, L., Harrington, K., Elander, J., Sinfield, S., Lusher, J., Reddy, P. *et al.* (2005). Supporting students to improve their essay writing through assessment criteria focused workshops. In C. Rust (ed.) *Improving student learning: Diversity and inclusivity. Improving Student Learning 12: Proceedings of the 2004 International Symposium.* Oxford: The Oxford Centre for Staff and Learning Development.

O'Donovan, B., Price, M. & Rust, C. (2000). The student experience of criterion-referenced assessment through the use of a common criteria assessment grid. *Innovations in Learning and Teaching International*, *38*(1), 74–85.

Pittam, G., Elander, J., Lusher, J., Fox, P. & Payne, N. (2009). Student beliefs and attitudes about authorial identity in academic writing. *Studies in Higher Education*, *34*(2), 153–170.

Quality Assurance Agency Scotland (2007a). *Integrative assessment: Monitoring students' experiences of assessment.* Enhancement Themes Guides to Integrative Assessment, No. 1. www.enhancementthemes.ac.uk/themes/IntegrativeAssessment. Accessed on 5 May 2009.

Quality Assurance Agency Scotland (2007b). *Integrative assessment: Balancing assessment* of *and assessment* for *learning.* Enhancement Themes Guides to Integrative Assessment, No. 2. www.enhancementthemes.ac.uk/themes/IntegrativeAssessment. Accessed on 5 May 2009.

Ramsden, P. (1992). *Learning to teach in higher education.* London: Routledge.

Ramsden, P. (2003). *Learning to teach in higher education* (2nd edn). London: RoutledgeFalmer.

Read, B., Francis, B. & Robson, J. (2001). 'Playing safe': Undergraduate essay writing and the presentation of the student voice. *British Journal of Sociology of Education*, *22*(3), 387–399.

Rust, C., Price, M. & O'Donovan, B. (2003). Improving students' learning by developing their understanding of assessment criteria and processes. *Assessment and Evaluation in Higher Education*, *28*(2), 147–164.

Ryan, C. (2001). Case study: How to get better essays while reducing your work and plagiarism. Economics Subject Network. www.economicsnetwork.ac.uk/showcase/ryan_essays.htm. Accessed on 6 May 2009.

Sadler, D.R. (1989). Formative assessment and the design of instructional systems. *Instructional Science, 18*(2), 119–144.

Samuelowicz, K. & Bain, J. (2002). Identifying academics' orientations to assessment practice. *Higher Education, 43*(2), 173–201.

Scouller, K. (1998). The influence of assessment method on students' learning approaches: Multiple choice question examination vs. essay assignment. *Higher Education, 35*(4), 453–472.

Sly, L. (1999). Practice tests as formative assessment improve student performance on computer-managed learning assessments. *Assessment and Evaluation in Higher Education, 24*(3), 339–344.

Snyder, B.R. (1971). *The hidden curriculum.* Cambridge, MA: MIT Press.

Stedmon, J., Wood, J., Curle, C., & Haslam, C. (2006). Development of PBL in the training of clinical psychologists. *Psychology Learning and Teaching, 5*(1), 52–60.

Thomas, J.W., Iventosh, L. & Rohwer, W.D. (1987). Relationships among student characteristics, study activities and achievement as a function of course characteristics. *Contemporary Educational Psychology, 12*, 344–364.

Trentin, G. (2009). Using a wiki to evaluate individual contribution to a collaborative learning project. *Journal of Computer Assisted Learning, 25*, 43–55.

Tynjälä, P. (1998). Traditional studying for examination versus constructivist learning tasks: Do learning outcomes differ? *Studies in Higher Education, 23*(2), 173–189.

Wingate, U. (2006). Doing away with 'study skills'. *Teaching in Higher Education, 11*, 457–469.

Yorke, M. (2003). Formative assessment in higher education: Moves towards theory and the enhancement of pedagogic practice. *Higher Education, 45*(4), 477–501.

# 9

# Onwards and Upwards
## *Teaching Postgraduate Students*

## Jacqui Akhurst

YOU WANT TO DO A POSTGRADUATE STUDIES "TO BECOME FAMOOS.. WEALTHY AND A LEADING ACADEMIC ..." IM NOT SURE ALL THREE ARE MUTUALLY COMPATIBLE ....

This chapter covers the following areas:

- the changing postgraduate psychology landscape in the UK and its impacts;
- factors contributing to cognitive and skill development of postgraduate psychology students;
- an exploration of competence-based training as a basis for postgraduate psychology programme development;
- forms of supervision and mentoring as important contributors to post-graduate students' learning;
- practice-based learning and the utilisation of technological developments to provide greater access and flexibility and promote reflexivity in students.

# Introduction

In recent years, there have been substantive changes in the social care and health systems in the United Kingdom (UK), and the changing employment landscape has required psychology postgraduate programmes to respond creatively. Postgraduate programmes are designed to cater either for the training of students in advanced research skills and consultation, or to equip candidates for professional psychology practice. In the latter case, many students will be aspiring to qualifications recognised by the Health Professions Council (HPC) and may wish to apply for chartered psychologist status in one of the divisions of the British Psychological Society (BPS). Each year, the list of postgraduate programmes at master's and doctoral level in the UK grows, with new programmes being developed to meet workplace requirements and ever-broadening applications of psychology.

In 2007, the BPS published a report on the findings of a project group entitled *New ways of working for applied psychologists in health and social care* (BPS, 2007). The working group considered what 'roles, career structures, training and supervision arrangements should be available to psychology graduates' (p.2). The report notes that 14,000–15,000 psychology students graduate with honours degrees in the UK each year; however, there are very limited places on applied doctoral training programmes (for example only around 550 places are available on funded clinical psychology programmes; and recent funding restrictions for educational psychology trainees has led to a reduction in student numbers on some programmes). The report notes that the BPS-accredited first degree 'provides a good grounding in psychological theory and concepts' (p.10), and recommends the development of postgraduate programmes at certificate, diploma and master's levels to equip people in new roles including the Primary Care Mental Health Worker (PCMHW) and the Psychology Associate. Whilst the report focused on the important employment contexts of the National Health System (NHS) and related social care, it is also likely to have implications for other contexts such as education, the prison services and the commercial and independent sectors, for example developing role requirements and the provision of short courses at postgraduate level.

Changes in the status and remuneration of applied psychologists with doctoral degrees mean that the newly qualified will need to take leadership roles from the start, with increased supervisory and consultative requirements. In the past such roles were gradually adopted once the person had been in post and had gained experience in the system. Postgraduate programmes have therefore needed to respond to the following challenges: preparation of students for supervisory roles, the need for psychologists to continue with lifelong learning through Continuing Professional Development (CPD) and the ongoing expansion in access to communications technology.

With the increasing evidence-base highlighting the importance of psychosocial factors in the aetiology and treatment of physical disease, psychology is being applied in a greater number of primary care treatment settings to respond to both mental health and physical problems (Cummings, 1995; Pruitt *et al.*, 1998). The number of psychologists working in non-psychiatric settings has gradually increased, where psychologists' roles are often to design and deliver educational, preventative and developmental initiatives. Such psychologists may be community-based, and their challenge is to shift from their traditional medical training models (with a central focus on individuals and families) to working in more collaborative and 'bottom-up' ways, including community groups and their representatives.

Postgraduate students often foreground their needs to develop practice-based skills, with academic and research-related skills not having as much emphasis. Since programmes are located in university settings where academics are likely to be more focused on research development, it is necessary for programme developers to weave these different 'threads' together. It is important to consider the impacts of integrating both practice-based and academic skills on students' time and work management.

An important role for graduates of research master's and PhD programmes is that of research consultation. Many qualified postgraduates work in social science and applied research roles in both governmental and private agencies (e.g. those providing market research). These roles require individuals to be able to apply their knowledge of psychological theories and research methods and techniques to promote better understanding of problems in society and the design of appropriate interventions. Graduates need to be able to function as independent professionals, often leading multidisciplinary teams, to analyse situations, make decisions about courses of action and to evaluate these. One of the aims of this chapter is to consider processes to facilitate the development of such skills in postgraduate programmes.

Psychology postgraduate programmes need to utilise both teaching and learning processes as well as experiential learning opportunities to prepare students for effective functioning in a variety of workplaces. Van Deventer *et al.* (2007) note the shifts required by educators in higher education to be responsive to the work-based demands: 'Whereas in the past universities guided students along protracted, predictable ... trajectories from knowledge consumers to knowledge producers, now universities need to function as brokers, providing networks of expertise within which students can pursue real-world knowledge projects.' Such changes have implications for academics and the nature of the work they undertake.

The above changes highlight the importance of equipping students to make valuable contributions to future workplaces, and to do so through utilising diverse methods to promote learning. Teaching postgraduate students feels qualitatively different to undergraduate teaching. With an increasing number of postgraduate courses in psychology in the UK, both new and experienced lecturers may be embarking on such teaching with little specific training. Such teaching is likely to raise a number of teaching challenges not experienced in undergraduate teaching, due to the diversity of demands made both upon the students and their lecturers and the increasing time constraints resulting from limited resources in departments. However, since one is dealing with motivated adults, often with clear career-related goals, this teaching has the potential to be a very rewarding experience. Thus, it is necessary to adapt and broaden one's approach to teaching to include a variety of both traditional and innovative practices.

In this chapter, the focus is on overarching themes relevant to many postgraduate programmes, rather than on the particular concerns of one part of applied psychology. The chapter will consider aspects of and factors contributing to cognitive and skill development of postgraduates, the move toward competence-based training and assessment, the central role played by various forms of supervision and mentoring, work-based experience and service-user involvement and the utilisation of problem-based learning and virtual learning environments. It will conclude with the mention of two specific issues concerning postgraduate students: their role in providing teaching assistance in departments and their preparation for the viva voce examination.

## Cognitive Development Considerations

Whilst undergraduates are often in a transition process towards becoming adult learners, the principles that have been identified as characterising adult learning are of great relevance to postgraduates. These principles should be used to guide the design of teaching approaches and interactions with postgraduates. Postgraduate students are likely to have a much greater sense of their own personal responsibility for their learning, and will benefit from more collaborative approaches and the incorporation of practices linked to the workplace. In a survey of colleagues' opinions, Grover *et al.* (2006) identified the following qualities of successful postgraduates: they were found to be hard working, motivated and easy to teach; they received feedback well; they showed qualities of dedication, determination and persistence; and had well developed critical thinking abilities and demonstrated creativity. Postgraduate programmes should thus seek to encourage the development of these qualities in students. This section describes some of the features of the adult learner, and considers ideas related to enhancing cognitive and skill development.

Drawing from extensive research into adult learning, Knowles and his collaborators identified the following central characteristics, taking a learner-centred perspective (Knowles *et al.*, 2005, p.4):

- the learner's need to know: Why? What? How?
- the self-concept of the learner: autonomous; self-directing;
- prior experience of the learner: as a resource; existent mental models;
- readiness to learn: life-related; developmental task;
- orientation to learning: problem-centred; contextual;
- motivation to learn: intrinsic value; personal pay-off.

These characteristics emphasise the adult learner's curiosity and sense of self, the likelihood of greater reflection on and critique of material, the learner's intrinsic interest in the work and the desire to apply learning to real-life and work contexts. Knowles *et al.* conceptualise these characteristics as being central, but always subject to the impact of individual and situational differences, and a clear expression of the goals and purposes of the learning. Postgraduate students are thus more likely than undergraduates to be interactive and engaged in the classroom, with a desire to work with material that they believe to have real-world relevance and application.

Since many postgraduate students will be returning to study after one or often a number of years of work experience, with many being funded by themselves or their employers, they show high levels of commitment and motivation. Lieb (1991) lists the following factors that need to be considered in relation to adult learners' motivation:

- social relationships;
- external expectations;
- altruistic purposes related to social justice;
- personal advancement;
- stimulation and cognitive interest.

Postgraduate students' motivations for taking on and continuing their studies is often a combination of specific aspects of these factors. There are likely to be important individual differences between students' motivation, both in terms of the factors contributing to their choice of study direction and related to their achievement motivation. Dweck (1986) differentiated between mastery-oriented motivation, where the individual is focused on skills acquisition, and performance-oriented student motivation, which is concerned with evaluation by others. Such differences will impact on the students' ways of undertaking tasks, and their need for feedback. Postgraduates who have recently completed undergraduate study may appear to be overly concerned with evaluation and external mark-related performance, and this has potential to impact on relationships with both peers and lecturers.

A useful way of conceptualising the postgraduates' developmental process as they begin to engage with professional psychology, and are gradually drawn in to the relevant practice skills, comes from the apprenticeship learning model, as explained by Lave and Wenger (1990) in their 'Situated Learning Theory'. At the start of any programme, students are likely to feel on the periphery 'looking in', and learning and work opportunities that draw them inwards in increasingly participative ways need to be structured into a programme. Brown *et al.* (1989) explore the idea of cognitive apprenticeship which 'supports learning in a domain by enabling students to acquire, develop and use cognitive tools in authentic domain activity' (p.39). These ideas are drawn from and emphasise the importance of social interaction and the social construction of knowledge as a basis of the advancement of learning. Wenger (1998) emphasises the building of a 'community of practice' to support and facilitate cooperative learning processes, where learners share joint responsibility for activities, contributions and products. Postgraduate students appreciate approaches based on mutual respect, which encourage their contributions and impact positively on their levels of motivation and feelings of self-worth.

Rosenberg (2006) writes of the following issues that need consideration when planning schedules and activities to promote the transfer of learning in postgraduate programmes: the learner's cognitive load (including the degree of complexity and volume of knowledge to be processed); the processes of assimilation and accommodation related to existing schemas; students' levels of attention and the challenges of sustaining this over long periods; and distinguishing between declarative and procedural knowledge. Whereas in much undergraduate teaching, the emphasis is on developing the students' declarative knowledge (i.e. that which the student has assimilated and is able to access and articulate), the focus in postgraduate work often shifts to procedural knowledge where knowledge needs to be applied in flexible and contextually appropriate ways.

In the context of the training of counselling psychologists, Strasser and Gruber (2004) note: 'Apart from the acquisition and accumulation of declarative knowledge, individuals acquire expertise as they participate in episodes of knowledge application that are personally meaningful to them. Thus, acquisition of expertise usually is embedded in natural situations of great relevance that are closely related to subjects' knowledge, motivation, and emotions' (p.9). They emphasise the role played by incorporating systematic reflection activities in supporting the learning process. It is therefore important to include frequent opportunities for students to engage in reflective practice, and these activities work best when they are carefully structured (as in peer group supervision to be described later in this chapter). Providing opportunities for students to consider 'both the mental representation of problems and the associated reasoning processes' is therefore recommended. Ronnestad and Skovholt (2001) note the enhancing role of 'seminars focusing on the interface between personal and professional development issues' (187), and Lieb (1991) emphasises the need to encourage and facilitate the transfer of knowledge and skills from one context or situation to the next.

Postgraduate students returning to study after many years in the workplace may suffer a crisis of confidence, and may feel anxious about their abilities to cope again with academic work. Drawing from the work of Bandura, Huss *et al.* (2002) note that 'a host of research has shown that both general academic self-efficacy and domain-specific academic efficacy predict academic persistence and performance above and beyond objective ability' (p.276). It is thus important for lecturers to be sensitive to challenges to their self-efficacy that postgraduates may experience, and Huss *et al.* recommend identifying 'graduate students who do not feel well prepared' in order to 'direct them toward experiences' (p.280) that provide support and affirming feedback. Students' coping skills may be developed through supportive interactions with teaching staff and mentors as well as engagement in practical research activities. Grover *et al.* (2006) found that being assigned a faculty mentor from early on promoted success and this is regarded as good practice in postgraduate psychology programmes. A useful resource to help students with the transition to postgraduate study is provided by Becker (2004).

To summarise, O'Byrne *et al.* (1997) emphasise the way that postgraduates learn through 'doing'. Supportive programming will include activities designed to build students' confidence, enabling them to link prior knowledge to the tasks at hand and to assist them gradually to become more confident in tackling novel problems. It is therefore important to explicitly cover problem solving procedures within an environment where students can learn from people with more expertise, as well as each other. Regular opportunities for exploration and discussion of the applications of declarative knowledge to practice need to be incorporated from early on, with judicious use of opportunities for feedback and self-reflection. Therefore, a variety of didactic environments need to be utilised, from highly structured classroom settings to more informal exchanges of information in seminars and group tutorials. Participation in professional meetings and developments towards the presentation of posters and then papers at conferences should be encouraged, both for the skills acquired through such activities and the associated opportunities for networking. The postgraduate lecturer needs to develop and enhance skills of facilitating learning by drawing from student experiences, utilising stories and case studies and sharing in the practice of generating different ways to address recurring problems. Such engagement requires an investment of time and is built on sustained interactions.

## Lecturer–student relationships

A clear theme that emerges from the literature is the importance of the relationship built between postgraduate students and their lecturers, tutors and mentors. Lammers and Smith (2008) found that variables related to the lecturer were rated as the most important influence on the learning environment. These include enthusiasm, knowledge of and interest in the material, approachability and responses to questions.

Lucas and Bernstein (2005), writing about undergraduate teaching, note the following issues that are also relevant to postgraduates: the ethical use of teacher power; classroom climate; dealing with student needs; enhancing students' motivation to learn; and ethical relationships. Lecturers are 'vested' with authority and thus need to consider the views they express and uphold the ethical standards of the profession. It is necessary to consider the learning environment that one creates – a comfortable climate, where people feel valued and respected – is seen to be most conducive to the enhancement of learning. Promoting inclusiveness and the use of diverse examples will contribute to the students' sense of being accepted. Particular sensitivity is needed when dealing with controversial topics. As in all teaching, dealing with students in a fair and even-handed way is important, including following university and departmental procedures for such issues as late work, assessment and feedback.

Whilst the underlying principles and philosophy upon which the BPS ethical code is based should guide the conduct of research, practice and the professional relationships built between lecturers and students, many university psychology lecturers are not registered with the BPS and may not be familiar with the ethical expectations related to teaching. Broadly, the BPS receives queries and complaints most often about the following areas and, though they most directly relate to psychologist–client interactions, they may also be applied to the lecturer–student context:

- multiple relationships – where the psychologist owes an allegiance to several different stakeholders;
- personal relationships – where the psychologist infringes or violates the trust of a client or clients;
- unclear or inadequate standards of practice – where the psychologist is unaware of or disregards the current systems in use by peers or others in similar work;
- breaches of confidentiality – where rules and constraints are broken or not clarified in advance with stakeholders;
- competence – where excessive or misleading claims are made or where inadequate safeguards and monitoring exist for new areas of work;
- research issues including falsifying data, failing to obtain consent, plagiarism or failing to acknowledge another's work or contribution;
- health problems affecting performance or conduct;
- bringing the profession or the Society into disrepute (BPS, 2006, p.7).

It is therefore important that programme directors alert both staff and students to the BPS ethical code and to the requirements not to engage in dual relationships or behaviour that in any way abuses power or might be viewed as a conflict of interests. This includes the maintenance of professional boundaries and censure of any behaviour that might be construed as harassment or intimidatory.

A theme that recurs in various publications is the discouragement of lecturers and students dating each other. Lucas and Bernstein (2005) note the potentially coercive elements of such relationships, with the associated loss of respect and the risk of undermining relationships with the rest of the group. A survey of postgraduates conducted in the USA found that some students were not satisfied that they had received adequate ethical training in this regard (Zakrzewski, 2006). Both staff members and students need to be familiar with the procedures that would be followed in cases of ethical misconduct. A UK-produced video/DVD entitled *Ethical issues in clinical supervision* (Green, 2003) may be a useful training resource for postgraduates, since one of the vignettes covers the issue of dual relationships and professional boundaries in supervision, which may be applied more broadly to lecturer–student relationships.

Programme directors should also scrutinise the accuracy of information provided to students; setting up assessment requirements beforehand in module handbooks, with all expectations specified. They should also specify lecturers' availability outside of the classroom, e-mail conventions and etiquette and the parameters of off-campus interactions. Since the lecturer–student relationship has been identified as such a central element in students' success, ways of encouraging productive and positive relationships should be a core consideration in the resourcing and management of postgraduate programmes.

## Competence-Based Training and Assessment

In the UK, much effort has recently gone into developing, articulating and implementing competence-based assessment for some postgraduate applied psychology programmes. In 2003, the BPS Division of Clinical Psychology adopted a competence-based training model including: psychological assessment, formulation, intervention, evaluation, research, personal and professional skills, communication, teaching and service delivery. In an overview of applied psychology training in the UK, Kinderman (2005) notes how confusing the various subdisciplines' training and professional practice guidelines must seem to employers and people outside of the discipline. He supports the move towards defining competences shared between subdisciplines as a means of greater communication and integration of training. Elander *et al.* (2007) also state that such moves will promote the internationalisation of psychologists' training.

Elander *et al.* (2007) describe the differences between 'competence' and 'competency', since both terms have 'been used to refer to behaviours, performance, knowledge, skills, capability and other qualities and states of the "competent" person' (Short, in Elander *et al.*, p.74). One of the ways to select the term to be used is to consider the required focus. When the focus is behavioural, with an emphasis on the job to be done, 'competences' are used. These should be operationalised in order to measure performance. A criticism of such an approach is that long lists of competences may then

| | | Individual and cultural issues | Scientific knowledge and methods | Reflective practice / self-assessment | Relationships | Ethical and legal standards / Policy | Interdisciplinary systems |
|---|---|---|---|---|---|---|---|
| **Functional competency domains** | Management/ Administration | | | | | | |
| | Supervision/ Teaching | | | | | | |
| | Research/ Evaluation | | | | | | |
| | Consultation/ Facilitation | | | | | | |
| | Assessment / Diagnosis / Conceptualisation | | | | | | |
| | Intervention | | | | | | |

Foundational competency domains

**Figure 9.1**   Competency matrix for psychology education

result, leading to a fragmentary and contextually bound approach. A focus on the underlying attributes of the person leads to a 'competency'-based approach, which is seen to be more generic; however, these are more difficult to assess, and may be based upon assumptions of transferability which may not be valid. Thus, in practice a combination of the approaches may be used where a competence basis is used for formal assessment of a first stage of training, followed by a second stage where the focus shifts to the integration of academic theory and practical professional attributes.

Working in the context of the USA, Rodolfa *et al.* (2005) developed a visual representation of competency development for psychology education that may be useful for programme developers as the basis of such considerations. This work resulted from cooperative work by a number of trainers of professional psychologists. It responds to the need for greater accountability of service-providers and the need to be more focused on the outcomes of training provision. An adapted form of the matrix is illustrated in Figure 9.1.

In the above model, the foundational competencies of the professional are represented by the columns. These result from the building of knowledge, skills, values and attitudes. The functional competencies or job-related roles and activities are shown in the rows. This matrix then becomes useful as a means of considering learning outcomes of various aspects of a post-graduate programme. A third dimension representing CPD and lifelong learning could be added later, forming a cube-shaped model. Rodolfa *et al.* (2005) state that 'within each professional stage ... specialty education ... can be visualized through the parameters of practice ... populations served, problems addressed, procedures of theoretical orientation and settings' (p.350). An example of the application of this model to health psychology training in the USA may be found in France *et al.* (2008).

A competence-based approach strives to make explicit the complexity of demands faced by the developing professional. Psychologists in training experience rich and profound experiences that have the potential to impact on their levels of competence, and Ronnestad and Skovholt (2001) empha-sise the importance of reflecting and processing in both training and prac-tice. However, the fast pace of working that is expected today, and the 'multiple demands to be productive' (p.186), have the potential to work against psychologists having the time to do the necessary cognitive and emotional processing.

Competence-based assessments of skills specify criteria against which postgraduates might be evaluated. A criticism of training in applied psy-chology has been of limited feedback to students (e.g. Akhurst and Kelly, 2006); thus matrices developed from the approaches described above may be helpful tools to articulate and communicate the development of profes-sional competences.

## Supervision and Mentoring

Different forms of supervision and mentoring are a central aspect of post-graduate programmes, both to provide tailored and intensive professional and research development and to support individual students' learning. Much has been written about both practice and research supervision, and Zinkiewicz (2004) provides a UK-based review of practice (available at www.psychology.heacademy.ac.uk). The intention of the section that fol-lows is therefore to select some aspects of individual and small-group prac-tice for consideration by programme developers.

Supervision of practice has an important monitoring and case manage-ment role, where the supervisor takes on responsibilities to ensure the safety of clients. This may particularly be true in placement supervision. The term itself implies that the supervisor has advanced skills and takes an overview of the trainee's practice. Traditional models of supervision thus emphasised a top-down and managerial focus, but this may feel like surveillance to trainees, rather than an activity with the positive enhancement of learning as its focus.

Over many years, Ronnestad and Skovholt (2001) have studied the professional development of psychologists, and they note that 'observing and interacting with respected and trusted seniors appears to be an integral part of being a student …' (p.184). Various forms of observation of skilled practitioners at work need to be structured into training programmes, particularly at the earlier stages, and reflection upon such exposure might then be covered in individual or small-group supervision. This may involve reviewing videotapes of the supervisee's interactions with clients, as well as actual shadowing of the supervisor at work. Supervision thus has a didactic role to play, enabling trainees to develop and hone their skills. In this type of supervision, it is helpful to recognise and draw from the postgraduates' previous work experiences, and to work towards the transfer of skills from one situation to the next.

Garcia-Shelton and Vogel (2002) note the modelling of professional roles that occurs in supervision. They also describe ways that the supervisor helps the supervisee to evaluate the limitations of psychological beliefs and systems, develop change strategies for those situations where this might be appropriate and deal effectively with time-limited or scope-limited contacts. To enhance trainees' skill development, exposure to a variety of practice supervisors during a programme is recommended, so that they can experience different models of practice. This might include collaborative professional engagement with support groups or organisations, and consultation with community agencies.

Forms of supervision and mentoring also play an important personal support role for the trainee. Zinkiewicz (2004) draws attention to the stressful nature of the changes that may be experienced by postgraduates during their studies, and mentions the role of personal tutors and mentors, with examples from some UK postgraduate psychology programmes (pp.13–17). The shift from being a consumer of knowledge to being a practitioner, able to utilise psychological skills and interventions in an applied setting, is demanding for the trainee. The skills and aptitudes required are often different to those required in other work and life contexts, and trainees might find the learning process to be personally challenging and anxiety-provoking. Supervisors need to provide a safe space to enable such needs to be addressed. The provision of support may be either

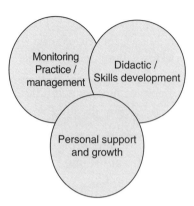

**Figure 9.2**    Roles and functions of supervision

face to face or online to enable trainees to adjust and cope with the stressful nature of the content and processes inherent in postgraduate training.

It is useful to keep in mind the three important roles and functions of supervision as represented in Figure 9.2.

There have been recent initiatives to develop courses to train supervisors in the UK, recognising both the complexity of the supervisor's role and the way in which such skills have been learnt 'on the job' in the past. Green and Dye (2003) undertook research amongst clinical psychology supervisors and found general consensus on the nature of such training. They emphasise the ethical importance of each of the elements of supervision noted above, and that the systematic provision of feedback on performance benefits both trainees and supervisors. A recent review of 11 studies of supervisor training (Milne *et al.*, in press) provides evidence-based support for such training, and identifies important elements, including corrective feedback, educational role-play and observational learning.

With the increasing availability of e-mail and hand-held communication devices, supervision at a distance becomes a possible option, especially when placements are at a distance away from the university. Kanz (2001) explores ideas of online supervision and concludes that it is potentially useful, but needs to be firmly based on an existent supervisor–supervisee relationship. Furthermore it is important to consider carefully the ethics related to confidentiality, considering protection of both the client(s) and trainee.

One of the consequences of the NWW (referred to in the introduction to this chapter) is that newly qualified psychologists may be required to take on supervisory responsibilities from the start. Such responsibilities may also necessitate work in multidisciplinary teams. Recent cohorts of trainees have reported not feeling ready for such roles, and there has been pressure on training courses to better prepare trainees in these roles (Green, personal communication, 19 March 2009). Whereas in training, students generally receive supervision from senior colleagues, they have little exposure to delivering supervision themselves. This led to a recent research project and production of a DVD exploring the potential use of peer group supervision for trainees and the newly qualified, to be described below (Green and Akhurst, 2009).

## Peer group supervision

Peer supervision has been used extensively during the development of practice in psychotherapy and counselling, and it would appear that around two thirds of psychologists use some form of peer supervision, though this tends to be informal. Although there has been increasing research into various forms of supervision over the past two decades, much less research evidence has been gathered about peer and peer group supervision in comparison with individual dyadic supervision. The ways in which interactions with peers enhance learning have been of interest to researchers in adult learning, and the value of collaborative learning has been established. Discussions with peers form part of one's professional practice, and when one's peers are at the same stage of development, the sharing of challenges and concerns can prove beneficial. Peers are often able to identify with each other because they experience similar situations and need to respond with comparable levels of skill. Descriptions of theoretical understanding and step-by-step explanations of strategies, in language that makes sense, promote this type of learning from each other (see Akhurst and Kelly, 2006).

Collaborative learning in a group has benefits for the postgraduate. Each member of the group has the potential to add value to discussions, through more than one mind being applied to casework. A well-managed group can be experienced as supportive and, since a peer group is not expert-driven or hierarchical, it promotes more honest and open communication. For trainees, a structured form of group interaction may be preferable because the structure itself enables the group members to feel more secure. Since group members' skills in group facilitation are in the process of developing, an underpinning structure enables the group to have a solution focus.

As noted previously, research into supervision has highlighted the potential for it to have both supportive and educative functions, and it is these two functions that peer group models serve. As psychologists develop as professionals, cognitive schemas develop, derived from supervisory dialogues, becoming a kind of 'internal supervisor'. The discussions in peer group supervision have the potential to enrich the 'internal supervisor', and appear to work well in tandem with individual supervision. Overall, the process is designed to develop a greater sense of autonomy in trainees.

The peer group (PGS) model demonstrated on the DVD (copies available free from www.heacademy.psychology.ac.uk) has been derived from a structured model that includes aspects of a reflecting team approach. The structure itself was originally written about by Wilbur *et al.* (1991), with various refinements over the years, and they noted its potential for use by peers without a more experienced supervisor present. The reflecting team approach was developed particularly in the context of family therapy, and has been recommended for use by solution-focused therapists. In the PGS model, aspects of a reflecting team are evident in the discussion phase. Whilst the model has a clear solution focus, it is not confined to one form of therapeutic or other psychological intervention, and may also be useful for multidisciplinary teams to enable professionals to learn from each other.

Forms of group supervision are popular in training; however Enyedy *et al.* (2003) highlight the sorts of problems that might emerge. These include potential conflicts between members, logistical constraints related to meeting regularly, poor management of time during group interactions and supervisee anxiety. Such issues need consideration, along with ways of managing the resultant power dynamics where a supervisor is present in a group.

### Preparing students for the viva

Hartley and Jory (2000) investigated the experiences of the viva (or viva voce) of UK postgraduate psychology students. Candidates noted the importance of preparation for the experience, and mock vivas are relatively common practice. There are specific texts that may be useful as preparatory tools (for example, Eley and Jennings, 2005; Wisker, 2005) and online/video productions are also available. Examiners are obliged to follow standard procedures (see Zinkiewicz, 2004; BPS 2008b).

## Work-Based Experience and Collaboration

In some UK universities, there is a rich tradition of building partnerships with workplaces through the provision of work placements of varying length. In the recent past there has been increased governmental support for employer engagement, and acknowledgement of the role of HE in workforce development. Nixon *et al.* (2006) report on an extensive survey of practice across UK institutions, and highlight some of the pedagogical and policy-related issues that emerge. They provide a number of pointers towards good practice with some examples from the health sciences, and highlight key issues and challenges when crossing the 'cultural bridge between learning and work' (p.5).

There have been noteworthy changes in psychology training in the past decade, with expanding placements in nontraditional workplaces (e.g. community and primary care settings) and the potential for interdisciplinary work. This has challenged psychologists to consider their roles and the nature of their interventions, with the need for increasing development of their collaborative working skills and understanding of the contributions of other professionals. For example, in the US context, Garcia-Shelton and Vogel (2002) draw attention to the differences in psychology practice when compared to medicine, such as in the role and use of both time and power. They note the value of collaborative work to provide integrated and comprehensive care to clients, but that such work has implications for training.

Many postgraduate master's programmes in the UK are offered in either full-time or part-time modes. There are instances of people already working in an assistant psychologist's role whilst receiving training. There are clear benefits to making links between the workplace and the student's academic work, but there are also potential conflicts between the demands of both roles as well as different practices being promoted by the two places.

Schmaling *et al.* (2002) write about the importance of training in interdisciplinary work for psychologists working in medical settings. They describe the way in which consultation and liaison were added to an internship programme, and the nature of the preparation needed for such work. Since it is acknowledged that psychologists often play such a role in multidisciplinary teams, facilitating communication and the passing on of relevant patient-related information, it is important to facilitate such training. The authors found that the trainee psychologists added to the capacity of such a team.

With regard to students' work experiences, one of the challenges to be resolved relates to the role of the practice-based supervisor, who may or may not have a role within the training programme. Where such a person has an appointment to the programme, there is likely to be a greater understanding of the ethos and guidelines that exist, and greater levels of communication with university-based lecturers. However, conflicts of interest such as the different roles associated with the assessment of academic work and supervision of practice must be considered. Workplace-based supervisors and tutors who take on the role less formally may need careful induction into the programme, and regular communication is advised (perhaps with a member of staff having liaison responsibilities). Such partnerships are important, and need careful nurturing, and a document that may be useful as a basis of training of or consultation with practice-based supervisors has been constructed by Allin and Turnock (2007). There appears to be the need for investigations of ways of promoting practice-based supervision in the UK context, with Harrison *et al.* (2009) providing an example of research into the support of primary care mental health workers.

## Service-User Involvement

A number of divisions of the BPS have incorporated service users in the training of psychologists. Goodbody (2003) writes of the 'need to respond to the invitation to work in new ways with people who use the services we provide, so that it becomes an inherent part of mainstream practices rather than a fringe activity or an "optional extra"' (p.9). She notes that this movement has evolved both from the recognition of the rights of the service user to be incorporated into practice as well as a holistic view of the person and the social context of each one's lived experience. She notes the following questions that need to be explored to enable psychologists to work effectively with service users:

- the status of professional expertise, and how can it be used to best effect in these new contexts of practice;
- the consequences of the centrality of the scientist-practitioner model and objectivity in our profession's justificatory accounts;
- current learning and teaching practices in clinical psychology;
- what unlearning is needed, and what other knowledge bases should be part of our … training (p.12).

A group of trainers explored such issues, in order to assist them to integrate service users' voices in a more central and respectful way. They noted the difficulty of shifting perspective, especially when the dominant discourse of psychology remains focused on individualistic conceptualisations of mental illness. It requires considerable skill to develop truly collaborative methods, given the entrenched power differentials that exist.

In the past decade, there have been a number of initiatives directed towards more central and respectful incorporation of service users in training. An example is the work of Hayward *et al.* (2008), where mental health service users became involved in mentoring the placement activities of trainees. The aim was to facilitate the development of trainees' capabilities for partnership working. The project was reportedly successful as an influence on learning and practice. It highlighted the resource needs of such initiatives, both in terms of payment of participants and the time and organisation required.

Also in 2008, the BPS produced *Good practice guidelines: Service user and carer involvement within clinical psychology* (available online from www. bps.org.uk). This document integrates the findings of a number of programmes and covers different ways of including service users and carers. It also highlights such issues as leadership, differing needs and aspirations, training, representation and evaluation, and includes possible questionnaires for use. A support network for workers in HE who engage in user and carer involvement has been developed by the Mental Health in Higher Education (MHHE) group (see www.mhhe.heacademy.ac.uk/networks/ducie/), and resources are available from this website.

## Problem-Based Learning

A further recent development has been the move towards various forms of 'problem-based learning' (PBL). This approach has been used in medical training across a number of settings in the past decade, and its success has led to broadened applications. It has been used far less in psychology training (Hays and Vincent, 2004), but certain programmes in the UK have been exploring its potentials (e.g. a group of educational psychology trainers from across the UK).

The value of the approach is the use of real-life practice scenarios in ways that engage groups of students in actively solving the problems. Such an approach requires the learners to be self-directed and to articulate the rationale for decisions that are made. Through PBL, learners become aware that there may be different ways of approaching a problem successfully, and that some problems may not be easily resolved. PBL mimics the real practice of practitioners more closely than traditional teaching methods and has the potential to enhance transfer of skills and students development of self-confidence. It is also more suited to the features of the adult learner as described earlier in the chapter. Hays and Vincent (2004) found that postgraduates preferred a PBL approach, that it promoted staff-student interactions; enhanced knowledge acquisition, critical thinking and research skills, as well as their ability to make oral presentations. They acknowledged the increased workload that resulted, though.

Some of the important features to be considered when developing this approach are:

- the need for 'buy in' from the programme team, and the organisational and planning support that will be needed;
- the staff development needs of the lecturers involved;
- the grading of student activities towards fully-fledged PBL, developing learner skills, confidence and group work;
- that lecturers need to articulate a clear understanding of the learning processes they are striving to facilitate;
- the degree of involvement of 'expert' or 'non-expert' tutors in the group processes.

A number of online resources are available to assist lecturers wishing to explore PBL and psychology-related learning scenarios. Two of these include a valuable DVD of a keynote presentation introducing the approach and principles by Schwartz (2004) and a resource pack by Norton (2005), both available online from www.psychology.heacademy.ac.uk. Norton provides brief text-based vignettes or case study scenarios which have been useful for the teaching and assessment of students. The scenarios provide an introduction to fully-fledged problem-based learning, and may be used flexibly. A group of UK educational psychology trainers have recently worked on a shared online virtual learning environment taking a PBL approach; however no publications on the efficacy of the approach are available at this stage.

## Virtual Learning Environments

Virtual Learning Environments (VLEs) have become ubiquitous in UK psychology teaching in the past decade, with undergraduate teachers having access to these resources as a repository for material. The more interactive aspects of VLEs tend to be used more sparingly, to some extent because of the time and resource-intensive nature of the development and maintenance of such work. VLE-based teaching and learner engagement at postgraduate level has also varied in its uptake; however, it has great potential to be useful to promote distance learning.

A recent project has developed a VLE as the basis of blended learning and the mediation of workplace learning within the three-year Educational Psychology training programmes. The VLE is a shared resource between more than 10 of the programmes and was developed collaboratively to meet the needs of both students and workplace-based supervisors. The material includes models of practice supervision, including both videotaped and PowerPoint demonstrations, discussion of the contracting processes in supervision and a collection of relevant documentation from a variety of sources, and a section on the use of PBL in the supervisory context.

This VLE illustrates the potential to pool expertise and material in a way that would not have been possible in individual programmes and underlines the value of cooperative work across different universities. The developers commented on the benefits of having had discussions about the underpinning pedagogy, both in the VLE and in the material, with spin-offs to other aspects of their programmes. Evidence on the uptake and responses to the initiative are being collected, and preliminary research reports students' engagement in and evaluation of learning via such means (Morris, personal communication, 30 June 2009).

## Postgraduates Who Teach Psychology

In many universities, postgraduates are valued for their contribution to aspects of undergraduate teaching and many postgraduates aspire towards an academic career. Teaching of psychology may even be a requirement of some postgraduate programmes as a means to both increase students' factual knowledge of psychology and their ability to integrate material (McElroy and Prentice-Dunn, 2005). Furthermore, many psychologists may need to play a psychoeducational role. Therefore, an important aspect of postgraduate skill development relates to developing presentation and teaching skills. Postgraduates need exposure to the development of such 'teaching' skills as establishing appropriate goals, defining measurable objectives, setting realistic outcomes, presenting the material and undertaking assessment. Burgess and Buskist (2006) report on a programme that encourages postgraduates to become engaged in the scholarship of teaching, i.e. researching aspects of teaching practice, which may be very useful to those who go on to academic positions.

Lantz *et al.* (2008) surveyed postgraduates across UK psychology departments, exploring experiences of teaching, training and support, as well as the balancing of teaching and research activities. The findings showed that most had good experiences, but many expressed concerns about marking, preparation, time management and being able to deal with difficult students. Time issues related to marking and preparation, and there were associated difficulties with adequate remuneration for the time spent on these activities. Postgraduates reported that clearer and more realistic guidance would be helpful. Respondents at institutions established after 1992 were more likely to report teaching more than their assigned teaching hours.

Postgraduates may be provided with in-house training at their universities (often linked to staff development departments), and some may also embark on a postgraduate teaching certificate. However, postgraduates may not receive as much support as they desire in smaller universities or departments where there are smaller numbers. The issues raised by postgraduates led to the formation of a psychology Postgraduates who Teach (PGwT) Network in the UK. This network is hosted by the Higher Education Academy Psychology Network and comprises regional groups covering most parts of England, Wales, Scotland and Northern Ireland. The PGwT offers support through workshops, e-mail discussion lists, and internet-based resources.

# Conclusion

In the UK, lecturers have been encouraged to learn from and contribute to each other's development due to the changes discussed in this chapter and recognition of common challenges for postgraduate programmes. There has also been valuable communication between applied psychology divisions of the BPS, such as the Health, Forensic, Clinical, Educational and Counselling Divisions. Sharing of good practice in such realms as competence-based training and assessment, VLE and PBL development, and broadly in promoting good supervision and mentoring of trainees, will all benefit the psychology profession. This is especially so given the recent introduction of HPC regulation of a number of branches of applied psychology in the UK, and ongoing university-based discussions on the nature, form and purpose of the doctorate in the UK (see Park, 2007).

Psychology has become an increasingly popular subject for study, and has the potential to be utilised in a wide range of service-related settings. As the marketplace for psychologists changes and grows, many exciting and challenging possibilities will also arise. In order to meet these practice opportunities, well-trained psychologists will be needed. To provide for better accountability, a competence-based model has been described to assist in articulating the sequence of skills and attributes applicable to professional psychology. Trainers of psychologists are encouraged to develop programmes that utilise a range of teaching methods designed to capitalise on the attributes and motivations of adult learners and facilitate their engagement and development.

## Key Messages

- Teaching postgraduates requires in-depth engagement with participatory methodologies to deepen students' learning and enable transfer of material.
- The need to underpin programmes with considerations of the cognitive, emotional and motivational aspects of postgraduate student development.
- The need to incorporate adequate coverage of ethical issues and articulate appropriate staff–student relationships.
- Adopting innovations related to peer learning, online communication and developing communities of practice enables shared responsibilities for learning outcomes and student empowerment.
- The importance of facilitating and maintaining relationships between programme teams and employers, and the value of work placements, to enhance student skill development.

## Research Questions

1. How do student expectations and perceptions of their skills change over the course of a postgraduate psychology programme?
2. What are the experiences, utility and limitations of using virtual learning environments in programmes catering for practice-based postgraduate psychology students?
3. What have been the contributions and challenges of implementing competence-based training and assessment in professional postgraduate psychology programmes?
4. How do teaching staff experience postgraduate psychology teaching in comparison to undergraduate teaching?
5. Which teaching methods best promote the development of ethical practice in postgraduate psychology students?
6. What are the ways of promoting practice-based supervision in applied psychology programmes?

# References

Akhurst, J.E. & Kelly, K. (2006). Peer group supervision as an adjunct to individual supervision: Optimising learning processes during psychologists' training. *Psychology Teaching Review, 12*(1), 3–15.

Allin, L. & Turnock, C. (2007). *Reflection on and in the workplace.* Retrieved on 15 July 2009 from www.practicebasedlearning.org/resources/materials/docs/Reflection%20Work%20Based%20Supervisors.doc

Becker, L. (2004). *How to manage your postgraduate course.* Basingstoke: Palgrave Macmillan.

BPS (British Psychological Society) (2006). *Codes of ethics and conduct.* Leicester: British Psychological Society. Retrieved on 1 May 2009 from www.bps.org.uk/downloadfile.cfm?file_uuid=5084A882-1143-DFD0-7E6C-F1938A65C242&ext=pdf

BPS (British Psychological Society) (2007). *New ways of working for applied psychologists in health and social care.* Leicester: J.L. Taylor & T. Lavender.

BPS (British Psychological Society) (2008a). *Good practice guidelines: Service user and carer involvement within clinical psychology.* Leicester: British Psychological Society retrieved on 1 May 2009 from www.bps.org.uk/document-download-area/document-download$.cfm?file_uuid=DE688754-1143-DFD0-7E15-0-DEEB1F678F9&ext=pdf

BPS (British Psychological Society) (2008b). *Guidelines for the assessment of the PhD* (revised version). Leicester: British Psychological Society retrieved on 1 May 2009 from www.bps.org.uk/document-download-area/document-download$.cfm?file_uuid=D56FD52E-1143-DFD0-7E63-4E6A57285D72&ext=pdf

Brown, J.S., Collins, A. & Duguid, S. (1989). Situated cognition and the culture of learning. *Educational Researcher, 18*(1), 32–42.

Burgess, S. & Buskist, W. (2006). An effective model of engaging graduate students in the scholarship of teaching. *Teaching of Psychology, 33*(2), 140–142.

Cummings, N.A. (1995). Impact of managed care on employment and training: A primer for survival. *Professional Psychology: Research and Practice, 26,* 10–15.

Dweck, C. (1986). Motivational processes affecting learning. *American Psychologist, 41,* 1040–1048.

Elander, J., Fox, P. & Towell, T. (2007). Competence-based training and assessment by portfolio: The health psychology model. *Psychology Learning and Teaching, 6*(2), 73–79.

Eley, A.R., & Jennings, R. (2005). *Effective postgraduate supervision: Improving the student/supervisor relationship.* Maidenhead: Open University Press.

Enyedy, K.L., Arcinue, F., Puri, N.N., Carter, J.W., Goodyear, R.K. & Getzelman, M.A. (2003). Hindering phenomena in group supervision: Implications for practice. *Professional Psychology: Research & Practice, 34,* 312–317.

France, C.R., Masters, K.S., Belar, C.D. *et al.* (2008). Application of the Competency Model to clinical health psychology. *Professional Psychology: Research and Practice, 39*(6), 573–580.

Garcia-Shelton, L. & Vogel, M.E. (2002). Primary care health psychology training: A collaborative model with family practice. *Professional Psychology: Research and Practice, 33*(6), 546–556.

Goodbody, L. (2003). On the edges of uncertain worlds: People who use services, clinical psychologists and training. *Clinical Psychology, 21*, 9–13.

Green, D.R. (2003). *Ethical issues in clinical supervision.* Leeds: University of Leeds/ Higher Education Academy. Retrieved on 1 May 2009 from www.psychology. heacademy.ac.uk/docs/pdf/p20030610_ethics_flyer.pdf

Green, D.R. & Akhurst, J.E. (2009). *Structured peer group supervision.* York: Higher Education Academy Psychology Network.

Green, D. & Dye, L. (2003). How should we best train clinical psychology supervisors? A Delphi survey. *Psychology Learning and Teaching, 2*(2), 108–115.

Grover, C.A., Leftwich, M.J.T., Backhaus, A.L., Fairchild, J.A. & Weaver, K.A. (2006). Qualities of superstar graduate students. *Teaching of Psychology, 33*(4), 271–273.

Harrison, N., Lyons, C., Baguley, C. & Fisher, D. (2009). An educational evaluation of supervisor and mentor experiences when supporting Primary Care Graduate Mental Health Workers. *Journal of Psychiatric and Mental Health Nursing, 16,* 416–423.

Hartley, J. & Jory, S (2000). Lifting the veil on the viva: The experiences of psychology PhD candidates in the UK. *Psychology Teaching Review, 9*(2), 76–90.

Hays, J.R. & Vincent, J.P. (2004). Students' evaluation of problem-based learning in graduate psychology courses. *Teaching of Psychology, 31*(2), 124–125.

Hayward, M., Cooke, A. & Riddell, B. (2008). *Influencing practice: The involvement of service users and carers within the placement activity of clinical psychology trainees.* York: Higher Education Academy draft report.

Huss, M.T., Randall, B.A., Patry, M., Davis, S.F. & Hansen, D.J. (2002). Factors influencing self-rated preparedness for graduate school: A survey of graduate students. *Teaching of Psychology, 29*(4), 275–281.

Kanz, J.E. (2001). Clinical-Supervision.com: Issues in the provision of online supervision. *Psychology: Research and Practice, 32*(4), 415–420.

Kinderman, P. (2005). The applied psychology revolution. *The Psychologist, 18,* 744–746.

Knowles, M., Holton, E. & Swanson, D. (2005). *The adult learner* (6th edn). London: Elsevier.

Lammers, W.J. & Smith, S.M. (2008). Learning factors in the university classroom: Faculty and student perspectives. *Teaching of Psychology, 35*, 61–70.

Lantz, C., Smith, D. & Branney, P. (2008). Psychology postgraduates' perspectives on teaching-related support and training. *Psychology Learning and Teaching, 7*(1), 37–45.

Lave, J. & Wenger, E. (1990). *Situated learning: Legitimate peripheral participation.* Cambridge, UK: Cambridge University Press.

Lieb, S. (1991). *The principles of adult learning.* Retrieved on 29 April 2009 from http://honolulu.hawaii.edu/intranet/committees/FacDevCom/guidebk/teachtip/adults-2.htm

Lucas, S.G. & Bernstein, D.A. (2005). *Teaching psychology: A step by step guide.* Mahwah, NJ: Lawrence Erlbaum.

McElroy, H.J. & Prentice-Dunn, S. (2005). Graduate students' perceptions of a teaching of psychology course. *Teaching of Psychology, 32*(2), 123–125.

Milne, D.L., Sheikh, A.I., Pattison, S. & Wilkinson, A. (in press). Evidence-based training for clinical supervisors: A systematic review of 11 controlled studies. *The Clinical Supervisor.*

Nixon, I., Smith, K., Stafford, R. & Camm, S. (2006). *Work-based learning: Illuminating the higher education landscape.* York: The Higher Education Academy, retrieved on 26 June 2009 from www.heacademy.ac.uk/assets/York/documents/ourwork/research/wbl_illuminating.pdf

Norton, L. (2005). *Psychology Applied Learning Scenarios (PALS): A practical introduction to problem-based learning using vignettes for psychology lecturers.* York: Higher Education Academy Psychology Network, retrieved on 1 May 2009 from www.psychology.heacademy.ac.uk/docs/pdf/p20040422_pals.pdf

O'Byrne, K., Clark, R.E. & Malakuti, R. (1997). Expert and novice performance: Implications for clinical training. *Educational Psychology Review, 9,* 321–332.

Park, C. (2007). *Redefining the doctorate.* York: Higher Education Academy, retrieved on 15 July 2009 from www.heacademy.ac.uk/assets/York/documents/ourwork/research/redefining_the_doctorate.pdf

Pruitt, S.D., Klapow, J.C., Epping-Jordan, J.E. & Dresselhaus, T.R. (1998). Moving behavioral medicine to the front line: A model for the integration of behavioral and medical sciences in primary care. *Professional Psychology: Research and Practice, 29,* 230–236.

Rodolfa, E., Bent, R., Eisman, E., Nelson, P., Rehm, L. & Ritchie, P. (2005). A cube model for competency development: Implications for psychology educators and regulators. *Professional Psychology: Research and Practice, 36,* 347–354.

Ronnestad, M.H., & Skovholt, T.M. (2001). Learning arenas for professional development: Retrospective accounts of senior psychotherapists. *Professional Psychology: Research and Practice, 32*(2), 181–187.

Rosenberg, J.I. (2006). Real-time training and transfer of knowledge. *Psychology: Research and Practice, 37*(5), 539–546.

Schmaling, K.B., Giardino, N.D., Korslund, K.E., Roberts, L.J. & Sweeny, S. (2002). The utility of interdisciplinary training and service: Psychology training on a psychiatry consultation–liaison service. *Professional Psychology: Research and Practice, 33*(4), 413–417.

Schwartz, S. (2004). *Beyond teaching: Changing the paradigm for university learning.* York: The Higher Education Academy Psychology Network. Retrieved on 30 April 2009 from http://ltsnpsy.york.ac.uk/ltsnpsych/plat2004/Zimbardo_Presentation/Plat_2004_HTML/p3204ss_files/intro.htm

Strasser, J. & Gruber, H. (2004). *The role of experience in professional training and development of psychological counsellors* (Research Report No. 11). Regensburg: Universität Regensburg. Retrieved on 29 April 2009 from www-campus.uni-regensburg.de/edu3/images/stories/PDF/Forschungsberichte/fb11.pdf.

Van Deventer, V., Segalo, P., Fourie, E., Grieve, K. & Terre Blanche, M. (2007, 22–23 March). Facilitating learner independence. Paper presented at *Teaching of Psychology in South Africa* conference, Bloemfontein.

Wenger, E. (1998). *Communities of practice: Learning, meaning, and identity.* Cambridge, UK: Cambridge University Press.

Wilbur, M.P., Roberts-Wilbur, J., Morris, J.R., Betz, R.L. & Hart, G.M. (1991). Structured group supervision: Theory into practice. *The Journal for Specialists in Group Work, 16*(2), 91–100.

Wisker, G. (2005). *The good supervisor: Supervising postgraduate and undergraduate research for doctoral theses and dissertations.* Basingstoke: Palgrave Macmillan.

Zakrzewski, R.F. (2006). A national survey of APA student affiliates' involvement and ethical training in psychology educator–student sexual relationships. *Professional Psychology: Research and Practice, 37*(6), 724–730.

Zinkiewicz, L. (2004). *Postgraduate supervision and support in psychology: A review of good practice.* York: The Higher Education Academy Psychology Network.

# 10

# Spreading the Word
## *Teaching Psychology to Non-Psychologists*

## Dominic Upton

IM GIVING A SERIES OF PSYCHOLOGY LECTURES AS PART OF A CIRCUS
PERFORMERS COURSE....

This chapter covers the following areas:

- the difficulties faced in developing psychology within non-psychology based curricula;
- the importance of psychology for non-psychology professional groups;
- the views on what should be included in a psychology curriculum;
- the challenges faced when attempting to teach psychology to non-psychologists;
- potential developments to enhance the teaching of psychology to non-psychology groups.

There is now considerable evidence from a range of sources to indicate the importance of psychology in a number of professional activities. For example, in teaching there is a considerable history on the value of psychology in the profession; in the late 19th century James Gibson Hume lectured on 'The Practical Value of Psychology to the Teacher' (Green, 2001), whilst the publication in 1899 of 'Talks to Teachers on Psychology', a series of lectures by William James, is commonly credited as the first educational psychology textbook. Consequently this is now reflected in the training of many professions and psychology is now included specifically as a topic on a range of professional and vocational courses at both undergraduate and postgraduate level. An unpublished audit of higher education institutions (HEIs) previously undertaken by the British Psychological Society's committee on the 'Teaching of Psychology to Other Professions' (TOPTOP, now renamed as Psychology Education to Other Groups – PEOG) during the 1990s received a number of responses from professions as diverse as commercial management, electrical engineering, accountancy, sport science, marketing, teaching, social work and business management. These courses also included a number of healthcare professional courses such as those for nurses, medics, physiotherapists, occupational therapists, and other healthcare professionals. This survey highlighted the broad extent of psychology being taught to non-psychologists. However, what was (and is) uncertain is what form of psychology is taught, who it is taught by and how it is taught.

This survey and subsequent informal discussions led to the development of a series of seminars and articles (e.g. Mathieson, 2007; Upton, P., 2007) on the teaching of psychology to healthcare professionals, computer scientists (Taylor, 2007) and teachers (Upton, D., 2007). These articles and seminars raised a number of issues that were summarised by Upton (2008):

- There is little if any information on the nature of the psychology material being taught to other groups;
- There is little information on why this information is being taught;
- There is a perceived need for the development of core curricula in psychology for different professional groups;
- There was no community spirit and a feeling of abandonment – psychologists felt they neither fitted with the psychology nor specific professional community.

As a consequence seminars were held on the nature of the psychology curriculum that should be included and this joined a number of other discussions, articles and contributions that have also been presented, for example within the medical literature (e.g. the work of BeSST – Behavioural & Social Sciences Teaching in Medical Education or Mayo, 2004) or within social work (Mayhew, 2000). Although psychology is taught in a number of different settings to a number of different groups at a number of different academic levels, the chapter will attempt to constrain the discussion and focus on the presentation of psychology content to non-psychologists at an undergraduate level to the major professional groups in which there is a psychology element – healthcare professionals. However, other professions will also be included to ensure coverage and to provide examples of some of the key issues and some of the key solutions. A number of fundamental questions will be addressed:

- What psychology material should be included in the professional curriculum?
- What particular challenges face the lecturer when presenting psychology to the non-psychology student?
- And, importantly, how can these be overcome?

## What Should Be in the Psychology Curriculum?

The first question – what should be included in the psychology curriculum? Should there be a 'core psychology curriculum' that should be included in all professional courses? Should psychologists take the lead in developing the curriculum or should this be left to the individual professions? Are there key psychological principles that need to be included in all courses? Is there any specific material that needs to be included for individual professions?

At its most simple, the overall purpose of the vocational course should determine the psychological content for the course. It would not be sensible to deliver the same content for dentists as it would for, say, engineers. However, it has to be noted that there may be core psychological theories or principles which may be applicable to both but the application may be different. For example, it may be that both engineers and dentists may need to have a discussion about the psychological principles of communication, but the application may differ between the different groups. Conversely, you would not expect there to be a need for the engineers to discuss pain management or how to deal with phobias but these topics may be relevant (and, indeed, essential) within a dental curriculum.

If you ask a group of psychologists to suggest topics for certain professional curricula then they will come up with a considerable list of essentials. However, despite the relevance of most of these topics, not all of them (or indeed, any of them) may be included! As Litva and Peters (2008) have discussed with regard to the medical curricula, the struggle to embed psychology has been long and hard. Building on their previous work, they describe the transition required as moving psychology from something that is 'nice to know'– an interesting but non-essential component – to one that is described as a 'need to know' (Peters & Litva, 2006). Despite some progress, de Visser (2009) suggests that, although there has been some movement, 'different medical schools decide which aspects of psychology they will teach, and incorporate in different ways' (p.20) and expresses a view that '*all* students need to understand the importance of psychological knowledge' (p.21).

Although (outside of teaching) the literature on the psychological components of the medical care/healthcare curricula is probably the most complete of all the vocational courses, the literature is comparatively small, as is the literature on the effective, evidence-based approach to teaching of effective healthcare professionals. As Jansen and Nicholl (2007) note, there is no guidance from the main professional psychology bodies (the American Psychological Association (APA) or the British Psychological Society (BPS)) on what psychology should be included in the nursing curriculum, a message that could be applied to many other professional courses (e.g. Mayhew, 2000; Painter & Lemkau, 1992).

This is of note since there is an acknowledgement that undergraduate health professionals should be taught what is relevant for *effective* professional practice. The importance of behavioural factors in health and illness has been recognised not only by students, researchers, and practitioners but also by government and policy makers (Abraham & Michie, 2005; Thirlaway & Upton, 2008; Wanless, 2004). Indeed, de Visser (2009) states 'To practise effective evidence-based medicine, doctors must know how psychological and behavioural factors influence health and illness' (p.20). It is obvious that psychology has a role in medicine and health, and by natural progression, in the training and education of healthcare professionals, but there is no research on what or how psychology should be incorporated into the professional curricula (Jansen & Nicholl, 2007).

Professional and regulatory bodies that oversee the educational requirements of the individual professions may suggest key topics and curriculum content that have to be both studied and completed in order for the individual student to be considered a proficient practitioner in that area. Many of these regulatory frameworks and guidance notes from the professional bodies mention the need for psychology to be contained within the educational experience. For example, the dietetic student is expected to 'understand sociology, social policy, *psychology*, public health and educational methods relevant to the dietetic management of individual clients or groups' (HPC, 2003).

Another form of guidance for healthcare professional educational programmes are the benchmark statements produced by the Quality Assurance Agency (QAA). Subject benchmark statements set out expectations about standards of degrees in a range of subject areas. They describe what gives a discipline its coherence and identity, and define what can be expected of a graduate in terms of the techniques and skills needed to develop understanding in the subject. So, for example, the occupational therapist student is expected to understand 'the relevance of the social and psychological sciences to health and healthcare' (QAA, 2001a). Similarly, students of prosthetics and orthotics are expected to 'have an awareness of the psychological and cultural factors affecting his/her patient's rehabilitation. If these factors adversely affect the treatment plan the graduate should be able to recognise the necessity to refer on to other disciplines' (QAA, 2001b).

From a psychology perspective, it is positive to see that the need for the subject to be incorporated within the heathcare curriculum is stressed (although, as we will see, there is a debate about whether it is integrated) and that this appears across a broad range of professional groups educated within the higher education sector. However, the statements provided by the QAA, Health Professions Council (HPC), General Medical Council (GMC), Nursing and Midwifery Council (NMC) and various other professional bodies are relatively broad and there is little specific material or detail. The guidance is provided in general terms and thus allows for the individual educational provider to interpret this into specific psychological topics. Because it is devolved to individual academic providers (at both an institutional and individual tutor level), then there is considerable disparity in the nature and provision of material (de Visser, 2009). Furthermore, the demands of the different topics within the professional curriculum can be considerable and there is a need for psychology to compete for space with other important topics.

Curriculum content, at a broad level, can be defined as the amount of time allocated to areas such as basic sciences, professional skills, sciences, communication skills, research methods, social sciences or, indeed, psychology. Although when asked which is the most important topic to a member of the public, a client, patient, student, practitioner or educator, the answer will probably be 'all of them' (there is no evidence that this question has ever been asked), there may be indirect ways of assessing this.

For example, the total amount of time allocated, or the proportion of the total curriculum time for each area, is one way to measure the relative emphasis on different content areas. So, for example, if we discover during the first year of a three-year degree course that 25 per cent is devoted to research, 25 per cent to psychology and communication skills and the remaining 50 per cent to the basic core aspects of the topic (e.g. engineering, computing, dietetics, physiotherapy), then both the tutor and the student can see how the importance has been defined by course designers. This is obviously at a broad level and it could be refined to a more discrete level. We could differentiate 'biology' into anatomy, physiology and biochemistry, for example. Alternatively, we could examine the years of a course in which particular topics are delivered and assessed. For example, is psychology simply taught in the first year and does not count towards the final degree classification? Is anatomy taught across all three years? Again, it is not difficult for the student or tutor to see the relative importance of these topics.

The dominance of anatomy, biochemistry and other basic science disciplines in the early years of the undergraduate health curriculum arose partly as a consequence of the research developments in these areas, and the promise that they would have a significant impact on healthcare delivery. Whether this amount of curriculum content is necessary is now the source of considerable debate. Do students *want* this much information on these topics, do they *need* this much information on these topics? Similarly, do patients want information on anatomy and biochemistry, do they need this information? Would they prefer a consultation with a practitioner that could communicate, rather than one that knew the physiological or biochemical processes underlying the condition but could not communicate? Returning to our dental example given at the outset of this chapter, we could argue that psychology and behavioural medicine are fundamental yet these were not fully *integrated* into the dental curriculum until relatively recently. For example, Pine and McGoldrick (2000) commented on dental education and noted that, although the behavioural sciences had become a requisite subject of the undergraduate curriculum since the 1990s, the subject matter and its integration varied from university to university.

Curriculum content is important for a number of reasons. At the outset, and most simply, it is reasonable to assume that undergraduate curriculum content (along with the process) will influence how well professionals are prepared for their professional roles (Schofield *et al.*, 1994) – one would hope so at least! Hence, the curriculum content would impact on how much they know their levels of clinical competence, and their beliefs about what is important for the provision of good clinical care. Furthermore, content areas allocated more time in the curriculum are likely to be perceived by students as more important than those allocated a lesser amount of time.

It also has to be noted that the unintended curriculum has important implications for practice and for patient care. Ewan (1998) reported that there was a relationship between time at medical school and an inability to see the importance of psychosocial factors in health and illness – explained by the predominantly biomedical clinical experience. Hafferty (1998) maintains 'Not all of what is taught during medical training is captured in course catalogues, class syllabi, lecture notes and handouts ... a great deal of what is taught – and most of what is learned – in medical school takes place not within formal course offerings but within medicine's hidden curriculum.' The hidden curriculum includes those elements of education that implicitly impact on students' attitudes. Hence, if the timetable is structured in such a way as to denigrate the importance of psychology, then this will communicate the relative importance to the student.

One example of this tension was the move to include social and behavioural sciences in undergraduate medical curricula in the 1970s on the back of the research evidence linking these disciplines to explaining health and illness. The introduction of these new professional groups proved difficult to achieve and highlighted a number of issues (Sanson-Fisher & Rolfe, 2000). For example, the established disciplines (e.g. those within the basic and clinical sciences) were reluctant to relinquish time or resources within the curriculum since it was perceived that these 'softer sciences' carried a low educational priority. In consequence, student access time was difficult within an already crowded curriculum and the new study areas were relegated in importance and time. This had a further implication: there was a limited staff base, given that access to students was limited. Given that the new disciplines were usually small, there was limited capacity to undertake a substantive programme of research quickly. The small discipline resource base, limited teaching allocations, lack of research prominence and the dissatisfaction expressed by some members of traditional disciplines may have reinforced impressions that behavioural sciences were not as important as the more traditional disciplines. Although this highlights the historical perspective of a medical education curriculum, this has occurred both within medical education and other professional curricula (e.g. Clancy *et al.*, 2000; Pine & McGoldrick, 2000).

Although it would be expected, and hoped, that curricula are based on some evidence, preferably research based (Davies, 1999), in reality this is often not the case and much of the curricula content is based on personal preference and individual idiosyncrasy.

Not only is this important, however, but changes in curriculum content can have an impact on resources at a number of levels whether these be human resources, physical resources, research facilities or the more nebulous 'power base'. It is likely, therefore, that there will be continual political struggles in the curriculum with those currently predominating fighting for the status quo and, some would argue, irrespective of the educational need. Hence, those that teach psychology will have fewer resources since they are seen as less important and this situation will continue since the status quo will remain. Therefore, it is important for psychologists to fully appreciate their importance (surely not difficult!), argue their case and discuss and develop appropriate strategies to ensure that psychology takes its rightful place in the professional curriculum.

Although professional teaching staff are increasingly trained to make decisions based on available evidence, when they put on their teacher's hat they seem to abandon their critical thinking about 'what works'. For example, a search of the databases using the descriptors of behavioural health education, curriculum content, evidence-based teaching and teaching strategies in behavioural health yields almost no articles. There are a few articles theoretically supporting reflective learning and the importance of teaching critical appraisal skills, for example. However, there is few, if any, relevant literature relating to the content of the professional curriculum.

Rolfe *et al.* (2002), in a survey connected with the medical curriculum, reported on a survey of recently qualified medical practitioners in New Zealand. This explored the necessity of knowing what medical conditions needed to be understood and what skills were needed in the clinic, but again no psychology was included. Interestingly, in terms of core practice, the graduates felt that the most important things to learn about (along with medical examination techniques of various conditions) were 'Managing a violent or uncooperative patient' (74.8%), 'Handling difficult patients' (64.2%), and 'Obtaining consent to manage an incompetent patient' – there was little mention of communicating with the normal (sic) patient, or with the patients' relatives, or the importance of psychological techniques in clinical practice.

This being said, however, the study highlighted some interesting findings, not the least of which was the fact that newly qualified medics were able to discriminate among their learning needs and identify many areas which they think need improvement. Indeed, the respondents identified a number of learning needs which may imply that medical students feel they are inadequately prepared for practice. Furthermore, it was of interest that the emphasis from the recent students was that they felt unprepared in how to deal with communication and psychological issues, surely an indication of a need to increase or improve in this area? Hence, it appears that the true value of psychology is only seen after graduation once in practice.

The optimal way of determining curriculum content would be to use an evidence-based approach (Davies, 1999). But where should we derive our evidence from? The strength of evidence can be viewed at a number of different levels – the highest level being the summarised results from a series of Randomised Controlled Trials (RCTs). However, there are no such studies available exploring the value of psychology and other topics in the healthcare professional curricula. In the absence of *any* evidence, it may be necessary to use opinion-based processes to decide on curriculum content. We should, of course, be wary of assuming that expert opinion is our best or only option for decision-making in the field of health education. However, in all opinion-based approaches, the results depend on who is included and who responds.

Current students are the most obvious consumers of an undergraduate course. However, they may not be aware of the tasks that will confront them as clinicians so may not be able to make an informed judgement. Although there is considerable time, effort and resources currently being invested in obtaining student views on the learning experience, this has mainly focused on the process rather than the content. An alternative is to seek the views of recently graduated professionals as they will have the most recent perspective on their undergraduate experience, their current clinical role and the potential marriage between them. Rolfe *et al.* (2001) have reported on a survey of 400 recently qualified medics and suggested that they are able to nominate and prioritise areas that they consider are required for practice.

An interesting finding has been reported by D. Upton (2007) in a study of dietetic students across the four years of their study, and subsequent first year of practice. The study asked for the value of psychology and of various other topics in the dietetic timetable to be rated on value to the student. The results, as highlighted in Figure 10.1, indicate that at the outset students did not consider psychology to be of value whereas biochemistry was considered far more important. However, during the years of study there was a change in opinion: students came to recognise the value

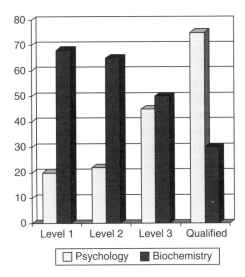

**Figure 10.1**    Value of psychology and biochemistry across the years of study

of psychology and thought that the biochemistry was of less value. An interpretation of this result is that at the outset psychology was not seen as value due to the timetable commitments and the 'hidden' curriculum as indicated above. The timetable, which was heavily loaded in favour of biochemistry (three times as much time compared to psychology), indicated to the students the perceived value of biochemistry compared to psychology and this was reinforced by educators and timetable designers. However, as the students progressed through the course and became more involved in clinical activity, the students appreciated the value of psychology in their communication and dealing with patients and clients. Again, the relevance of psychology only became clearly apparent after the event.

An alternative interpretation (which is discussed in more detail below) is that the dietitians (and medics) only appreciated the relevance of the theoretical aspects of psychology once it had become integrated with their professional practice. This is a common finding and one that has been discussed in a number of professional settings (e.g. Mowforth *et al.*, 2005; P. Upton, 2007).

There has been little previous research in the development of the specific psychology curricula. Mowforth *et al.* (2005) do report on student nurses' views on the relevance of psychology in their curriculum (along with sociology and biology) and noted that students perceived topics as important to understand the concept of health and illness. Furthermore, student nurses appreciated the relevance of psychology but mainly *after* their practical placement when they appreciated how psychology could provide insight into both patient problems and care. Similarly, Jansen and Nicholl (2007) report on the challenges of introducing psychology into the (nursing) curriculum and stress that it is essential for psychology to be appropriately integrated into the curricula in order that students can apply their psychological knowledge to their practice.

One study (Upton & Mansell, 2008) does report on a survey of the healthcare professional courses to explore what psychology is taught on such courses, how it was taught and what concerns were raised. There were a number of concerns that were brought up about the teaching of psychology. (For examples, see Table 10.1.).

Finally, one comment appeared to sum up some of the responses received throughout: 'Whilst we view psychology and the supplementary topics as being equal value, we feel that this may not be the case for some students' (Upton & Mansell, 2008). Obviously it is up to the tutors and the psychology community in general to promote the value of psychology and demonstrate its importance to students.

Psychology may be included within the curriculum in an integrated manner rather than as a separate entity (e.g. Mowforth *et al.*, 2005). Some courses stated psychology was not taught as a separate unit, so was therefore not able to be assessed individually. On the one hand, this can be viewed positively in as much as the application of psychology can be viewed within a professional context. However, others may argue that the underlying principles of psychology are probably best taught prior to the clinical application so a fuller understanding of the value and limitations can be appreciated. However, which approach is 'best' is a matter of personal opinion until appropriate research evidence is developed and supported by empirical studies. Certainly, the research evidence presented to date (e.g. Jansen & Nicholl, 2007; Mowforth *et al.*, 2005) suggests that integration within the curriculum is complex and requires clarification. If there was a clear understanding about what integration within the curriculum was available, then clear strategies could be developed that would enhance and ensure that psychology was running throughout and was not diluted or marginalised in any way.

Obviously, psychology is not just taught on health courses; there are a range of other courses in which it plays an important, if not essential, element. We might consider another student group and look at what they need – engineering and computing students. Taylor (2007) has outlined

**Table 10.1**   Issues raised about the teaching of psychology to non-psychologists

| *Issue* | *Detail* |
| --- | --- |
| Loss of depth due to teaching mode | Attempting to integrate psychological principles and the use of applied texts may mean that there is a greater focus on breadth and application rather than depth and clear psychological understanding. |
| Difficulty in demonstrating link with clinical skills because taught in isolation/difficulty with integration | The dilemma between presenting the material in module-sized chunks which means that it will be seen in isolation compared to attempts at integration with the problem of maintaining depth. |
| Difficulties in engaging healthcare students or in students seeing relevance of subjects | Students may have come to study the other subject – their core area of study. If they get taught other areas which do not appear applied in nature, then they will not see the relevance and become tired and disappointed. |
| Difficulties in presenting material due to lack of time | Given the pressures on the psychology lecturer attempting to deal with the 'service teaching', there was felt to be a disproportionate pressure on an individual's time. This came when attempting to input into more than one course. |
| Better interaction with psychology colleagues required | Psychology lecturers felt that they were alone and isolated in the professional settings. They were not seen as professional nurses, dietitians, engineers or so on and were often seen as outside of the 'core team'. |
| Too much information had to be presented | The demands of teaching psychology and the relevance of much of the material meant that psychology lecturers were attempting to present considerable information in a limited amount of time. |

the role of psychology in computing. She suggests that there is a symbiotic relationship between computing and psychology: psychologists have helped in many ways to understand the way that computer systems are developed and used, but also an understanding of computers has helped psychologists to model and investigate human cognitive and social processes.

The extent of psychology is quite broad, of course, and contains many areas and subdisciplines. Selecting course content in psychology can prove even more daunting in terms of what should be included and excluded. Certain psychologists might argue that social psychology and interpersonal skills should predominate, whereas others think that motivation, personality, or individual differences should be the key focus. Furthermore, for health-care professionals, the sub-area of health psychology could be included – yet this also includes many sub-areas which could be specified. If we explore this in relation to computing and engineering, then we see that certain key psychological principles can have a major role in their professional education.

The designing, development and evaluation of technology require students to understand and consider how people perceive, remember, feel, think and solve problems, i.e. the domain of cognitive psychology. It is also important for students to consider individual differences and social behaviour if effective interaction between people and the technological systems is to be achieved, i.e. the domain of personality and social psychology. An understanding of these topics in psychology enables engineering, computing and other technology students to consider the potential capabilities and limitations of users and helps them to design systems that are more effective (useable) and affective (enjoyable). Applied psychologists have been involved in these areas for many years and often work in departments other than psychology (e.g. human computer interaction (HCI), human factors or ergonomics, engineering). In addition to covering the foundation areas of psychology and HCI, it is also important that students are taught evaluation methods and that they are able to consider the social impacts regarding the implementation and use of systems in organisations and society.

After covering the major topics within social psychology (conversation and communication; group processes; interpersonal perception and attraction; social influence; attitudes, and conflict), applied topics can be covered, such as:

- Computer-mediated communication: for example, the ways that online group discussion, using bulletin boards and video conferencing, can impact on interaction and decision-making and how to make online meetings as effective as face-to-face meetings.
- Affective computing: covering the role of emotion in computing systems and how to design systems that are effective and affective – this is a rapidly expanding topic in HCI and one in which many students have little background understanding; therefore this lecture provides a review of emotion involving definitions and early and current research directions.

- New technology and organisational change: covering the role of occupational psychologists in computer system implementation (e.g. the
  issues for the management of staff working online and remotely) as well
  as internet-based methods for recruitment and selection of personnel
  and training employees.

Although undergraduate engineering students often have considerable
research teaching, much of this will be concerned with the technical aspects of
their degree programme: exploring their physical systems, their engineering
developments, for example. However, they may have little understanding
regarding the way empirical methods (an integral part of all psychology degrees)
can be used to evaluate human interaction with their developed systems.

A range of empirical methods can be taught to such students, but ideally
students (as with all students) need to experience these methods; therefore
it is helpful if the teaching experience includes case studies and practical
workshops with associated scientific reports as coursework. For example,
workshops which compare qualitative methods (e.g. observation, focus
groups) and quantitative methods (e.g. questionnaires and performance
scores) to evaluate the use of computer and engineering systems have been
used and this has illustrated the different methodological approaches well.

Still on the topic of methods, using the internet to conduct research
receives less coverage on computing degrees than might be expected. As with
traditional experimental design, designing an internet-based experiment or
survey requires careful consideration. Although computing lecturers have
the technical skills to conduct online surveys, they often have less understanding of experimental design and what can be done with the data.

Feedback from students indicated that they appreciated the 'academic'
approach, where practical ideas were grounded in psychological research.
Also, postgraduate students were more interested, compared to undergraduate students, in the philosophical debates regarding the psychological
implications of internet use.

## So What Should Students Study?

From these broad examples of course provision, what can we conclude about
psychologists involvement in the development of other courses? The selection of course content for the whole programme is beset with difficulties at
a practical, political and strategic level. The curriculum content can indicate

to students, tutors and clients what is perceived as important and what is not. This can, in the long term, lead to differential allocation of resources and an impact on the educational provision in the degree programmes. Given the competing demands on the student curriculum, there is a need to clearly identify the syllabus for psychology content and its application to the core subject. Psychologists need to be aware of the core topic and the applicability of psychology to it. However, they also need to consider the strategic development of the subject. They need to fight for psychology's inclusion within the overall course curriculum and be able to demonstrate the relevance, strength and applicability of the subject to the core topic.

The percentage of time spent within the psychology curriculum also requires clarification. What from across the psychology domain is included and, just as importantly, what is excluded? Should there be a foundation year of psychological theory before being applied more specifically in subsequent years? Or should the application be evident from the first year? The answers to these questions will differ according to the nature of the students, the culture of the HEI and the skills, abilities and preferences of the individual lecturer. However, these questions have to be asked and addressed to ensure that a quality experience is delivered and experienced by students and staff alike.

## Issues in Delivering Psychology Content
## to Non-Psychologists

Once the course has been developed and its place within the curriculum focused, there is the need to deal with the delivery. What issues face the psychology lecturer when delivering the psychology content to non-psychologists? Although the literature on this is not extensive, and the empirical research even less so, there are a few reviews and opinion pieces on the pains and pleasures of teaching psychology to non-psychology groups (e.g. de Visser, 2009; Mayhew, 2000; Mowforth *et al.*, 2005; Upton, 2008).

### *Individual differences in the student cohort*

Firstly, there is the nature of the student cohort. Psychology students (and healthcare professionals) are usually female and may have a higher proportion of mature people (i.e. over 21 years of age) than some other groups. Whilst this is a sweeping generalisation, of course, the statistics (see Table 10.2) do indicate that engineering or computing degrees, for example, have a greater proportion

**Table 10.2**  Data taken from HESA (2007) comparing males and females for computing-related and psychology-related subject areas

| HESA subject area | Females % | Males % |
| --- | --- | --- |
| Computer Science | 21 | 79 |
| Engineering and Technology | 16 | 84 |
| Biological Science | 65 | 35 |
| Subjects Allied to Medicine | 82 | 18 |
| Social Studies | 59 | 41 |

of male school-leavers in the cohort. This may mean that the individual lecturer needs to tailor their approach to characteristics of individual cohorts.

As mentioned, the composition of most psychology and engineering/computing degree courses are significantly skewed, with females making up the majority of psychology degrees and males making up the majority of computing/engineering degrees. Table 10.2 presents data taken from the Higher Education Statistical Agency (HESA, 2007) comparing males and females for engineering/computing-related and psychology-related subject areas. There are no specific figures given for psychology separately as a discipline, therefore Table 10.2 shows the three subject areas where psychology degree data are included by HESA, depending on the focus of the degree.

Does having a greater proportion of males (or females) in the cohort alter the teaching practice of the individual lecturer? Whilst the evidence on this in psychology is slim, there is some indication that the performance of males and females on psychology courses can differ and that different approaches may be needed in both teaching and assessment (e.g. Sander & Sanders, 2007). Whilst the full implications of such studies needs to be further explored, it is important that the lecturer is aware of potential differences in learning dependent on individual differences. This is important given the widespread indication of gender differences in learning style and outcome (e.g. Breckler *et al.*, 2009; Slater *et al.*, 2007).

### Age

Psychology degrees tend to attract a significant number of mature entrants who have frequently been employed in other careers, have many life experiences or are returning to work after raising a family. Similarly, those undertaking social work or health professional courses attract a relatively high proportion of more mature entrants. In contrast, more 'traditional' science-based subjects such as, for example, computing and engineering degrees tend to attract direct-entry A-level students. Consequently, it is important to consider students' ages when developing and delivering course material. The cognitive development and life experiences may differ between cohorts and this may impact on the design of your curriculum (see also chapter 2). For example, an environment needs to be created that allows students to safely reflect on and explore ethical beliefs relative to the current psychological issues in computing, engineering, social work or health professional courses. Furthermore, age may have an impact on the ambiguity inherent in psychology.

A further problem may confront the individual psychology lecturer when dealing with different age groups with different life experiences. Some may argue that psychology is 'all common sense' or may argue that they know it all, or that their profession does not allow for that form of psychological intervention. The psychology lecturer has to be able to think on their feet and to provide concrete examples on how psychology can be applied to the individual profession or at least facilitate the learning of the student so they can apply their psychological knowledge to their individual practice (see below).

## Motivation to study and learning style

Although there is limited research evidence, personal experience from many psychology lecturers would comment that many psychology undergraduate students enrol on such a programme in order to develop an understanding of both themselves and others by developing 'people' skills that may be of use in a range of future careers. In contrast, engineering students may wish to develop employment in more technically based careers. One particular study cited by Taylor (2007) is that of Radford and Holdstock (1995, p.163) who reported on the differences between student choices for selecting either computing or psychology degrees. The results showed that the most important items differentiating the two fields were those indicated in Table 10.3.

It is important to recognise that students undertaking courses other than psychology but undertaking a psychology component may be taught in different ways and may approach studying in different ways, compared to those studying for single honour psychology degree students. For example, Taylor (2007) suggests that engineering and computing students want definitive answers to specific questions, whereas psychology students are

**Table 10.3**   Most important reasons for selecting undergraduate degree

| *Computing* | *Psychology* |
|---|---|
| Develop problem-solving and computer skills | Development as a person |
| Clear, logical thinking | Understanding other people |
| Increasing future earning power | Understanding oneself |
| Practical, work-related experience | Greater personal independence |

more accustomed to discussing the relative merits of a debate to provide a considered response. Similarly, Jansen and Nicholl (2007) suggest that nurses prefer unambiguous information and clear direction on what is right and wrong so that clear decisions can be made. They highlight the fact that nursing students may be frustrated by the open and questioning nature of psychology and may ask 'why have so many theories, wouldn't one be enough?' (p.268). Consequently, for students not only is there the issue of learning psychology whilst it is not their core topic of study but there is also the problem of attempting to deal with the uncertainty of psychology and a different style of learning and assessing. Hence, there can be a juxtaposition between the technical requirements of the professional course and the need for a psychological mindset.

## Applying the material

A key issue for lecturers attempting to teach psychology to non-psychology students is that the students did not select psychology – their interests lie elsewhere. The students may not be expecting psychology, and some students may consider it irrelevant to their own study. Consequently, they may view psychology as a 'bind', as something 'to be passed' or even 'something to be endured'. In order to overcome this, the lecturer must ensure the material is presented appropriately and is relevant to the student. One way of doing this is to ensure that all materials are adapted so that they provide an effective link to the discipline. Hence, there is a need to appreciate the context in which the psychology will be used. This does not mean that the individual psychology lecturer needs to be a qualified engineer, health professional, nurse or whatever but they do need an overview of the profession. Of course, the lecturer can ask the student what the core issues are that face them and their profession. Another option is to try and explore a particular situation – a clinical consultation or a computer or engineering system – and investigate how psychological principles can be applied, for example, as Taylor (2007) suggests, exploring a system where psychological principles have not been applied and where it has gone wrong. Or, when asking podiatrists how to get their patients to follow their advice, students responded (on one occasion) simply 'tell the patients what to do and they will do it'. This opens up a discussion on adherence, communication and compliance and the psychological research that underpins this.

In the discussion on curriculum content a number of issues were raised and the importance of developing appropriate content for students was stressed and the need to apply this to the individual student's core subject specialism was demonstrated. For example, in nursing the psychology content at first-year level may include basic psychological theories. However, not all of these are relevant or practical for nursing and it will be up to the individual lecturer to ensure that they get the right material and apply it within an appropriate context (Jansen & Nicholl, 2007).

*Correct level*

As with all the courses it is important to deliver the content at the correct level in order to take account of the intended learning outcomes and educational stage. Obviously this may not always be the same for a non-psychology student as it would be for a psychology student. For psychology students, there may be a greater presentation of the psychology research, how it was conducted, what the conclusions were and how the theoretical principles underpin the research. A non-psychology student may just want to understand the principles and how they can be applied.

It is important not to overwhelm students with psychological content but to provide references and supporting material to encourage further reading to reinforce the concepts being covered. This raises another important issue: what texts to use. There are a range of appropriate introductory texts for psychology students (e.g. Passer *et al.*, 2008), amongst which there are some for individual courses (e.g. Rana & Upton, 2008; Upton, 2010). The difficulty in selecting which text to use, however, brings up a dilemma. On the one hand, the psychology texts designed for psychologists contain considerable information and are well produced and present comprehensive material in a readable and informed way. However, some of this will not be relevant and will not be applicable to the particular profession. As Mayhew (2000) states: 'The average academic text in psychology presents students, particularly those who look for application of knowledge, with several serious problems' (p.141).

In contrast, the psychology-specific nursing textbooks may demonstrate the relevance of psychology to nursing practice and the theory to specific situations. This may be of benefit since learning can be facilitated when students take and apply experiences to the psychological content they are covering. However, there may be a problem, as Mayhew (2000) points out in his discussion of psychology teaching for social workers. He suggests that providing one example of how psychology can be applied to social work practice might be self-limiting. Applying theory in one situation can be restricting in terms of the way in which the theory is understood and evaluated. Mayhew (2000) suggests that the simplification of psychological theory can result in interpretation of complex realities in overly simplistic and naive understanding and application which then does not allow for sufficient breadth and hence allow for sufficient, informed decision-making in social work practice. Hence, there is a need for texts where student nurses, social workers, medics (or whatever) can integrate their complete practice in multiple theoretical perspectives.

### *Dealing with preconceptions*

It is important to recognise that all students will have a certain perception of what psychology covers (see chapter 3). The knowledge and expectations of all students of the discipline of psychology has changed significantly – quite possibly as a result of the media representation of psychology and psychologists. As a result, it is useful at the start of any contact with any students to briefly cover what is psychology and what is not and to differentiate between academic psychology and 'pop' psychology. This helps to contextualise the wider role of psychologists in the many areas of modern life relating to computing and technology.

## Assessing Students

An issue that arises from the content is how best to assess the student outcomes. The most obvious and common practice is that learning is assessed by formal examination or written assignments. This may not be the best way of assessing the application of theory to practice and this may be through the assessment of practical scenarios, case-based approaches (Mayo, 2004) or other practical assignments. Although the basic knowledge or underlying principles could be assessed through formal examinations (e.g. multiple choice questions), the application of these may not be fully realised until they are seen in the context of professional practice. Hence, if this is the case, then the integration of practice with psychological principles can be assessed through portfolios. Until integration takes place, the students may view the psychological content as extraneous and distinct from practice.

In other areas of professional practice, there may be the need for 'real answers'. Taylor (2007) highlights that computing or engineering students may want the definitive 'one answer' (akin to the nurses reported by Jansen and Nicholl (2007) wanting 'one theory') which in a discursive and critical subject as psychology may not sit comfortably.

## Conclusion

A fundamental issue that all psychology lecturers must address when teaching non-psychologists is to ensure, as has been emphasised throughout this chapter, that the psychological material is relevant: 'the content must have occupational and professional relevance and be educationally credible and worthwhile' (Greaves, 1987, p.6).

## Key Messages

- Psychologists need to be active contributors to the development of psychology within non-psychology curricula.
- The relative importance of psychology can be perceived by its contribution to the overall course curriculum.
- Involve your students in the development of their psychology learning.
- Applying psychology to specific topics can enhance the student learning.
- Confront and manage the ambiguities inherent in psychology for the non-psychologist.

## Research Questions

1. What is the value of psychology in professional curricula and how is this perceived by students, tutors, educationalists and users?
2. What topics in psychology should be taught in different professional curricula?

3. Are any particular learning styles associated with non-psychology groups compared to psychology groups?
4. How can you enhance *your* teaching practice with particular non-psychology groups?
5. Are there any specific techniques, improvements or activities that actively engage non-psychology students in psychology?

# References

Abraham, C. & Michie, S. (2005). Contributing to public health policy and practice. *The Psychologist, 18*, 676–679.

Breckler, J., Joun, D. & Ngo, H. (2009). Learning styles of physiology students interested in the health professions. *Advances in Physiological Education, 33*, 30–36.

Clancy, J., McVicar, A. & Bird, D. (2000). Getting it right? An exploration of issues relating to the biological sciences in nurse education and nursing practice. *Journal of Advanced Nursing, 32*, 1522–1532.

Davies, P. (1999). What is evidence-based education? *British Journal of Educational Studies, 47*, 108–121.

de Visser, R. (2009). Psychology in the medical curricula: 'Need to know' or 'nice to know'? *The European Health Psychologist, 11*, 20–23.

Ewan, C. (1998). Social issues in medicine: A follow-up comparison of senior year medical students' attitudes with contemporaries in non-medical faculties. *Medical Education, 22*, 375–380.

Greaves, F. (1987). *The nursing curriculum*. London: Chapman and Hall.

Green, C.D. (2001). Classics in the history of psychology. An internet resource available at http://psychclassics.yorku.ca/Hume/teacher.htm

Hafferty, F.W. (1998). Beyond curriculum reform: Confronting medicine's hidden curriculum. *Academic Medicine, 73*, 403–407HESA (2007).

HESA (Higher Education Statistical Agency) (2007). Qualifications obtained by students on HE courses at HEIs in the UK by level of qualification obtained, gender and subject area, 2002/03 to 2005/06. Retrieved on 22 January 2007 from www.hesa.ac.uk/sfrs/sfr107/sfr107_6.pdf

HPC (2003). *Standards of proficiency dietetics*. HPC: London.

Jansen, P. & Nicholl, H. (2007). Challenges in teaching undergraduate psychology to nursing students. *Nurse Education Today, 27*, 267–270.

Litva, A. & Peters, S. (2008). Exploring barriers to teaching behavioural and social sciences in medical education. *Medical Education, 42*, 309–314.

Mathieson, I. (2007). The value of psychology in heath professional education: A health professional's view. *Psychology Teaching Review, 14*, 13–20.

Mayhew, J. (2000). Teaching psychology to social workers: Dilemmas in programme design. *Journal of Social Work Practice, 14*, 135–148.

Mayo, J. (2004). Using case-based instruction to bridge the gap between theory and practice in psychology of adjustment. *Journal of Constructivist Psychology, 17*, 137–146.

Mowforth, G., Harrison, J. & Morris, M. (2005). An investigation into adult nursing students' experiences of the relevance and application of behavioural sciences (biology, psychology and sociology) across two different curricula. *Nurse Education Today, 25*, 41–48.

Painter, A. & Lemkau, J.P. (1992). Turning roadblocks into stepping stones: Teaching psychology to physicians. *Teaching in Psychology, 19*, 183–184.

Passer, M.W., Smith, R.E., Holt, N., Bremner, A., Sutherland, E. & Vliek, M. (2008). *Psychology: The science of mind and behaviour*. Oxford: McGraw-Hill.

Peters, S. & Litva, A. (2006). Relevant behavioural and social sciences for medical education. *Medical Education, 40*, 1020–1026.

Pine, C. & McGoldrick, P. (2000). Application of behavioural sciences teaching by UK dental undergraduates. *European Journal of Dental Education, 4*, 49–56.

QAA (2001a). *Subject benchmarks: Occupational therapy*. London.

QAA (2001b). *Subject benchmarks: Prosthetics and orthotics*. London.

Radford, J. & Holdstock, L. (1995). Gender differences in higher education aims between computing and psychology students. *Research in Science and Technological Education, 13*(2), 163–176.

Rana, D. & Upton, D. (2008). *Psychology for nurses*. London: Pearson Educational.

Rolfe, I.E., Pearson, S., Sanson-Fischer, R.W. & Rigland, C. (2001). Identifying medical school learning needs: A survey of Australian interns. *Education for Health, 14*, 395–404.

Rolfe, I.E., Pearson, S.-A., Sanson-Fischer, R.W., Rigland, C., Bayley, S., Hart, A. & Kelly, S. (2002). Which common clinical conditions should medical students be able to manage by graduation? A perspective from Australian interns. *Medical Teacher, 24*, 16–22.

Sander, P. & Sanders, L. (2007). Gender, psychology students and higher education. *Psychology Learning and Teaching, 6*, 33–36.

Sanson-Fisher, R. & Rolfe, I. (2000). The content of undergraduate heath professional courses: A topic largely ignored? *Medical Teacher, 22*, 564–567.

Schofield, M.J., Walsh, R. & Sanson-Fischer, R. (1994). Training medical students in behavioural and cognitive strategies. *Behavioural Change, 11*, 6–18.

Slater, J.A., Lujan, H.L. & DiCarlo, S.E. (2007). Does gender influence learning style preferences of first-year medical students? *Advances in Physiological Education, 31*, 336–342.

Taylor, J. (2007). Teaching psychology to computing students. *Psychology Teaching Review, 14*(2), 21–29.

Thirlaway, K. & Upton, D. (2008). *The psychology of lifestyle: Promoting health behaviour*. London: Routledge.

Upton, D. (2007). Psychology teaching to healthcare professionals: Who, what, how and why? *Health Psychology Update, 1–2,* 14–25.

Upton, D. (2008). Teaching psychology to others – the pains and the potential. *The Psychologist, 21*(11), 950–951.

Upton, D. & Mansell, H. (2008). The teaching of psychology on healthcare professional courses. *Psychology Teaching Review, 14*(2), 84–93.

Upton, D. (2010). *An introduction to psychology for nurses and health care professionals.* London: Pearson Educational.

Upton, P. (2007). Teaching Granny (and Grandpa) to suck eggs: Psychology and the practicing teacher. *Psychology Teaching Review, 14,* 30–37.

Wanless, D. (2004). *Securing good health for the whole population.* London: HMSO.

# Psychology
## *Past, Present and Future*

## Dominic Upton and Annie Trapp

I have to leave it switched on ... I'm in the middle of an on-line tutorial with one of my students in England

Given the substantial growth of psychology in UK higher education, it is surprising that there have been relatively few resources dealing with the teaching of the subject. However, this has progressed of late with the development of a number of supporting resources. These include two specific UK journals dedicated to teaching and learning in psychology (*Psychology Teaching Review* and *Psychology Learning and Teaching*), outputs from the Higher Education Academy Psychology Network including its newsletter and website with associated resource guide (www.psychology.heacademy.ac.uk/), and a growing number of texts (e.g. this one!). Other, more diverse resources are highlighted throughout this text and, in particular, in the Resource Guide. However, these positive developments are growing at a time of flux for psychology education in the UK and for higher education in general.

For example, the undergraduate curriculum is currently accredited by the British Psychological Society which is itself guided by the QAA Benchmark Statements (2007). The BPS accredits undergraduate programmes according to a set of criteria (e.g. topic coverage, resource statements) and students who achieve a 2:2 or above attain Graduate Basis for Registration (GBR). Until recently the acquisition of GBR was the required route for graduates to progress to postgraduate studies in preparation for Chartership from the BPS in order to practise as a professional psychologist in the health service, forensic or business arenas. Consequently, there was considerable weight on the BPS accreditation of undergraduate degrees as a gateway into professional practice.

However, from 1 July 2009 all of this changed. The Health Professions Council (HPC) now regulates professional psychology. They set the standards for entry to the professional register and do not involve themselves with undergraduate psychology degrees. As a consequence, admission requirements to postgraduate degrees will be up to individual postgraduate programmes in the higher education sector rather than the collective BPS professional body. GBR will cease to exist (although it will be replaced with the Graduate Basis for Chartership – GBC). The transfer of responsibility from the BPS to university programmes around admission standards will lead to the weakening of the professional body's influence over the undergraduate degree. This is a position favoured by many, but mourned by others. How this impacts on the psychological curriculum and the teaching of psychology students (at both undergraduate and postgraduate level) remains to be seen but we can expect some evolution in the undergraduate programme, the HE sector and the relationship between the BPS and the universities.

The future of psychology teaching is more than simply the future role of the British Psychological Society, of course. The economic climate, changes in government policy and funding and shifting university infrastructures will also bring turbulence and change in the teaching landscape to which all lecturers will need to adapt.

What is certain is that there will be more students of psychology. The inexorable growth in students wanting to study psychology (in one shape or another) shows no signs of waning and hence all lecturers, and potential lecturers, need to be well prepared for teaching, guiding and facilitating learning. This may be in the classroom, in the seminar group, in a research project, a one-to-one situation or online. It may be to undergraduates or to postgraduates, to psychologists or non-psychologists. This book has, hopefully provided you with an overview and a perspective on each of these areas and many more.

The worldwide recession, trends of globalisation, increased access to information and social and environmental challenges bring a set of additional responsibilities for university lecturers – what are we educating our students for? In order to address this question, we need to consider who our students are (and will be), what their employment prospects and needs are (and will be) and how our current educational provision can best fit these needs and aspirations.

This text was not intended to be a book full of tips for practice, or 'How to' guides. It was supposed to be a considered, evidence-driven resource on current issues relating to psychology teaching in the UK together with thoughts on how the current provision could (and should) be organised and delivered in the UK. It was about addressing these central questions. The contributions from all the authors within this text have attempted to address these questions and have reviewed the current literature and presented material in a helpful manner for the increasing number of postgraduates who are involved in teaching, the new lecturer, the experienced lecturer and for lecturers from abroad who want to learn more about teaching psychology in the UK. However, the authors do not have all the answers – despite their experience and undoubted expertise – but they have raised a number of common themes that are worthy of further consideration in attempting to address these questions.

Firstly, engaging students is essential. With a subject like psychology, this should be relatively easy – the topic itself is so fundamentally interesting that it would be tricky to make some of it uninteresting and tiresome, no matter how much some people try. However, is this true? Is it true for all areas of psychology? Could all of us agree that all of psychology interests us all of the time? If the answer to this is no, which it surely is, then we have to consider that it will also be true of students. Students may consider certain elements of their undergraduate degree to be boring, irrelevant and not worthy of inclusion on the curriculum and they will need to be engaged. Furthermore, some students (I know it is difficult to appreciate) do not come to university to study psychology but undertake, because of their professional qualifications, psychology modules.

But what exactly is engagement and how do we increase it? Some researchers have tried to conceptualise engagement within an educational context although it will not come as a surprise that the effects of increasing engagement have not been empirically tested within an ecologically valid setting appropriate for psychology teaching in the UK. This is despite student engagement being generally considered to be among the better predictors of learning and personal development (Carini *et al.*, 2006). The premise is simple and self-evident: the more students are engaged, the more they study or practise a subject, the more they learn about it. The very act of being engaged adds to the foundation skills of successful study and future employment. That is, those that are actively engaged or involved in educationally productive study are developing habits that will prepare them well for their future careers.

A number of examples have been provided within these chapters on how to engage students. Many of these examples are based on 'expert opinion' ('it works for me!' approach), but others are based on empirical research. There is a need however for further ecological valid studies in psychology which empirically assess the value of suggested engagement practice to see what works and what doesn't. However, perhaps more importantly, there needs to be recognition of, and an active appreciation of, existing research on student engagement by lecturing staff.

In the same way as the growth of evidence-based medicine has led to agreed guidance and manuals of effective practice, there is a need for similar material to be developed around evidence-based teaching. Obviously, there are two issues that need to be highlighted: first, there is good practice out there (see the Resource Guide), but lecturing staff need to engage with it. Secondly, the concept of 'evidence-based practice' is not without its detractors who argue that it is shallow, does not allow for individual expertise and is not objectively formulated (e.g. Glasby & Beresford, 2006).

Another common, related theme in this text serves to highlight that, although psychologists may be good at designing, implementing, conducting, analysing and reporting studies related to psychology, there does not appear to be the same methodological rigour applied to their everyday teaching practice. Hence, there is still the need to move from the research data to the evidence base sufficient to inform practice. Although this is a concern, we should remember that some 10–20 per cent of medical practice (Shojania & Grimshaw, 2005) is reported as not actually evidence based, so we are in good company! However, we have the techniques, the methodological toolbox and the psychological theories to develop, implement and (most importantly) evaluate approaches to enhancing learning and teaching.

Another common theme arising from the chapters is the need to prepare our students for work, for their career and for their productive contribution to society. Most of the authors here have stressed that the skills learned during the psychology degree are as essential as the psychology content itself. These skills can be developed both implicitly and explicitly during a psychology degree. Students can increase their own awareness of their acquired skills through the use of Personal Development Plans (PDP) but some PDP provide only objective markers that fail to capture the skill set of individual students adequately. Growth in skills, competencies, personal developments – call them what you will – is fundamental to the student learning experience in higher education and can (and should) be influenced by the university lecturer. Not just through the presentation in the classroom (or through any other media) but through the way the lecturers interact with students and peers, how they present the content and what they expect of their students. During these times of economic recession and the growing pessimism over student job prospects, all lecturers owe it to their students to develop these skills as consistently and as explicitly as possible. Again, how this is achieved is largely based on suggestion rather than on empirically driven evidence. It may be through the use of appropriate resources, through assessment or through the design of the module or course curricula. This text has presented some of these methods but there will be many more that have been used by individuals and seem to be successful. These methods need to be shared, promoted and evaluated to ensure that the benefits can be maximised.

Another consideration is what the university will look like in the future. More students are undertaking their initial higher education in local further education colleges and as a result there are stronger regional linkages between higher education and further education. The brick-and-mortar campus will remain (although there may be fewer of them) in combination with the transformation of learning through technology. This transformation will not, as previously heralded, be through a rapid expansion in online learning. There is increased understanding that students now want (and in some cases demand) online material, but prefer a blended approach – face-to-face and online material combined for their benefit. The transformation is more likely to be brought about by the technological capabilities of the internet and communication technologies in the same way as e-mail and the web have transformed education in recent decades.

In this text we have not presented chapters on specific areas of teaching. For example, there are no dedicated chapters on 'online learning', 'teaching large groups' or 'learning in seminars'. This was intentional. The nature of teaching psychology requires the lecturer to be master of all trades, equipped to use a range of approaches in a variety of contexts, and often as not these are a consequence of personal preference and the demands of the subject. There are, of course, excellent elements throughout this text on dealing with groups and dealing with student issues (see chapter 2) but these are intended as signposts and encouragement rather than diktats.

We also need to explore the 'place of psychology' as prompted by an article by Radford (2008a) resulting in a series of responses in the subsequent journal issue. In his article Radford raised a number of questions and issues about the place of psychology in higher education, spanning, as 'only an Emeritus professor can', UK psychology from A-level and Scottish Highers through to employment. In a wide series of responding articles there was no clear consensus but some clear indicators that many could agree with: psychology had a place on nearly all undergraduate programmes; research should underpin our activities and psychology has a great value as a subject, profession and discipline. There is a need for psychology to reflect on its past, its current position and its direction of travel.

We are not alone in taking a reflective stance towards psychology education at this time. In 2008, psychology educators across the US met to discuss a blueprint for psychology education in the future. A publication based on this meeting (Halpern, 2009) examined 'what students need to know to be psychologically literate citizens of the contemporary world, caring family members, and productive workers who can meet today's challenges'. The book arose from recognition that US psychology graduates should be educated in a way that will give them the knowledge, skills and abilities to address the social problems in America such as heart disease, cancer, drug addictions, racism, environmental pollution, violence and terrorism, and child abuse. This mirrors the view of leading psychologists such as Bandura, Seligman and Zimbardo, all passionate advocates for psychological research and practice to focus more on contemporary social and community issues. Similar trends can be seen elsewhere, for example, Silbereisen (2008), President of the International Union of Psychological Sciences, highlights the 'dramatic gap between what is known from basic and applied science, and what social policy makers and those responsible for programming are aware of and utilize' and 'governments [that] are not aware of the potential contribution of psychological research and its application to major social problems in their countries'.

Psychology, however, does not speak with one voice, and this is a fundamental problem for psychology education. As in other developed countries, there is considerable fragmentation of psychology as a discipline within the UK and little appetite for open debate about the purpose of undergraduate psychology education in the 21st century, although the Radford article (2008a) and subsequent debate (Radford, 2008b) have started a process that may lead to this being redressed. There is a need for a sensible, informed debate about what psychology undergraduate education is for, who it serves and how best to achieve these aims. Given the current environmental flux, now might be an opportune time for this debate to commence.

A final theme highlighted by many of the contributors was the need to dispel misconceptions amongst students. Whenever a 'psychologist' appears in fiction, professional psychologists have two competing thoughts. On the one hand, most are pleased that the subject is getting the appropriate consideration and exposure it deserves. On the other hand, the heart may sink as the psychologist may be portrayed as a solver of all ills, as somebody that can read minds, can solve unsolvable crimes and can understand all the intricacies of the human condition. It is therefore not surprising that students arriving at the undergraduate psychology induction want to know where the first-year modules on 'Introductory criminological psychological investigation' or 'Analysis of *Big Brother*, seasons 1–4' or 'Dealing with clinical problems, A–S' are. Some are shocked (and potentially stunned) to find that they have to complete modules on statistics, research methods and maybe cognitive psychology and biopsychology. Of course, students are right to recognise a psychological dimension in the above examples but they need to learn what it is to study such applied examples with 'a psychologist's scientific toolkit'. This problem is not insurmountable but, if we are really interested and willing to start from the point that students are currently at, then we need more creativity and flexibility in the design of undergraduate programmes.

There may also be some misunderstanding about study requirements. A common moan from lecturers is that students are not like they use to be (are they ever?). They no longer enjoy studying for the sake of studying, but are more performance orientated. Of course we all hope that students want to learn something about psychology – they have selected this course at great costs to themselves (and probably their significant others) in terms of time, emotional commitment and (of course) finance – but we have to appreciate the reality of the situation. Students will need to pay for their studies in the future so it is not surprising that they have become more focused on the outcomes of their study. They need the grades to progress in an increasingly competitive marketplace. Of course, the best way of achieving a positive outcome is to become actively engaged in the material, but focusing on the outputs means that lecturers need to become more creative and active in guiding student learning.

This text has been about prompting us all to reflect on our own practice to review how it can be improved and developed on the basis of research evidence, whether this be our own or from others. The growth in university student numbers over the past decade or so has been considerable, and this has been matched and exceeded by those studying psychology. Accompanying this growth has been the (rightful) expectation from students of a high-quality learning experience that prepares them well for their future professional lives and lifelong learning. It is incumbent upon university psychology lecturers to continue to rise to this challenge to ensure that through turbulent seas of professional body unrest, economic turmoil and future insecurities, psychology as an undergraduate degree continues to offer students knowledge, skills and experiences that prepare them well for the uncertainties to come.

## References

Carini, R.M., Kuh, G.D. & Klein, S.P. (2006). Student engagement and student learning: Testing the linkages. *Research in Higher Education, 47,* 1–32.

Glasby, J. & Beresford, P. (2006). Commentary and issues: Who knows best? Evidence based practice and the service user contribution. *Critical Social Policy, 26,* 268–284.

Halpern, D. (2009). *Undergraduate education in psychology: A blueprint for the future of the discipline.* Washington, DC: American Psychological Association.

Quality Assurance Agency for Higher Education (2007). *Psychology.* Retrieved on 4 July 2009 from www.qaa.ac.uk/academicinfrastructure/benchmark/statements/Psychology07.pdf

Radford, J. (2008a). Psychology in its place. *Psychology Teaching Review, 14,* 38–50.

Radford, J. (2008b). A place for everything, and everything in its place. *Psychology Teaching Review, 14*(2), 58–61.

Shojania, K.G. & Grimshaw, J.M. (2005). Evidence-based quality improvement: The state of the science. *Health Affairs, 24,* 138–150.

Silbereisen, R. (2008). Message from IUPsyS President Rainer Silbereisen. Retrieved on 11 July 2009 from www.am.org/iupsys/presidents-page/Silbereisenwebletter.pdf

# Resource Guide

## Books about teaching psychology

Benjamin, L. (2008). *Favorite activities for the teaching of psychology*. Washington, DC: The American Psychological Association.

Buskist, W. & Davis, S. (2005). *Handbook of the teaching of psychology*. Wiley-Blackwell.

Dunn, D., Smith, R. & Beins, B. (2007). *Best practices in teaching statistics and research methods in the behavioral sciences*. UK: Psychology Press.

Goss-Lucas, S. & Bernstein, D.A. (2005). *Teaching psychology: A step by step guide*. Mahwah, NJ: Lawrence Erlbaum.

Griggs, R.A. (2002). *Handbook for teaching introductory psychology, Vol. III*. New Jersey: Lawrence Erlbaum Associates.

Jarvis, M. (2006). *Teaching post-16 psychology*. UK: Nelson Thomes.

Lucas, S.G. (2008). *A guide to teaching introductory psychology*. Malden, MA: Blackwell.

Perlman, B., McCann, L, & McFadden, S. (Eds.) (1999). *Lessons learned, Vol. 1: Practical advice for the teaching of psychology*. Washington, DC: Association for Psychological Science.

Perlman, B., McCann, L. & McFadden, S. (Eds.) (2004). *Lessons learned, Vol. 2: Practical advice for the teaching of psychology*. Washington, DC: American Psychological Society.

Perlman, B., McCann, L. & McFadden, S. (Eds.) (2007). *Lessons learned, Vol. 3: Practical advice for the teaching of psychology*. Washington, DC: Association for Psychological Science.

Ware, M. & Johnson, R. (Eds.) (2000a). *Handbook of demonstrations and activities in the teaching of psychology, Vol. 1: Introductory Statistics, Research Methods and History* (2nd edn). Mahwah, NJ: Erlbaum.

Ware, M. & Johnson, R. (Eds.) (2000b). *Handbook of demonstrations and activities in the teaching of psychology, Vol. 2: Physiological-comparative, learning, cognitive, and developmental* (2nd edn). Mahwah, NJ: Erlbaum.

Ware, M. & Johnson, R. (Eds.) (2000c). *Handbook of demonstrations and activities in the teaching of psychology, Vol. 3: Personality, abnormal, clinical-counseling, and social* (2nd edn). Mahwah, NJ: Erlbaum.

# E-mail lists related to teaching psychology

PsyTeach: Psyteach@Listserv.gsu.edu. A very active list for psychology instructors mainly from the US.

Psychologynetwork@jiscmail.ac.uk. UK list with members in all UK psychology departments.

Teaching in the Psychological Sciences: tips@acsun.frostburg.edu. Another active US list.

# Websites of organizations focusing on psychology teaching

Europlat: www.europlat.org.uk

Higher Education Academy Psychology Network: www.psychology.heacademy.ac.uk

Quality Assurance Agency (subject benchmarks for psychology): www.qaa.ac.uk/academicinfrastructure/benchmark/honours/psychology.pdf

The National Institute on the Teaching of Psychology: www.nitop.org

The Society for the Teaching of Psychology: http://teachpsych.org/

# Grant and project funding for teaching

Association for Psychological Science Fund for the Teaching and Public Understanding of Psychological Science: www.psychologicalscience.org/teaching/

Higher Education Academy Psychology Network: www.psychology.heacademy.ac.uk

Joint Information Systems Committee: www.jisc.org.uk

National Teaching Fellows: www.heacademy.ac.uk

Many universities offer grants for teaching innovation

# Organisations and networks with relevance to teaching psychology

Association for Psychological Science: www.psychologicalscience.org/teaching

British Psychological Society Division of Teachers and Researchers: www.bps.org.uk/dtrp/dtrp_home.cfm

British Psychological Society Postgraduate Affairs Group: www.psypag.co.uk/index.html

British Psychological Society Student Member Group: www.bps.org.uk/smg/

Higher Education Academy with links to the 24 discipline-based subject centres: www.heacademy.ac.uk

Higher Education Academy Psychology Network: www.psychology.heacademy.ac.uk

Office of Teaching Resources in Psychology: http://teachpsych.org/otrp/index.php

Society for the Teaching of Psychology (Division 2 of the American Psychological Association): http://teach psych.org

UK Regional network for postgraduates who teach: www.psychology.heacademy. ac.uk/html/postgrads_who_teach.asp

## Publications relevant to teaching psychology

ESRC Teaching and Learning Research Programme: www.tlrp.org/

*Psychology Learning and Teaching* (PLAT) journal: www.psychology.heacademy.ac.uk

*Psychology Network Newsletter*: www.psychology.heacademy.ac.uk. Published quarterly, this free newsletter contains short articles and features relating to psychology teaching.

*Psychology Teaching. Encouraging Student Attendance*: www.psychology.heacademy. ac.uk/html/psych_teaching.asp. Published by the Psychology Network twice a year.

*Psychology Teaching. Large Group Teaching*: www.psychology.heacademy.ac.uk/ html/psych_teaching.asp

*Psychology Teaching Review*: www.bps.org.uk. Official journal of the British Psychological Society's Division of Teachers and Researchers in Psychology.

*Teaching of Psychology*: http://teachpsych.org/top/topindex.php. Official journal of the Society for the Teaching of Psychology.

## Looking for learning materials to use in teaching psychology?

Useful resources can be found at www.psychology.heacademy.ac.uk. A few examples are shown below:

All in the Mind: www.bbc.co.uk/radio4/science/allinthemind.shtml. Podcasts of the BBC programme that explores the limits and potential of the mind.

BBC Science and Nature: Surveys and Psychological Tests: www.bbc.co.uk/science/ humanbody/mind/index_surveys.shtml

BPS Research Digest: bps-research-digest.blogspot.com/. A compilation of public-friendly press releases about recent published research.

CETL: Centre for Excellence in Interdisciplinary Teaching and Learning in Mental Health: www.ceimh.bham.ac.uk/

Child Development Assets 1: www.open.ac.uk/observationskills/p2_3shtml. CD containing videos showing children of different ages taking part in classic Piagetian assessments, post-Piagetian assessments, executive function assessments, pre-verbal infants 'Theory of Mind' tasks.

Cognitive Daily: http://scienceblogs.com/cognitivedaily/. Cognitive psychology entries exploring recent psychological themes, research and news nearly every day.

Internet Psychologist: www.vts.intute.ac.uk/he/tutorial/psychologist. A 'teach yourself' tutorial for students, lecturers and researchers who want to make more use of the internet.

Introduction to Psychology from MIT: http://ocw.mit.edu/OcwWeb/Brain-and-Cognitive-Sciences/9-00Fall-2004/CourseHome/

Intute: www.intute.ac.uk/socialsciences/psychology/

Neuropod: www.nature.com/neurosci/neuropod/index.html A neuroscience podcast from *Nature*.

OpenLearn: www.open.ac.uk/openlearn/home.php. The Open University has freely available OU course materials.

Psychological Image Collection (PICS): http://pics.psych.stir.ac.uk/. This database is a collection of images including faces and objects.

Psychology Matters: www.psychologymatters.org. This is a web-based compendium of psychological research that demonstrates the application and value of psychological science in our everyday lives.

Psychology Practicals: www.psychologypracticals.com/. This site provides access to materials and resources to support student practical work and the teaching of research methods within psychology at undergraduate and postgraduate level.

Psychological Test Resource: www.psychologypracticals.com/html/details.asp?id=516/. This database contains the details of just over 1500 public domain tests for use by both undergraduate and postgraduate level students in their research work.

Social Psychology Teaching Resources: www.socialpsychology.org/teaching.htm

Uniview: www.uniview.co.uk/. Video and learning and teaching resources.

Viperlib: http://viperlib.york.ac.uk/. A web-based resource library for visual perception.

## Additional resources relating to book chapters

### *Chapter 1*

*American Psychological Association Task Force on Internationalizing the Undergraduate Psychology Curriculum: Report and Recommended Learning Outcomes for Internationalizing the Undergraduate Curriculum* (November 2005): www.acenet.edu/AM/Template.cfm?Section=Home&Template=/CM/ContentDisplay.cfm&ContentFileID=1383

*European Psychologist*: www.hogrefe.com/index.php?mod=journals&action= 1&site=ep

European Psychology Learning and Teaching: www.europlat.org

International Psychology: Annotated Bibliography, Relevant Organizations, and Course Suggestions (2002). Society for the Teaching of Psychology (APA Division 2) Office of Teaching Resources in Psychology (OTRP): http:// teachpsych.org/otrp/resources/resources.php?category=International%20 Psychology

## Chapter 2

Card Sort for Psychology: www.psychology.heacademy.ac.uk/CardSort/CardSort_ Psychology/index.htm. This card sort has been designed to contribute to students' PDP by enhancing their reflection on the skills and knowledge gained through studying psychology.

Grover, C.A. (2006). Teaching and mentoring non-traditional students. In W. Buskist & S.F. Davis (Eds.) *The handbook of the teaching of psychology* (pp.149–152).Oxford: Blackwell.

Improving Provision for Disabled Psychology Students: www.psychology.heacademy.ac.uk/ipdps/ipdps.asp

Inclusion and accessibility: www.psychology.heacademy.ac.uk/networks/sig/index. asp. Key information relating to competence standards, inclusive teaching practice, inclusive curriculum, student engagement, inclusive assessment and inclusive technology.

Lantz, C., Moysey, L., Dean, L., Tawse, I. & Duncan, A. (2008). *The psychology student employability guide.* Higher Education Academy Psychology Network. Retrieved on 27 January 2009 from www.psychology.heacademy.ac.uk/docs/ pdf/p20080915_Employability_Guide.pdf

National Centre for Tactile Diagrams: www.nctd.org.uk/

## Chapter 3

BPS Careers video:

www.bps.org.uk/careers/careers-videos/careers-videos_home.cfm

www.bps.org.uk/careers/careers-in-psychology---gcse-a-level-and-equivalents/ careers-in-psychology---gcse-a-level-and-equivalents_home.cfm

www.bps.org.uk/careers/careers-in-psychology---undergraduate/careers-in- psychology---undergraduate_home.cfm

www.bps.org.uk/careers/careers-in-psychology---postgraduate/careers-in- psychology---postgraduate_home.cfm

Dunn, D. & Chew, S.L. (Eds.) (2006). *Best practices for teaching introductory psychology.* Mahwah, NJ. Lawrence Erlbaum.

Lantz, C., Moysey, L., Dean, L., Tawse, I. & Duncan, A. (2008). *The psychology student employability guide.* Higher Education Academy Psychology Network.

## Chapter 4

## Teaching psychology conferences

A full list of North American teaching conferences: http://teachpsych.org/conferences/conferences.php

International Conference on Psychology Education: biennial conference. http://icope2010.psy.unsw.edu.au/index.html

International Conference for the Scholarship of Teaching and Learning: www.issotl.org/

National Institute on the Teaching of Psychology (US): www.nitop.org

Psychology Learning and Teaching: www.psychology.heacademy.ac.uk

Society for Teaching Psychology Best Practices Conference (US): http://teachpsych.org/conferences/bp/index.php

European Association for Research on Learning and Instruction: www.earli.org/

Research Fortnight Opportunities. A fortnightly listing of research opportunities, a few of which are relevant to teaching. Register at http://new.researchresearch.com

## Chapter 5

Halpern, D. (2009). *Undergraduate education in psychology: A blueprint for the future.* Washington, DC: American Psychological Association.

Marsella, A.J. & Pedersen, P. (2004). Internationalizing the counseling psychology curriculum: Toward new values, competencies, and directions. *Counselling Psychology Quarterly, 17*(4), 413–423.

Norton, L. (2002). *Psychology Applied Learning Scenarios (PALS): A practical introduction to problem-based learning using vignettes for psychology lecturers.* York: LTSN Psychology.

Silberman, M. (1996). *Active learning: 101 strategies to teach any subject.* Boston: Allyn & Bacon.

Teaching Psychology for Sustainability: A Manual of Resources: www.teachgreenpsych.com/

## Chapter 6

Chance News: http://chance.dartmouth.edu/chancewiki/index.php/Main_Page. A useful source for interesting examples of media bloopers involving probability, maths and statistics.

Consortium for the Advancement of Undergraduate Statistics Education: www. causeweb.org/. A collection of wide-ranging resources including fun statistics-related songs, cartoons, poems, jokes and videos (I kid you not).

Discovering Statistics Using SPSS: www.uk.sagepub.com/field3e/default.htm. Support materials include PowerPoint slides, instructional flash moves, flashcard glossaries, MCQs, self-test questions, answers to tasks in the textbook and study skills.

Andy P. Field's website: www.statisticshell.com/. This contains free handouts for a range of statistical techniques.

David C. Howell's website: www.uvm.edu/~dhowell/StatPages/StatHomePage. html. Some useful materials.

Higher Education Academy Psychology Network resources page: www.psychology. heacademy.ac.uk/html/resources.asp. A searchable database of statistics links.

David Kenney's website: http://davidakenny.net/kenny.htm. A wide range of instructional tutorials.

StatNotes: http://faculty.chass.ncsu.edu/garson/PA765/statnote.htm. A wide range of extremely good tutorials on (typically more advanced) statistical techniques.

## Chapter 7

Field, A. & Hole, G. (2003). *How to design and report experiments.* London: Sage Publications.

Forshaw, M. (2004). *Your undergraduate psychology project: A BPS guide.* Oxford: Blackwell.

Guidelines for the Supervision of Undergraduate Qualitative Research in Psychology. LTSN Report and Evaluation series No. 3, May 2003: www.psychology. heacademy.ac.uk/docs/pdf/p20030626_ltsn_report_3_text.pdf

Koocher, G.P. & Keith-Spiegel, P. (2008). *Ethics in psychology and the mental health professions: Standards and cases.* New York: Oxford University Press.

TQRMUL: www.psychology.heacademy.ac.uk/html/qual_res_methods.asp. Supporting the teaching of qualitative research methods at undergraduate level.

## Chapter 8

### Books

Bloxham, S. & Boyd, P. (2007). *Developing effective assessment in higher education: A practical guide.* Maidenhead, UK: Open University Press.

Brown, S. & Glasner, A. (1999). *Assessment matters in higher education: Choosing and using diverse approaches.* Guildford: Society for Research in Higher Education and Open University Press.

Bryan, C. & Clegg, K. (Eds.) (2006). *Innovative assessment in higher education.* London: Routledge.

Ramsden, P. (2003). *Learning to teach in higher education* (2nd edn). London: Routledge Falmer. Revised and updated new edition of the classic text on principles and practice of effective teaching in higher education. See especially chapter 10, 'Assessing for understanding', which includes a section on 'Fourteen rules for better assessment in higher education'.

## Guides

Essay writing: A guide for undergraduates: www.rlf.org.uk/fellowshipscheme/writing/essayguide.cfm

Collecting and using student feedback – a guide to good practice: www.heacademy. ac.uk/resources.asp?process=full_record&section=generic&id=352. This guide is based on a HEFCE funded project undertaken by the Centre for Higher Education Research and Information (CHERI).

## Websites

FAST (Formative Assessment in Science Teaching): www.open.ac.uk/fast/. This is the 'legacy' website of the FAST project which contains reports, papers, case studies, tools and other resources on the use of formative assessment to support students' learning.

Promoting Student Authorship: www.writenow.ac.uk/student_authorship.html. This project addressed the problem of unintentional plagiarism by developing teaching materials to help students develop their understanding of authorship and improve their own authorial identity. The project has focused on psychology students, and has also produced a questionnaire that can be used to measure student beliefs and attitudes to authorship and writing.

REAP (Re-Engineering Assessment Practice): www.reap.ac.uk/index.html. The REAP project has investigated how redesign of assessment using technology can lead to improved learning, increased student satisfaction and more efficient use of staff time. The focus has been on enabling students to monitor and self-direct their own learning in large first-year cohorts, and the website includes examples of redesigned modules.

SENLEF (Student Enhanced Learning through Effective Feedback): www.heacademy. ac.uk/ourwork/learning/assessment/senlef. The SENLEF project has developed case studies, good practice principles, teaching materials and web links in the area of formative assessment, all of which are available on this website.

## Chapter 9

Developers of User and Carer Involvement in Education (DUCIE) network: www.caipe.org.uk/news/developers-of-user-and-carer-involvement-in-education-ducie-network/. DUCIE aims to enhance the involvement of users and carers in learning and teaching through a support network for development workers promoting user and carer involvement within UK higher education institutions (HEIs).

*Good Practice Guidelines: Service User and Carer Involvement within Clinical Psychology Training*: www.bps.org.uk/downloadfile.cfm?file_uuid=DE688754-1143-DFD0-7E15-0DEEB1F678F9&ext=pdf

Making practice-based learning work website: www.practicebasedlearning.org/home.htm

*Postgraduate Supervision and Support in Psychology: A Review of Good Practice*. LTSN Report and Evaluation Series No 4, April 2004: www.psychology.heacademy.ac.uk/docs/pdf/p20040422_postgrad_sup_pro.pdf

*Promoting Good Practice in Peer Group Supervision for Trainee Clinical Psychologists* (DVD): www.psychology.heacademy.ac.uk/docs/pdf/p20090616_Issue52.pdf (p.5).

## Chapter 10

BESST in Medicine: www.heacademy.ac.uk/besst/index.asp. Forum for psychologists, sociologists and cognate disciplines involved in teaching, learning and research relating to the education of medical practitioners.

British Psychological Society Standing Committee: Psychology Education to Other Groups (PEOG): www.bps.org.uk/the-society/organisation-and-governance/psychology-education-board/standing-committee-for-psychology-education-to-other-groups.

# Index